The Five Weirs Walk

Sheffield East End History Trail 3

Text

Paul Griffiths

The **Hallamshire** Press 1999

COVER PICTURE: SANDERSON'S WEIR (KEN PHILLIP)

LORD MAYOR OF SHEFFIELD, COUNCILLOR PETER PRICE, WITH CHILDREN FROM THE BRIGHTSIDE JUNIOR AND INFANT SCHOOL, OPENING THE WEIRHEAD SECTION OF THE WALK, SPRING 1997. (PHOTOGRAPH BY CHRISTINE GODDARD.)

THE FIVE WEIRS WALK

Sheffield East End History Trail No.3

Paul Griffiths

© 1999 The Hallamshire Press Limited

**Published by
The Hallamshire Press Limited
Broom Hall
Sheffield S10 2DR**

Typeset by The Hallamshire Press Limited
Printed in Singapore

British Library Cataloguing in Publication
  A catalogue record for this book is available from the British Library

ISBN 1 874718 27 X

Contents

The Five Weirs Walk at Royds Mill, 1997.
(Sheffield City Council.)

PREFACE
weirs walk

The Five Weirs Walk is a 7.5 km footpath and cycleway which follows the River Don from Lady's Bridge in Sheffield City Centre to Meadowhall on the city's eastern boundary. This stretch of river incorporates five weirs which were built as part of Sheffield's industrial evolution, and which give the walk its name.

Since the late 1980s the East End of Sheffield has gone through a period of major regeneration. The redevelopment of derelict industrial land, together with significant improvements in the quality of the water in the river, has created an opportunity to reclaim the Don as a valuable environmental and recreational resource. To this end, the Five Weirs Walk Trust was established in 1987 to promote and construct access to the river between Sheffield City Centre and Tinsley. The Trust encourages responsible enjoyment of the river through a number of activities. It works with anglers, canoeists and other river users as well as running events, guided walks, clean-up sessions, and public lectures. The Trust also encourages river users to report pollution incidents, using the Environment Agency's 24 hour free emergency hotline number 0800 80 70 60.

The unique environment which presents itself as you progress along the Five Weirs Walk is not always beautiful, but is frequently surprising, impressive and fascinating.

The River Don alongside the walk is ideal in normal weather for the occasional canoeist and for less experienced groups. Between the weirs it flows gently with still waters above the weirs and more movement below.

All the weirs bar one can be walked around at normal water levels and portage points are described on the appropriate maps. In exceptional rain conditions the river can rise rapidly and in such conditions should only be attempted by experienced paddlers. Weirs should be inspected before launching.

All paddlers should understand and follow the British Canoe Union Code of Conduct. Further information from BCU on 0115 982 1100

Enjoy your journey.

INTRODUCTION
weirs walk

Sheffield owes its existence to the river system on which it grew up. Its history is rooted in the local land-form, but things are changing and, as the city goes through a period of massive regeneration, the links between past and present may not seem so apparent.

Nowhere has the process of change been more total than in what Sheffielders sometimes call the Lower Don Valley or East End—the city's industrial heartland. But if you want to understand the link between what Sheffield was and is, the East End is the place to go and look.

The Don, Sheffield's largest river, flows steeply south-eastward from its source on the gritstone moors above Penistone to the city centre where, at its confluence with the Sheaf, it turns sharply north-east into the wider, more gently sloping valley floor of the East End. From here it flows through the valley for 7.5 km before crossing the city boundary, just beyond Tinsley, on its way to the flat lands of the Humber. At this end of the valley the hill of High Wincobank rises from the north-west bank of the river. Standing on top of this hill, for instance on Jenkin Road (see map on page 13), near the ancient remains of a Celtic Brigante fort surrounded by modern houses, you can see the entire Lower Don Valley and comprehend its growth.

To the north and west, the city is ringed by the sharp edged plateaux of the gritstone moors. Five rivers rise from these moors and descend rapidly through steep wooded valleys to the city centre. It is in these valleys that the industrial history of Sheffield began. With the technical knowledge of monks who settled the area following the Norman conquest, the fast flowing water of the rivers became a power source for mills and forges, while the wood of the valleys provided fuel for heat. The first of around a hundred water-powered sites were well established by the fifteenth century, and from then onwards until the nineteenth century Sheffield existed as the centre of a collection of small villages strung along the valleys. Remnants of this village structure are still apparent in the present day suburban landscape.

THE CYCLOPS WORKS,1845 FROM CARLISLE STREET SHOWING THE NEW SHEFFIELD TO ROTHERHAM RAILWAY AND IN THE FOREGROUND THE FARMERS' FIELDS WHCH WERE FAST DISAPPEARING.

So how did the city evolve? The answer is contained in the view from High Wincobank. The narrow valleys that favoured industry did not favour transport. For many years it was hard to get goods in and out of Sheffield's steep valleys. All the national lines of transport lay in the flat lands to the east, and it was along the more gently sloping, wider floor of the Lower Don Valley that these lines of transport were accessed. First it was a packhorse road to the nearest inland port of Bawtry, then in 1732 the Don was made navigable to Tinsley and the road between Tinsley Wharf and Sheffield's centre (now Attercliffe Road) was turnpiked by the 1750s. The canal came to town through the valley in 1819, followed in 1838 by Sheffield's first railway line. These latter transport links, together with the development of steam power, crucible steel and Sheffield silver plate, were the major catalysts of Sheffield's industrial revolution.

Coal from mines to the east and iron ore from Sweden came up the new transport lines. Industry spread into the space between these lines to swallow the raw materials they carried, spitting them back as steel. By the late nineteenth century the revolution was complete. Sheffield was a city, and the East End was smothered by factories and houses.

The effect on the river was slow suffocation. Hidden behind factory walls, cloaked in smoke, the former source of power had less noble uses for a city now semi-detached from its landscape. For almost 150 years a river that once supported salmon was dead, killed first by the severance caused by weirs and lockgates and then by industrial effluent, dumped rubbish and human sewage.

Only the spectacular collapse of heavy industry (at least in terms of land occupied and numbers employed) in the early 1980s provided the ironic means by which life returned to the river. Recent improvements in sewage piping and treatment have enabled the river's new life to grow stronger but, despite the fact that the period of heavy industrialisation was quite short in relation to the history of human settlement in the area, it was a period that totally changed the river and valley as a whole. The emerging new environment is disturbed and dynamic, reflecting the turbulence of the city's industrial history.

Today's East End is a patchwork of old familiar structures, reclaimed derelict sites and new developments. The River Don is the strand that links this patchwork together and, as a constant feature in a changing landscape, it provides a vital focus to the process of regeneration and a benchmark for historians. Some of the newer developments, like the steelworks before them, may seem big, bold and a little alien. Nevertheless, they are there because the space and the transport links were there, and as such they are still rooted in the land-form. Some of the oldest developments, the weirs themselves, are perhaps the closest remaining link with the natural form of the valley. It is fitting, therefore, that they are once more accessible and visible and that the walk described in this guide should be named after them.

SECTION ONE
(see page 14)

SECTION TWO
(see page 26)

SECTION THREE
(see page 32)

SECTION FOUR
(see page 40)

SECTION FIVE
(see page 45)

SECTION SIX
(see page 52)

SECTION SEVEN
(see page 58)

SECT
(se

START

Lady's Bridge

Blonk Street Bridge

PH PH PH

PH

PH

SAVILE STREET

Park Square Roundabout

Victoria Quays

PH PH

Hyde Park

ATTERCLIFFE ROAD

SAVILE STREET EAST

PH

STEVENSON ROAD

River Don

BRIGHTSIDE LANE

NEWHALL ROAD

HAWKE STREET

PH

PH

PH

PH

PH

PH

ATTERCLIFFE COMMON

Attercliffe

DON VALLEY STADIUM

SHEFFIELD ARENA

PH

PH

Cricket Inn Road

Nunnery Square PARK and RIDE

Woodbourn Road

PH

PH

PH

Sheffield and Tinsley Canal

Arena/Don Valley Stadium

KEY TO MAPS

Public House	PH	**The Five Weirs Walk** • • • • • •
Refreshments	⍥	**Proposed Phase 6 of Walk** ○ ○ ○ ○ ○
Public Toilets	WC	Connecting footpaths /cycleways • • • • •
		The Sheffield and Tinsley Canal Trail • • • • •
		Canoe Portage Points ✈
		Supertram ⊡⊡⊡⊙⊡⊡

FIVE WEIRS WALK
RIVER DON SHEFFIELD

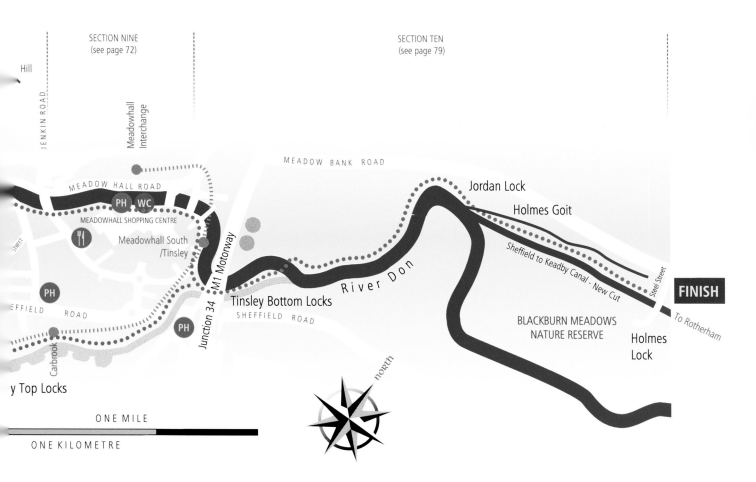

Hill

JENKIN ROAD

Meadowhall
Interchange

MEADOW HALL ROAD

PH   WC

MEADOWHALL SHOPPING CENTRE

Meadowhall South
/Tinsley

MEADOW BANK ROAD

Jordan Lock

Holmes Goit

PH

STREET

SHEFFIELD   ROAD

PH

M1 Motorway

Junction 34

Tinsley Bottom Locks

SHEFFIELD   ROAD

River Don

Sheffield to Keadby Canal - New Cut

Steel Street

FINISH

To Rotherham

BLACKBURN MEADOWS
NATURE RESERVE

Holmes
Lock

PH

Carbrook

y Top Locks

ONE MILE

ONE KILOMETRE

north

SECTION ONE

LADY'S BRIDGE TO WALK MILL WEIR
(WICKER)

The western end of Lady's Bridge (1) marks the formal start of the Five Weirs Walk. The bridge here has long been an important crossing point on the River Don, standing as it does on the original pack-horse route between Sheffield and the towns of Rotherham, Bawtry and Doncaster. The first bridge, probably a simple wooden structure, was built in the mid 1100s when William de Lovetot became the first Norman knight to make Sheffield his home by building a castle near by. During the reign of Henry VII (1485-1509) the bridge was completely rebuilt by the Town Trust. Widening took place on three occasions in 1761, 1865 and 1909 to cope with increasing volumes of traffic as Sheffield's industrial base expanded. The present bridge contains work from all three of these dates, and also some of the structure, with

LADY'S BRIDGE AROUND 1850, VIEWED FROM THE UPSTREAM SIDE WITH THE START OF THE WICKER ON THE LEFT. IN THE BACKGROUND CAN BE SEEN TWO CASTLE-LIKE BUILDINGS. THE NEARER IS THE WICKER TILT FORGE, OPERATED AT THE TIME BY HUNTSMANS, AND THE FAR ONE IS THE TOWER GRINDING WHEEL, LATER PART OF OSBORN'S STEEL WORKS—THE TURRETS WERE CHIMNEYS!

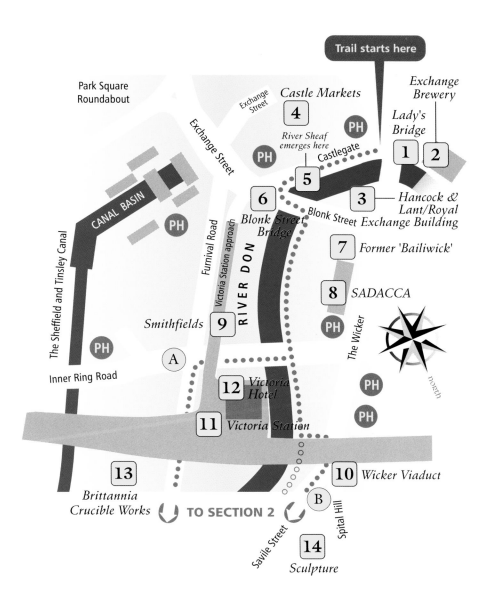

Trail starts here

Park Square Roundabout

Exchange Street

Castle Markets

Exchange Brewery

Lady's Bridge

River Sheaf emerges here

Castlegate

CANAL BASIN

4

PH

PH

1

2

5

3

Hancock & Lant/Royal Exchange Building

6

Blonk Street Bridge

Blonk Street

7 Former 'Bailiwick'

8 SADACCA

Furnival Road

Victoria Station approach

RIVER DON

PH

The Wicker

north

The Sheffield and Tinsley Canal

PH

Smithfields

9

Ⓐ

PH

PH

Inner Ring Road

12 Victoria Hotel

11 Victoria Station

13

Brittannia Crucible Works

Ⓑ

TO SECTION 2

10 Wicker Viaduct

Savile Street

Spital Hill

14

Sculpture

Start of Five Weirs Paddle is accessed from Blonk St/Wicker section.

distinctive pointed arches, from c.1500, is sandwiched in the middle.

The name Lady's Bridge derives from a small chapel dedicated to Our Lady which stood on the town side of the river. Here a priest would pray for the safety of travellers on the road, who in turn would give thanks for their safe arrival in the town. Sadly, the chapel was lost in the dissolution of the monasteries in 1536, but a similar arrangement remains on the Chantry Bridge in Rotherham. Happily, a safe journey through the Don Valley is now more assured than it was during the time of the chapel's existence.

The building to the north-west of Lady's Bridge is the former Exchange Brewery(2). Founded in 1852 by the Tennant Brothers, it was taken over by Whitbread's in 1962 but unfortunately it was closed in 1994.

Spanning the river just upstream of the bridge is the impressive crescent of Lady's Bridge Weir. This isn't one of the five weirs from which the walk takes its name, but nevertheless its history is well worth noting. Records from the Norfolk Estates indicate that a weir has been in existence at this point since at least 1581. Water from the weir was used to power two distinct sets of works. The first works, built in the late 16th century for the grinding of edge tools, were known simply as the Wicker Wheel, and they stood roughly where the Sheffield and District African Caribbean Community Association (SADACCA) building(8) is located on the present day Wicker. The second set of works, the Wicker Tilt Forge, didn't appear until the mid 18th century. They were built immediately downstream of the weir and Lady's Bridge in a building with castellations in homage to Sheffield Castle (see Fairbank's Map opposite).

Both sites were leased in 1785 by Benjamin Blonk and Co., who opened the first steam-powered grinding shop in Sheffield and gave the name to the nearby Blonk Street and Bridge. By 1870 a wire mill had been added to the tilt now operated by Huntsman & Co., originators of the crucible steel-making process. Today, the only visible remains of the waterpowered Wicker works are the weir itself and the start of the head goyt, which can be seen flowing under the eastern arch of the bridge. Other parts of the goyt system remain but are culverted beneath present-day buildings. A description of how a weir, goyt and waterwheel system works can be found on page 87.

The Wicker Tilt was demolished in 1901 and replaced by the attractive 'Flemish' style brick building(3) now occupied by Hancock and Lant.

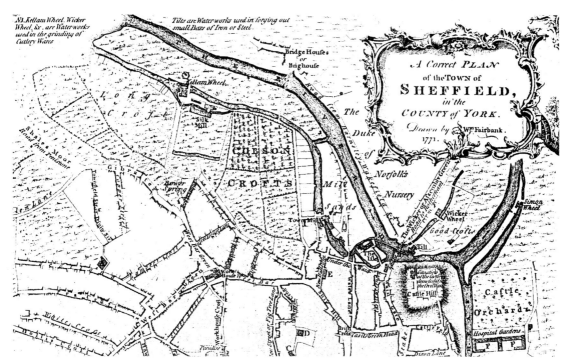

FAIRBANK'S MAP OF SHEFFIELD, 1771. NOTICE THE WICKER TILT AND WHEEL AND THE SIMON WHEEL BEING FED BY A GOYT FROM THE RIVER SHEAF.

It was originally built as a multi-storey stable for the care of the Midland Railway Company's dray horses by an enterprising vet named John Henry Bryars who also developed the two blocks of tenements on either side of the road, known as Royal Exchange and Royal Victoria buildings. Turning into Hancock and Lant's entrance down the side of Royal Exchange Buildings you can see the entrance to the vet's surgery, a doorway decorated with the medical motif of snake and sword, and horseshoes. The horses were stabled on four floors reached by ramps, and the building included a farriers shop

and a sick-bay. During the First World War the stables became home to Lizzy, Tommy Ward's now almost legendary elephant, acquired to replace cart horses commandeered by the army.

In 1928 the building was converted to Batchelor's first canning factory, and as such is reputed to be the birthplace of the mushy pea. The implications for river water quality at this time can only be guessed at.

From Lady's Bridge the Walk heads east along Castlegate. To the right, where Castle Market(4)

SHEFFIELD CASTLE (ARTIST'S IMPRESSION). TO THE LEFT IS LADY'S BRIDGE, ON THE RIGHT THE RIVER SHEAF. WHETHER THE TOPOGRAPHY WOULD HAVE ALLOWED A MOAT TO FLOW FROM ONE RIVER TO THE OTHER AS SHOWN IS DEBATABLE! (REPRODUCED BY KIND PERMISSION OF SHEFFIELD NEWSPAPERS LTD.)

now stands, was the site of Sheffield Castle. The first castle, of a wooden 'motte and bailey' construction, was built around 1150 by William de Lovetot, perhaps the true founder of the town of Sheffield. Standing as it did on a mound between the confluence of the rivers Sheaf and Don, the castle was easily defended and effective in controlling access to the Sheaf and Upper Don valleys.

Thomas de Furnival replaced the wooden castle with one built of stone in about 1270. In later years this was one of the prisons of Mary Queen of Scots, who was held either at the castle, Sheffield Manor or Chatsworth from 1570–1584 by George Talbot, 6th Earl of Shrewsbury, on behalf of Queen Elizabeth I. In 1644, during the English Civil War, the castle was besieged and conquered by a Parliamentary army led by John Bright of Carbrook Hall. The castle's defences proved ineffective against the artillery of the time, and it was subsequently demolished in 1648. All that remains is part of the dungeon and some foundations, now preserved beneath the floor of Castle Market.

Castlegate itself used to be the site of the town's slaughterhouses or 'shambles', built to serve the cattle market on the nearby Wicker. Waste from the slaughterhouses would be dumped straight into the river, adding to the gross industrial pollution of the late 19th century. This situation persisted until the late 1920s when Sheffield's first Labour Council opened the Corporation Abattoir, and Castlegate became the city's first purpose-built section of riverside walk, with some elegant cast-iron railings.

The river flows by Castlegate within a straight and narrow channel which doesn't create the best conditions for wildlife. However, the continuous tumbling of water over the weir stirs up the river bed sediment, and over the years this sediment has steadily settled out of the water to form a long thin island stretching from the weir to Blonk Street Bridge. Plants have been able to colonise this island. Among them is the common riverside tree, crack willow, which would have figured strongly in the pre-industrial landscape of the East End and still occurs frequently on the lower reaches of many water courses in Sheffield today. Despite being broken and contorted into sometimes fantastic shapes this willow is well able to withstand the river in flood, its roots help to prevent erosion of the banks and islands, and it provides good habitat for fish, insects and birds. The slender lower branches often trail in the

water, affording good cover to birds such as mallard and moorhen, but also presenting something of a management dilemma. Solid waste which is thrown into the river frequently gets caught on these branches. Not only does this look unsightly, but in some cases an accumulation of waste can begin to restrict the channel and increase the risk of flooding. If the branches are removed the channel remains clear, but valuable habitat for birds is then lost.

ROYAL EXCHANGE BUILDINGS, LADY'S BRIDGE—A BIT OF BRUGES BY THE DON? (PHOTOGRAPH BY SIMON OGDEN.)

An anonymous painting of the River Sheaf near its confluence with the Don, around 1825. Both the weir and bridge, which spanned the river at the foot of Dixon Lane, still exist within the culverted section of river which passes beneath the Sheaf Market. The conical roof of the old Shrewsbury Hospital is on the extreme left of the picture, standing on the site now occupied by Victioria Quays. On the right can be seen the castle-like walls of the town shambles or slaughterhouses. (Sheffield City Museums.)

Various plants can be seen growing from cracks in the river retaining walls, some of the most common being ferns, Oxford ragwort, and michaelmas daisy. Oxford ragwort was first introduced to this country last century and, being a native of the volcanic slopes of Vesuvius, it really likes disturbed ground, and so it quickly spread from its new home in the Oxford Botanical Garden along railway embankments between Britain's towns. Nowadays it is a common sight on many derelict sites in Sheffield, and it is extremely popular with the red and yellow caterpillars of the cinnabar moth. As well as plants, many dis-used drainpipes can be seen jutting from the walls. These provide very suitable secluded nest sites for kingfishers, a bird now frequently seen on the river (see page 88 for more information on weirs and wildlife).

At the junction of Castlegate and Blonk Street Bridge the River Sheaf(5) can be seen emerging from a tunnel mouth marked 'AD 1916', from where it flows into the Don. Sadly, the Sheaf is culverted all the way upstream from here to Granville Square, passing under the Sheaf Market, Ponds Forge Complex and Midland Railway Station. Before all this culverting, the confluence of the Sheaf and the Porter Brook created a natural floodplain where the railway station now stands, hence the local names Pond Street and Ponds Forge. Despite careful

THE VIEW FROM THE ROYAL VICTORIA HOTEL BACK TOWARDS BLONK STREET BRIDGE IN 1879. IN THE FOREGROUND IS THE SMITHFIELD CATTLE MARKET, IN THE CENTRE IS THE ALEXANDRA THEATRE AND CIRCUS AND THE CASTELLATED TOWN SLAUGHTERHOUSES BETWEEN WHICH FLOWS THE SHEAF. THE TOWER GRINDING WHEEL AND OSBORN'S STEELWORKS CAN BE SEEN ON THE RIGHT HAND BANK OF THE DON. IN THE BACKGROUND (FROM LEFT TO RIGHT) ARE THE CANAL BASIN (NOW VICTORIA QUAYS), THE GAS COMPANY OFFICES, AND THE SPIRES OF ST MARIES CHURCH (NOW CATHEDRAL), THE OLD TOWN HALL (ON WAINGATE) AND SHEFFIELD PARISH CHURCH (NOW CATHEDRAL).

management of river flows in this area, flooding has been known in the recent past.

The former banks of the Sheaf at the foot of what is now Commercial Street were probably the site of an Angle settlement in around 500 AD. The ancient name of this site 'SCEATH-FELD', literally meant field or clearing by the Sheaf, from which the name Sheffield was derived. When

A MORE RECENT VIEW ALONG THE FIVE WEIRS WALK TOWARDS BLONK STREET BRIDGE. THE CASTLE MARKET, ON THE FORMER SITE OF SHEFFIELD CASTLE, IS IN THE BACKGROUND TO THE RIGHT, AS IS THE SPIRE OF THE OLD TOWN HALL. (PHOTOGRAPH BY KEN PHILLIP.)

future redevelopment takes place in this area, it would be nice to think that the Sheaf could be uncovered and put back into the heart of Sheffield.

Blonk Street Bridge(6) was built in 1827 by the Duke of Norfolk, Lord of the Manor, when he decided to move the town's cattle market from its ancient site in the Wicker to the new 'Smithfields'(9), on the southern banks of the Don, now partly occupied by Bristol Hotel and a petrol station. The bridge allowed easy access to the new mart from the north. Up to the middle of this century Smithfields also served as the Town's Fairground.

The Walk continues at the opposite end of Blonk Street Bridge on the other side of the road. Opened in 1994, this section introduces the common features of the Five Weirs Walk, entrance arch, black railings and green name plaques. The site to the left of the path(7) was the location for the old town 'Bailiwick' or Assembly Green, closely associated with the castle. The Bailiwick was used for various purposes including archery matches, military training and witch ducking in the river! Later, it became the site of the Tower Wheel, another castellated pseudo-gothic building which appeared prominently on many 19th-century illustrations of Sheffield. This was an example of the new steam powered cutlery factories, where a number of individual 'little mesters' would hire their workspace and power.

Later the Tower Wheel and the old Wicker Wheel were all incorporated into Shortridges Steelworks, which in turn became Samuel Osborn's Dannemora Works, famous not only for steel but for their prize silver band. As the firm prospered the works overflowed its site and extended crazily on cast iron stilts out into the river.

Shortridge's splendid offices can still be seen on the Wicker, now serving as the African Carribbean Community Centre (SADACCA)(8).

Next door was the Capital Steelworks of Siebohm and Dieckstahl. Henry Siehbohm was an eminent Victorian birdwatcher who travelled the world seeking rare species (usually shooting and stuffing them!). Like other local firms founded by Germans, it fell foul of virulent xenophobia during the First World War and changed its name to that of the then Managing Director, Arthur Balfour.

The river here is wide and shallow as it curves to the north-east and accommodates the extra flow from the Sheaf. Large areas of stony river bed are exposed at times of low flow, and grey wagtails can often be seen flitting across the stones in search of midges and fly larvae to eat. In the summer months this is also a good place to watch house martins sweeping low over the water as they gather insects.

The flood margin between the path and the river is predominantly lined with willow and sycamore. Along the more open stretches however, the vegetation is dominated by two plants recently introduced to this country, Japanese knotweed and Himalayan balsam. As the river has improved over the past twenty years, these two plants have been quick to re-colonise the bare flood margins and banks, at the expense of native plant species. Their vigorous growth and resilience during floods has helped them to dominate large stretches of the riverside in the East End. The success of these and other introduced plant species has led to a mix of plants unlike anything you would see in the countryside. For more information on the effect of introduced plants on the wildlife of the river see page 89.

As well as the balsam and knotweed there are several native plants by this part of the river, including hedge garlic, with white flowers and leaves that smell of garlic when crushed, a plant attractive to the caterpillars of the orange-tip butterfly. Depending on the season, also look out for red campion, forget-me-not, bluebell, ramsons, lesser celandine, wood anemone and great reedmace (bulrush) in the muddy margins.

The end of this section of the walk is marked by the arches of the Wicker Viaduct(10). In 1849

[WICKER VIADUCT, SHEFFIELD.]

THE SHEFFIELD TIMES
AND ROTHERHAM AND
WORKSOP ADVERTISER,
OF SATURDAY, JULY 21ST, 1849,
WILL CONTAIN THE FULLEST PARTICULARS OF THE OPENING OF THE LINE AND THE
PROCEEDINGS AT WORKSOP
CONNECTED WITH THIS EVENT.
Sole AGENT for WORKSOP and the NEIGHBOURHOOD: ROBERT WHITE, PARK STREET.

the Manchester, Sheffield and Lincolnshire Railway extended their line across the Don Valley from Bridgehouses near Kelham Island all the way to Beighton Junction. In so doing they created the stone viaduct which spans the Wicker, the river and the canal, at the time the largest masonry viaduct in Europe.

Victoria Station(11) was built on a section of the viaduct to the south-east of the river in 1851. This station provided through services to London Marylebone until 1960. By 1965 only the service to Manchester via the Woodhead tunnel remained, and when this ceased in 1970 the station was closed, though a rail line still exists as far as Stocksbridge to the north-west.

In 1991 the Grade II listed viaduct was renovated and cleaned.

Completed in 1861 to serve the station, the Royal Victoria Hotel (12) (now a Holiday Inn) and its approach road still stand on the opposite side of the river.

The building of the viaduct and Victoria Station complex removed all traces of what was known as the Simon or Castle Orchards Wheel and dam. This grinding hull had existed in various guises since the early 1700s, and although it stood adjacent to the River Don it actually drew water from a goyt taken from the River Sheaf just above the confluence with the Don. The weir still exists on the last section of the culverted River Sheaf (see maps on pages 15 and 17). From here there is a choice of routes—A or B—until the final section of the Walk is built.

(A) The new Inner Ring Road bridge will take you over the Don to Furnival Road under the Station Approach. Turn left along Furnival Road and pass under the section of the Wicker Viaduct known as the 'Dark Arches'.
Close to the junction with Sussex Street and Effingham Street to the right of Furnival Road stands a chimney stack from a ten-hole crucible furnace(13). This was built around 1914 as part of the Britannia Works, and as such is a fairly late example. The building now houses a brass foundry. Continue along Furnival Road to where you can see the river on your left and the start of section 2 of the Five Weirs Walk (see below).

(B) Alternatively you can follow the river as far as the viaduct and then turn left to reach the Wicker. Follow the arrows on the pavement through the Wicker Arches. The nearest pedestrian arch contains a memorial to Great Central Railway employees who fell in the First World War, this memorial originally stood in Victoria Station. Part of the road arch on the far side has clearly been patched. This is the spot where a bomb hit the arch during the Second World War but fortunately failed to detonate.

Go through the pedestrian arch and along Savile Street. *Note that taking this route will involve missing almost all of section 2 described below, including Walk Mill Weir.*

The stainless steel sculpture(14) at the fork of Savile Street and Spital Hill occupies part of the site of Sheffield's first railway station. Built in 1838 by the Sheffield and Rotherham Railway, the Wicker Station was effectively at the end of a branch line from Rotherham, indicating the town's status at that time. The line itself ran between the Wicker and Rotherham Masborough Station. Indeed, it was the opening of this line which encouraged the first major industrial expansion into the Don Valley and the building of the great steelworks along its route. The station served passengers until the opening of the Midland Station in 1870, surviving from then on as a goods depot until its closure in 1965.

At the fork in the road keep right along Attercliffe Road. The office complex actually in the fork, known as 12 o'Clock Court, takes its name from the site of the 12 o'Clock toll bar and pub. Continue on Attercliffe Road until rejoining the river. Pass under the Midland railway bridge, cross Leveson Street and turn into Warren Street to return to the Five Weirs Walk proper, section 3.

WALK MILL WEIR TO NORFOLK BRIDGE

A 'walk mill' is another term for a fulling mill, meaning to cleanse and thicken cloth by beating or 'walking' it. Cloth-making was the biggest and most widespread industry of Mediaeval England. Walk Mill weir(15) is officially the first of the Five Weirs Walk. The earliest mention of its existence is in the records of the Duke of Norfolk Estates for 1581, which refer to a fulling mill and cutler wheel on the north bank (eventually to be known as Nether Walk Mill and Wheels), but the weir could well be older. By 1780 there was another cutler wheel on this site and a separate wheel had been installed upstream, known as Upper Walk Mill Wheel. By 1846 a bone mill and corn mill had been added

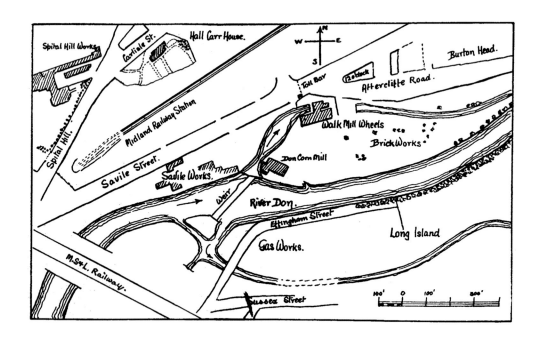

A PLAN OF THE WALK MILLS, BASED ON THE 1853 ORDNANCE SURVEY. NOTE THE 12 O'CLOCK TOLL, THE TWO WHEELS AND THE NEW GAS WORKS ON 'LONG ISLAND'. (REPRODUCED FROM VINE, 1936.)

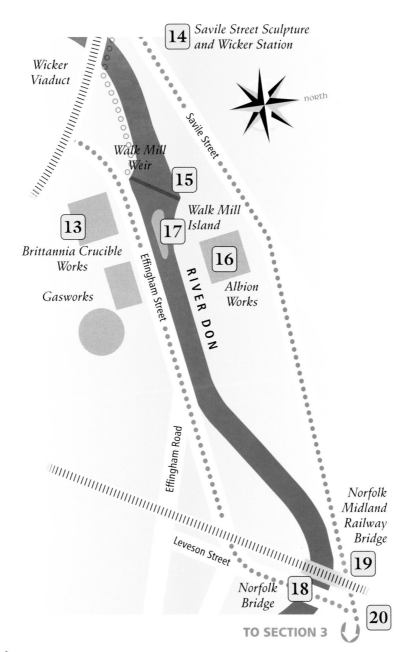

14 Savile Street Sculpture and Wicker Station

Wicker Viaduct

Savile Street

NORTH

Walk Mill Weir

15

13

Brittannia Crucible Works

Gasworks

Effingham Street

Walk Mill Island

17

16

Albion Works

RIVER DON

Effingham Road

Norfolk Midland Railway Bridge

19

Leveson Street

18

Norfolk Bridge

20

TO SECTION 3

 Walk Mill Weir: Portage to be constructed on Right via fishing platform.

to the complex, but by 1853 waterpower had ceased to be used. Shortly after this William Brown built his Albion Iron and Steel Works(16) on the site of the mills, one of the main products being crinoline wire. Perhaps as a result of changes in fashion this venture ended in bankruptcy by 1864.

Other industries followed until Thomas Ward's occupied the Albion Works in 1887. Thomas Ward's successful business ventures included scrap, dismantling, machinery, and roadstone, earning the works the title of 'swap-shop of the world'. The company still carries out some of these businesses in the Albion Works of today,

which can be seen on the opposite bank of the river. Albion House, built in 1901 on Savile Street, once contained panelling and fittings from some of the great ships Tommy Wards had broken up, but these were removed to London when the firm was taken over by RTZ. Albion House is now the headquarters of Sheffield Chamber of Commerce.

All that really remains of the Walk Mills today is the weir itself. There appears to be a blocked head goyt just upstream of the weir in the North bank, and two outfalls downstream which were probably an overflow and the tail goyt for the Upper Mill. There is no trace of the extensive Nether tail goyt.

The long island(17) downstream of the weir is particularly attractive. It supports a range of trees including crack willow, alder, ash and sycamore. The even stand of similar aged trees suggests that they grow well but are periodically wiped out by major

THE PRESENT DAY WALK MILL WEIR. (PHOTOGRAPH BY PAUL GRIFFITHS.)

floods before they reach any great age. None of the trees on the urban River Don are more than 60–70 years old.

Alder is a common waterside tree. In the past its wood was used to make gate posts and the soles of clogs because it didn't warp when it got wet. The roots of the tree contain nodules which gather nitrogen from the air, allowing it to thrive in nutrient poor and damp riverside soils. When the tree dies it releases its stock of nutrients which other plants can then utilise.

Mallard and moorhen are regularly seen on this stretch of river, along with grey wagtail, kingfisher, blue tit and wren, all of which nest in the channel walls. There is usually an abundance of Japanese knotweed just

RIVER DON AND ATTERCLIFFE ROAD LOOKING TOWARDS SHEFFIELD, ABOUT 1819, FROM A STANDPOINT NEAR THE PRESENT DAY NORFOLK BRIDGE. THE VIEW SHOWS THE APPROACH OF HEAVY INDUSTRY FROM SHEFFIELD INTO THE MEADOWS OF THE LOWER DON. ON THE SKYLINE ARE THE OLD TOWN HALL ON WAINGATE, THE PARISH CHURCH (NOW THE ANGLICAN CATHEDRAL) AND THE FORMER ST PAULS CHURCH. (DRAWING BY EDWARD BLORE.)

downstream of the weir, which you may see festooned with the white trumpet-shaped flowers of hedge bindweed if you visit in late summer. These flowers shouldn't be mistaken for the knotweed's own much smaller and stringier looking flowers. A variety of plants grow from cracks in the walls, including foxglove, ferns, ragwort and brambles. Many of the flowering plants provide nectar for insects such as hoverflies. Pondweed and water lilies can often be seen floating in the stiller water just upstream of the weir, especially in dry summers when the flow of water is low.

If the river is flowing strongly there may be a distinct smell of drains rising from the weir. This depends on the amount of sewage that is being discharged directly into the river from stormwater overflows. It is likely that sewage pollution will be reduced further in the future and, as water quality improves, there is evidence that the shallow waters downstream of the weir will support water crowfoot, a plant which creates a spectacular display when in flower.

THE NORFOLK BRIDGE PARAPET WITH INITIALS C.H.
(PHOTOGRAPH BY KEN PHILLIP.)

The river flows alongside Effingham Street in a straight-sided channel, getting steadily deeper and slower as it approaches Norfolk Bridge. The banks are confined on both sides by workshops and roads which offer a limited habitat for wildlife. Where the road forks the river bends slightly to the left. The Walk follows the left fork, but the river is temporarily hidden behind the workshops of the Tempered Spring Company. As you pass under the railway bridge notice the subtle shape of the brickwork in the roof of the arch, a beautiful example of Victorian engineering brickwork.

Through the arch to the right along Leveson Street can be glimpsed the former North Pole pub, now a printers. Originally this was the residence of the master of the Park Iron Works, and stood in a rural setting overlooking a large dam roughly on the triangle now bounded by Foley Street, Effingham Road and the railway. The blast furnaces of the Park Works were a prominent landmark, lighting up the night sky with their lurid flames.

In 1845 the site was taken over by the Davy Engineering Company which made the heavy machinery for other Sheffield steelmakers. Tempered Springs now occupy the old Davy works and a detour up Foley Street will reveal the steep drop into the works yard which probably represents the line of the old dam. Now turn back north along Leveson Street to Norfolk Bridge and Burton Weir.

Norfolk Bridge(18) was opened in March 1856. It was built by the Duke of Norfolk, at a cost of £3,000, to provide access between the growing industrial properties of the Norfolk Estate. Before 1856 there were no river crossing points between Blonk Street and Washford Bridges, so the building of Norfolk Bridge considerably improved transport in the area. In the centre of the ornamental ironwork panels that form the bridge parapets the letters 'CH' can be seen. These stand for Charles Howard, the then Duke of Norfolk. Just in case you have any remaining doubt that he was responsible for the building of the bridge, note the large letter 'N' carved on the outer faces of the stone abutments.

The larger stone arched railway bridge just upstream of Norfolk Bridge(19) was built in 1870 as part of the Midland Line from Tapton Junction (near Chesterfield) to Grimesthorpe Junction in the East End. This line, on which the Midland Station stands, gave Sheffield direct access to London St Pancras. It is now the main line through Sheffield.

On the opposite side of Attercliffe Road is Princess Street(20). It was on this street in 1925 that Jock Plommer was stabbed to death by members of the Garvin Gang or 'Park Brigade', an event which marked the bloody culmination of the Sheffield Gang Wars. A number of gangs were active in Sheffield in the early 1920s, each seeking to maximise their control of the gambling rings that were rife in the city during a period of acute hardship. As the income from gambling grew, so the methods the gangs employed became more brutal. Ironically, the man murdered as part of an intended revenge attack wasn't a member of any of the gangs. It was perhaps this fact that led to a severe police crackdown on the gangs' activities and their subsequent extinction.

At the time of the murder, Princess Street and Sutherland Street were packed with three-storey terraced back-to-backs. Only the former Norfolk Arms, now a café and sauna, recalls this domestic scale.

Cross onto the downstream side of Norfolk Bridge to see Burton Weir and to start the next section of the Walk.

SECTION THREE

NORFOLK BRIDGE TO WASHFORD BRIDGE
(SALMON PASTURES)

From the north end of Norfolk Bridge(19) turn sharp right into Warren Street. The entrance to Salmon Pastures is about 100 metres along on the right, marked by an arch incorporating a stainless steel salmon by David Mayne, donated by Ancon Clark plc. The Walk follows the ancient line of the head goyt from Burton Weir(21) to Royds Mill. The way is lined with discarded grindstones from the bed of the river. The building on the left side of the Walk was first known as Scotia Steel Works and renamed the Crescent Works(22) in 1901, by Walter Spencers, steel and file makers, later Spencer

PLAN OF BURTON WEIR FROM 1853 ORDNANCE SURVEY, REDRAWN BY GEORGE VINE. THE TRIANGULAR PARK IRONWORKS DAM AT BOTTOM LEFT IS ALREADY SILTING UP BUT THE GOYT SUPPLYING ROYDS WORKS AND ROYDS MILLS IS STILL IN USE. ATTERCLIFFE ROAD TURNPIKE IS SHOWN AS SHEFFIELD AND TINSLEY TRUST.

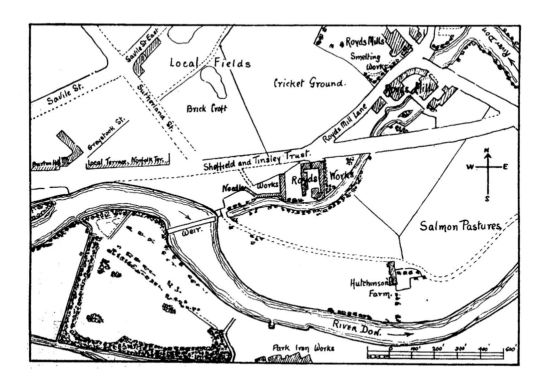

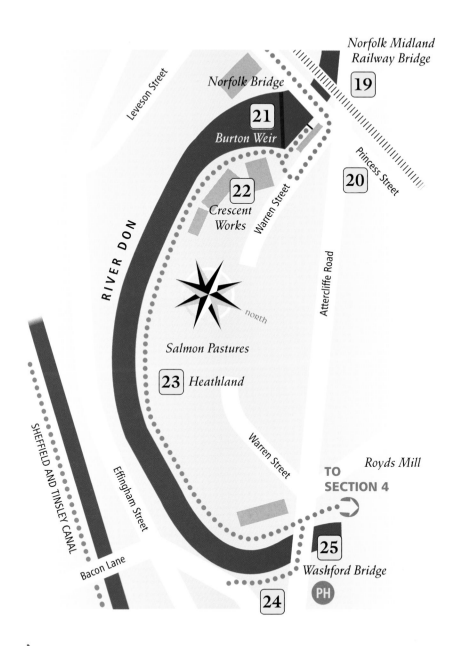

Norfolk Midland
Railway Bridge

19

Norfolk Bridge

21

Burton Weir

Leveson Street

Princess Street

20

Warren Street

Attercliffe Road

22

Crescent
Works

north

Salmon Pastures

23 Heathland

RIVER DON

Warren Street

Royds Mill

TO
SECTION 4

SHEFFIELD AND TINSLEY CANAL

Effingham Street

25

Washford Bridge

PH

Bacon Lane

24

Burton Weir: Portage Left egressing onto fishing platform and
walking to end of railing to relaunch.

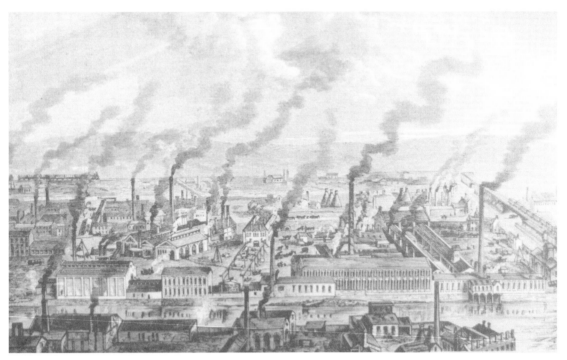

Scotia Works, 1864, showing Burton Weir Goyt, bottom left, Norfolk Bridge and the River across the middle of the picture, and the Park Ironworks on the far bank. Some of these buildings are still visible from the river.

Clarks and finally Ancon Clarks, who now occupy a modern plant nearby. The buildings are now used for an innovative materials recycling operation reusing building refuse.

At the end of the goyt you emerge on top of the weir. To the right is a fishing platform whilst the main walk goes to the left. The view, with the towering factory walls of the Park Iron Works, the noise of metalworking and the roar of the weir remains a classic East Sheffield scene. Burton Weir, the second of the Five Weirs, can be seen with the remains of a sluice gate. Water

from the weir was used to power a corn mill and cutler wheels known as Royds Mill and Wheels, which were located to the north of Attercliffe Road on the site now occupied by The Sheffield Smelting Company (THESSCO), of which more later (see section 4).

Salmon Pastures is probably the most 'natural' looking stretch of river in the East End, which is ironic given the level of industrial activity on both banks over the past 150 years, and the fact that the channel is almost entirely artificial. The island below Burton weir is short and wide, due

(Right) Salmon Pastures from the air in the late 1980s. The river stands out as a distinctive green corridor in an area still heavily industrialised. In the top right of the picture is the now demolished Salmon Pastures School. (Sheffield City Council Planning.)

weir is a favoured spot for mallard and, although it might be hard to imagine, the south-east facing side of Norfolk Bridge is a wonderful place to watch the sun rise on a crisp autumnal or winter morning.

Further along, the works are replaced by a stone wall and then trees. This is the site of the Salmon Pastures Coke Ovens(23) which were run by

(ABOVE) SALMON PASTURES IN 1959, LOOKING DOWNSTREAM BEFORE THE ALTERATION OF THE RIVER CHANNEL. THE SLAG HEAP GENERATED BY THE DUKE OF NORFOLK'S COKE OVENS CAN BE SEEN ON THE LEFT OF THE PICTURE. ON THE RIGHT IS EFFINGHAM ROAD (SHEFFIELD CITY COUNCIL PLANNING) • (BELOW) SALMON PASTURES IN 1960, LOOKING UPSTREAM FROM WASHFORD BRIDGE AFTER THE RESTORATION OF THE RIVER CHANNEL. THE NEWLY PLANTED TREES ON THE LEFT BANK HAVE GROWN CONSIDERABLY IN THE LAST FORTY YEARS. (SHEFFIELD CITY COUNCIL PLANNING.)

to its location on a shallow sweeping bend of the river. It is populated with a good stand of crack willow and sycamore, as well as the inevitable Japanese knotweed. To the north of the weir and just upstream of it, some of the few alders on the Salmon Pastures section can be seen against the buildings. It is hoped that more of this species will be planted as part of the construction of the Walk. The still water above the

ELIZABETH RODES' HOUSE AT WASHFORD BRIDGE, BUILT IN 1671. THE STONE RETAINING WALL WITH ITS SEVERAL STRING COURSES CAN STILL BE SEEN FROM THE WALK. (ILLUSTRATED IN 1877 BY W. TOPHAM.)

the Duke of Norfolk and supplied from his Manor and Nunnery Collieries by a tramway over the river. By the 1940s this was a desolate scene, the north bank was heaped high with slag from the 'beehive' coke ovens, whilst the south bank was a badly eroded soft cliff. In 1959 the City Council bought the slag heap and carried out a realignment of the river to the north. This is the reason why the present river banks are so high and the origin of its present green appearance. All the trees now lining the banks were planted or have self-seeded since 1959.

The mixture of sycamore, willow, alder, poplar, hawthorn and the odd oak supports nests for birds such as wren, greenfinch, robin and bluetit. On the Walk side of the river, the high

amount of cinder remaining from the slag heaps has created an area of acid heath(23), complete with heather and interesting insects. This area is now being colonised by birch trees, which are being managed to prevent the site reverting to woodland.

As you approach Washford Bridge you will see, set into the bank, the stone dedication panel for the former Salmon Pastures School, opened in 1908 and demolished in 1997.

The path on the opposite side of the river just above the bridge is called Don Terrace(24). Occupied by a line of houses until quite recently, this area is the former site of Elizabeth Rodes' house. Elizabeth was a widow and a prosperous 17th-century business-woman who ran the family farm and cutlery businesses (see next section) and built the house for her retirement. The house contained elaborate plaster fireplaces and ceilings similar to those in Carbrook Hall. Later it became the *Fleur de Lys* pub, but sadly was demolished late in the 19th century.

The 1877 illustration of the house shows part of the river retaining wall with string courses. When viewed from the Walk, string courses can be seen about two thirds of the way up the present day retaining wall. If this is the same

WASHFORD BRIDGE WITH WINCOBANK HILL IN THE BACKGROUND. THIS IS THE FIRST STONE BRIDGE, BUILT JUST UPSTREAM OF ELIZABETH RODES' HOUSE IN 1672. A CONTEMPORARY HEAVY GOODS VEHICLE CAN BE SEEN ON THE LEFT.

piece of wall as shown in the illustration, it demonstrates how much the river banks have been raised.

As the name Washford Bridge(25) implies, this was once a point where the river was forded. It is a long established crossing point, lying as it does on the line of an old packhorse, and later turnpike, road. Fording the river here must have been tricky at times of high flow, so it is not surprising that a wooden bridge had been built at least by 1535. The bridge was damaged in a small battle at the start of the Civil War, prior to the siege of the castle in 1644. The first stone bridge was built in 1672, a little upstream of where Elizabeth Rodes' house once stood, possibly where a line of stones can still be made out across the river. It was a narrow bridge, one cart wide with five arches. A second stone bridge was built about 60 metres downstream but this must have also been unsound because it only lasted five years.

The third and present bridge was built in 1794 and widened to accommodate trams in 1880. It consists of three arches of ashlar blocks made

CROZZIL EMPLOYED TO CAP A WALL

from honey coloured sandstone, giving an impressive appearance. The wooden gate in the parapet allowed snow to be shovelled off the road and into the river in the days before grit was employed.

If the river is low, you will be able to pass under the left arch of the bridge and straight onto the next section of the Walk. However, please take care, ensuring that no water is flowing beneath the arch and look out for mud and other debris. An alternative route takes you to a road crossing over the bridge itself.

If you have time, it is worth taking a quick detour to Don Terrace at the opposite end of Washford Bridge. At the far end of the terrace you will find a stone wall topped with 'crozzil'. Made of clay and wheel swarf from cutlers' wheels, crozzil was placed as an airtight crust over 'coffins' of iron and charcoal when making steel in conical cementation furnaces. It baked hard during firing to give the appearance of honey-combed volcanic rock . With some of the material within crozzil having been re-used twice, it is an excellent example of waste minimisation.

The next section of the Walk begins from the west end of Washford Bridge at the junction of Attercliffe Road and Windsor Street. There is also an opportunity to join the Canal Towpath at this point by crossing over Effingham Road and Bacon Lane Bridge (see *Sheffield East End History Trail 1*).

WASHFORD BRIDGE IN THE LATE 1800s. THIS IS THE BRIDGE, BUILT IN 1794, DOWNSTREAM OF ELIZABETH RODES' HOUSE WHICH IS JUST VISIBLE ON THE EXTREME RIGHT OF THE PICTURE.

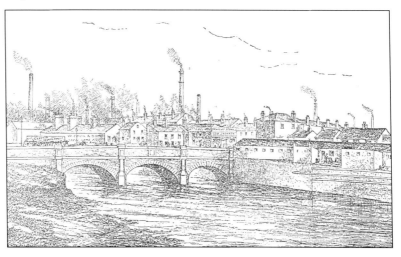

SECTION FOUR

WASHFORD BRIDGE TO EAST COAST ROAD (ROYDS MILL)

Note: For security reasons, this section of the Walk is closed during the hours of darkness.

Windsor Street now forms the entrance to the Sheffield Smelting Company (THESSCO), which occupies the former site of the Royds Mill mentioned in the previous section. The corn mill appears in the Earl of Shrewsbury's accounts as early as 1578 under the name Attercliffe Mill. In the Duke of Norfolk's rental records there are lease entries for John, Richard and widow (Elizabeth) Rodes dated 1604, 1624, and 1637, and it is possibly a corruption of 'Rodes' that led to the name Royds. In 1737 William Burton took out a 21-year lease for the mill and two cutler wheels, and in so doing gave his name to Burton Weir.

The last record of water power being used at Royds Mill was in 1907, but the dam could still be seen from Attercliffe Road in the 1920s and a waterwheel remained on the site until 1950.

In around 1787 John Read moved his silver refining and sweep-smelting business (re-cycling precious metals swept up from the workshop

(TOP) JOHN READ AND ANN READ.
(BOTTOM) WILLIAM WILSON AND HENRY JOSEPH WILSON.

floors and benches) from Green Lane in Sheffield to Royds Mill Farm, possibly to avoid the expense of the 12 o'clock toll bar. The business he started at Royds Mill was the forerunner of today's THESSCO.

From 1843 to 1923 the business was owned and run by the Wilson family, successors to John Read. They were an austere and passionate Congregationalist family, combining success in business with support for radical causes such as

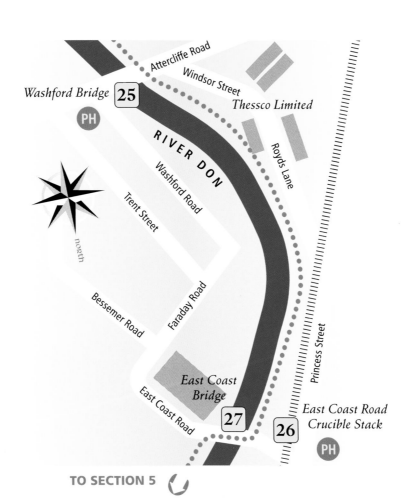

Washford Bridge **25**

PH

Attercliffe Road

Windsor Street

Thessco Limited

RIVER DON

Royds Lane

Washford Road

Trent Street

north

Faraday Road

Bessemer Road

Princess Street

East Coast
Bridge

East Coast Road

27

26

East Coast Road
Crucible Stack

PH

TO SECTION 5

temperance, pacifism, and even paid holidays for their workers! Members of the family were prominent in first the Liberal and later the Labour Party, numbering two MPs and two Lord Mayors among their ranks. As such, they were one part of the wider dissenting tradition in religion and politics in Attercliffe, a tradition which has influenced political life in Sheffield until very recent times (for more information, see *The Attercliffe Village Trail*).

The section of walkway heading downstream from Washford Bridge was built in 1991–1992. Here the river sweeps in a gentle curve from north-west to north-east, and the flow is smooth and slow. The margins of the opposite bank are a good place to look for waterbirds including mallard, moorhen, and little grebe, which have all bred here. In summer, swifts and housemartins can often be seen gliding low over the water as they gather insects. Also look out for grey and pied wagtails and kingfishers.

Some of the most mature and best examples of alder trees on the walk can be seen along this section, together with sycamore, crack and goat willow, and ash. In addition, oak, maple, hawthorn and wild cherry have been planted as part of the walk construction. These are trees that would have featured prominently in the

THE VIEW FROM THE PATH DOWNSTREAM. (SHEFFIELD CITY COUNCIL PLANNING.)

Looking upstream from East Coast Road in 1970 with Arthur Lee's Crown Works on both sides of the river linked by a small bridge. (Sheffield City Council Planning.)

The same stretch of river today, with the walk and fishing platform. (Photograph Simon Ogden.)

pre-industrial environment, but are less likely to regenerate naturally by the present-day riverside. Beneath the trees, common plants to be seen include red campion, garlic mustard, sweet cicely, lady fern, knapweed and yarrow, as well as the inevitable knotweed and balsam.

As you walk along this section notice the stretch of pergola which actually stands on stone filled baskets (gabions) within the river channel. The pergola has proved to be an attractive means of providing security to THESSCO. It is planted with climbers such as honeysuckle, vine and clematis, which have been joined by numerous self-seeding buddleia bushes.

After the pergola, the path runs into a small open section of meadowland which, until the 1970s, was Arthur Lee's wire mill. The flowering plants here help to attract butterflies including orange tip, common blue, meadow brown and wall brown. It is hoped that a careful grass cutting regime will increase the diversity of flowering plants, making the meadow even more attractive to butterflies and insects, the important components of the lower part of the food chain. As well as plants, animals sometimes seen on this section include rabbit, fox, water vole and the much maligned brown rat.

Much of the opposite bank on this section is occupied by scrap metal businesses, which provide an important source of raw material for the modern steel industry. Although it might look messy, this is recycling on a grand scale and, as such, it benefits the environment. The steelworks opposite the wheelchair anglers' platform is the Chantry Works. The railway embankment to the left of the walk carries the 1870 Midland Line again. The stone gateposts marking the end of this section were salvaged from Spear and Jackson's Aetna Works on Savile Street following demolition in 1991. Established in 1840, these makers of saws and tools were one of the first larger companies to move into the East End.

The Walk now emerges onto East Coast Road(27). A quick detour to the left under the railway bridge will reveal an old crucible stack on the building at the junction with Princess Street(26). The main route turns to the right and over the river. This rather functional looking bridge was built in 1898 by the Sheffield and District Railway (a branch of the Lancashire, Derbyshire and East Coast Railway) to provide access to their East Coast Goods Yard, situated at the other end of the bridge on the downstream side. Hence the name East Coast Road, and another reminder that the most important transport links lay to the east.

SECTION FIVE

EAST COAST ROAD TO STEVENSON ROAD (SANDERSON'S WEIR)

In 1990, this was the first stretch of the Five Weirs Walk to be opened. It is also one of the more natural looking stretches of the Walk, with no large buildings or roads in close proximity. The embankment to the right of the path forms the boundary with a large scrapyard. It is constructed in places with rubble filled gabions, with much of the rubble coming from houses demolished on the old Manor Estate. The trees and shrubs planted on the embankment include

A PLAN OF SANDERSON'S WEIR AND ATTERCLIFFE NETHER FORGE IN 1906, BASED ON THE 1906 ORDNANCE SURVEY. (REPRODUCED FROM VINE, 1936.)

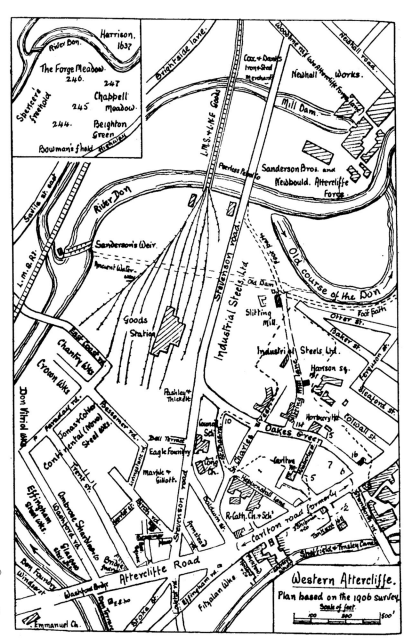

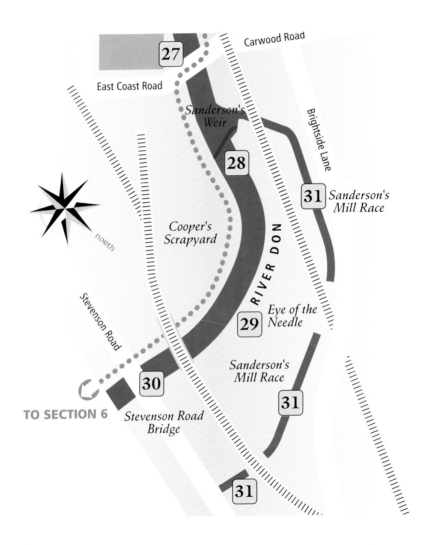

East Coast Road

Carwood Road

27

Sanderson's
Weir

28

Brightside Lane

31 Sanderson's
Mill Race

Cooper's
Scrapyard

R I V E R   D O N

north

29 Eye of the
Needle

Sanderson's
Mill Race

Stevenson Road

30

31

TO SECTION 6

Stevenson Road
Bridge

31

Sanderson's Weir: Portage Right, via fishing path and relaunching from foreshore below weir.

oak, ash, holly, hawthorn, wild cherry and maple. The riverbank to the left of the path is occupied by the familiar willow and sycamore along with a number of young alder trees and several clumps of rushes. Considerable amounts of sediment have been deposited at this point to make a wide flood margin. The lower path beneath the railings provides good access for anglers.

A little further on, the path reaches the broad sweep of Sanderson's Weir(28). The first weir at this location was built in the 1580s by George Talbot, the 6th Earl of Shrewsbury—perhaps best known as the husband of Bess of Hardwick and the gaoler of Mary, Queen of Scots from 1570–1584. George Talbot died in 1590 and is buried in Sheffield's Anglican Cathedral.

The weir powered two sets of works, known as the Upper and Nether Attercliffe Forges (or Hammers) arguably the first of Attercliffe's 'works'. The Upper Forge, which was the smaller of the two, was situated on the south side of the river, just to the west of where Stevenson Road now runs. In 1618 it became part of the Copley ironworks, the same Copleys that would later provide officers for Cromwell's army during the English Civil War of the 1640s. In the late 17th century the forge passed into the ownership of the Simpson–Heyford–Barlow partnership, in which John Fell was a clerk. It was to be his son, John Fell Jnr, who eventually took over the forge and built Attercliffe New Hall, of which more in the next section.

The output of the Upper Forge was often poor compared to its Nether partner, and in 1696 it actually closed for a time. It re-opened in 1715 as a cutler wheel, and was converted to a slitting

George Talbot's tomb in Sheffield Cathedral. (Drawing by Norah Rogerson.)

SANDERSON'S WEIR WAS RENEWED IN 1825, BUILT IN SANDSTONE WITH PANELS OF FURNACE SLAG. (PHOTOGRAPH BY KEN PHILLIP.)

mill in 1746 (slitting is the process of rolling thin strips of steel out of large bars). In 1775 the lease for the mill passed to Richard Swallow, an adopted family member of the Fells and another resident of the New Hall. Despite changes in use, profitability continued to be poor in relation to the Nether Forge, leading to abandonment, neglect and the filling in of the goyt and dam by 1818. The nearby Slitting Mill Lane is now the only reminder of its former existence.

Later, the site of the Upper Forge became the Old Forge Ground, home of Attercliffe Football Club. This was one of the leading clubs during the 1870s and 1880s before professionalism took over. 'Star' names from the club include W.F. Beardshaw of the Baltic Works, a co-founder of Sheffield United; and George and Tommy Crawshaw, the latter going on to play for Sheffield Wednesday and England, 1894–1908. The ground closed in the late 1890s to make way for the Sheffield and District Railway's East Coast Goods Yard, which was mentioned at the end of section 4.

The Nether Forge was situated to the north of the river, just upstream of the present day Newhall Road. Again, this forge was established by George Talbot, who proved to be a leading industrialist of the late 16th century with interests in iron, coal and lead as well as imprisoning monarchs. Having twice the

CONSTRUCTION OF THE WALK 1989. (PHOTOGRAPH SIMON OGDEN.)

capacity of its Upper counterpart, the Nether Forge was also leased by the Copleys in 1618, the Simpson–Heyford–Barlow partnership in 1683 (later dominated by the Fells and linked to the Spencer Ironworks), and Richard Swallow in 1775. In 1822 the forge was assigned to Naylor and Sanderson, they rebuilt the weir that stands today in 1825 and gave it the name Sanderson's Weir. It was this partnership that was the forerunner of the present day Sanderson Kayser Works (of which more in the next section).

The use of water power was recorded until 1895, and the weir and Nether Forge head goyt both remain today. Built from a curving framework of gritstone blocks over which the water flows smoothly, the face of the weir is infilled with lumps of furnace slag which, at times of moderate flow, causes the water to bounce and froth creating an attractive effect. The head goyt branches off from the opposite side of the weir, running east between the railway and Brightside Lane as far as Stevenson Road. From here the water enters a culverted drain leading under Sanderson Kayser Steelworks and back into the river.

Because the flow of water in the goyt is regulated, it is more like a long pond with an environment quite distinct from the river. Plants on the goyt include water plantain, common spike rush, iris, gipsywort, angelica and michaelmas daisy. Dragonflies and damsel flies are common in the summer, probably breeding here as well as in the nearby canal. Some 28 species of hoverfly have also been recorded. Downstream of Sanderson's Weir the island and stretch of shallow, choppy water is quite extensive. Once more, the familiar birds to look for are mallard, moorhen and grey wagtail. If water quality improves further and the insect population increases, this might prove a good site for the return of the dipper to the urban Don. Due to the absence of a retaining wall on

THE EYE OF THE NEEDLE AND SWEEPING BIRCHES BY DAVID NASH.

the path side of the river, the floodplain at this point is relatively wide. Sediment is constantly being stripped and redeposited along this floodplain, resulting in a variety of plants. Flowers such as red campion, cow parsley, celandine, wood anemone, garlic mustard, vetch, forget-me-not, birds-foot trefoil, buttercup, michaelmas daisy and gorse can all be seen here, depending on the time of year. All of these flowers are progressively crowded out by Japanese knotweed and Himalayan balsam as the season progresses. The familiar waterside trees have been supplemented by the planting of ceremonial oaks to mark the opening of the Walk.

Regular clean-ups now take place to maintain this stretch of riverside. Large amounts of junk have been cleared, including chairs, tyres, steel shafts and even half a car lodged in a willow tree. This demonstrates the unique and challenging nature of urban river conservation.

To the right of the Walk, you might notice a large wooden structure within Cooper's Scrapyard. This is a 'tupping pit', used for breaking up cast iron with a large steel ball. It was built by the Trust in order to prevent shrapnel being thrown over the Walk and river. A little further along is a state of the art

CHILDREN AT SANDERSON'S MILL RACE ECOLO PARK. (PHOTOGRAPH SIMON OGDEN.)

'fragmentiser', this reduces scrap cars to neat little piles of their constituent materials.

Before reaching the railway bridge, look out for the viewing point for the 'Eye of the Needle and Sweeping Birches' sculpture by David Nash, which is sited on the opposite bank(29). Erected in 1992, the needle itself was formed by carving and charring a thirty foot fallen oak from Ecclesall Woods in the south-west of the city. The principal tool for this sculpture wasn't a chisel but a chainsaw. In the words of the sculptor, the needle is meant to 'recall images from the surrounding environment, notably the fast disappearing industrial chimneys'. Birch trees have been planted around the needle. As they reach up they will become the dominant sculptural form. The centrepiece will change in scale, and, 'ironically preserved through burning, will form a still centre around which the rest of the world will change and grow'. Perhaps a fitting image of how the East End as a whole is regenerating.

The viewing point for the sculpture is a large metal plug weighing some ten tonnes, which may once have been the anvil of a large drop hammer. The sculptor found the plug blocking the site entrance on the opposite side of the river, and had it moved to its present position. Watch out for further pieces of art along the Walk, which will develop into a public art trail to be featured in a separate leaflet in the future.

The area behind the sculpture is Sanderson's Mill Race Ecology Park. Formerly a railway siding, the cinder in the soil of the park supports only sparse grass cover so allowing a variety of other plants to grow including soapwort, michaelmas daisy, common centaury, toadflax, great and rosebay willowherb. All these plants offer a good source of nectar and pollen which supports a diverse community of insects. The site is noted in particular for cinnabar and six-spot burnet moths. Trees such as birch and willow are slowly colonising the park along with numerous buddleia bushes—much loved by butterflies. Rabbits are regularly seen in the semi-light of dawn or dusk, and one of the more unusual sightings in the park is of a red-legged partridge.

The Ecology Park is a valuable educational resource in an area not noted for easy access to outdoor environmental education. It will help children who visit the park to understand how food webs work, how a site can change through time, and how people have an impact on their environment.

After the Eye of the Needle the path passes beneath the brick arch of a railway bridge, built in 1898 to serve the East Coast Railway goods yard. A line still connects Cooper's scrapyard with the main railway line at the end of Newhall Road because the yard has a contract to scrap old rolling stock. Stevenson Road Bridge (30), which marks the end of this section, was built by the Sheffield and District Railway at the same time as the adjacent railway bridge and goods yard.

The Walk continues straight over the road, but a detour of around 100 metres to the left will enable you to view part of the Nether Forge head goyt (31) as it disappears into Sanderson Kayser steelworks. The forge dam is now covered and filled in apart from a culverted drain, although its outline can be roughly traced on three sides by buildings. The goyt, or mill race, is much higher than the river and has an entirely different character—more like a canal.

SECTION SIX

STEVENSON ROAD TO NEWHALL ROAD
(HECLA AND ATTERCLIFFE CEMETERY)

The next two sections have a very different character. Starting between the river and Avesta alloy steelworks, the Hecla section quickly runs into an open area of redeveloped land(33). Away to the right and partially hidden behind brick and concrete retaining walls, it is possible to trace the line of a shallow sandstone cliff. This is the cliff from which Attercliffe, a corruption of

CHRIST CHURCH, ATTERCLIFFE, C.1845. THIS VIEW SHOWS THE OLD COURSE OF THE DON, AND DEMONSTRATES HOW MUCH LOWER THE BANKS WERE BEFORE INDUSTRIALISATION. (PAINTING BY I. SHAW, SHEFFIELD CITY MUSEUMS.)

Stevenson Road
Bridge

Hecla Site

33

Site of
Christ Church

35

Attercliffe Steel Works

32

Stevenson Road

RIVER DON

34

Attercliffe Cemetery

Liverpool Road

Newhall Road

New Hall Bridge **36**

TO SECTION 7

north

'at the cliff', probably derives its name. The original course of the river used to sweep in a wide bend at the base of the cliff. In 1884, the Norfolk Estate diverted and confined the river to its present course in order to create a site on which Robert Hadfield could expand his Hecla Works (named after an Icelandic Volcano), producing steel castings.

Robert Hadfield, the son of an Attercliffe vestry clerk of the same name, was born at nearby

Attercliffe Hill Top Vestry Hall in 1858. He served a brief apprenticeship at Jonas and Colver before joining his father's new steel making business as a metallurgist. He was only 24 when he discovered manganese steel, a tough, durable, non-magnetic alloy or 'special' steel, which became the foundation of Hadfield's (and Sheffield's) modern 'special steels' reputation. Of all the major names in steel making, Robert Hadfield was the only one born in the heart of the East End. He died in 1940, shortly after

gaining the freedom of the City.

The Hecla works closed in the 1980s, and the derelict part of the site was reclaimed by the Sheffield Development Corporation in 1992, creating this section of the walk in the process. The front offices of the Hecla Works can still be seen on New Hall Road.

The tight confinement of the river on both sides makes this one of the less interesting stretches for wildlife beyond the species most commonly encountered. However, the high retaining wall on the Walk side offers some potential for secluded nesting sites for birds such as the kingfisher. As the newly planted trees and shrubs mature this section will take on a somewhat softer feel.

The opposite bank is the former site of the Attercliffe Nether Forge(32). It is still the home of the Sanderson Kayser works, the oldest iron and steelmaking business in the East End.

This works was the first to export steel to the United States and such an example of global enterprise earned the company a mention in Karl Marx's 'Das Kapital'. None of the original forge buildings remain, and the Newhall Road frontage has recently been partly rebuilt and landscaped. About 25 metres upstream of Newhall Bridge it is possible to make out some stone arches in the retaining

CHRIST CHURCH CEMETERY, WITH THE RIVER AND SANDERSON KAYSER IN THE BACKGROUND BEFORE CONSTRUCTION OF THE WALK. (PHOTOGRAPH BY PAUL GRIFFITHS.)

SANDERSON'S ATTERCLIFFE WORKS IN THE MID-NINETEENTH CENTURY SHOWING TAIL GOYTS AND DISTINCTIVE STONE WALLS WHICH CAN STILL BE SEEN. REPRODUCED FROM THE 'HOUSE OF SABEN', SANDERSON'S OWN WORKS MAGAZINE.

wall, these being the points where the old tail goyts used to discharge into the river.

Before progressing to Newhall Bridge it is worth having a look around Attercliffe Cemetery(34), which can be reached by following the path leading to the right near the interpretive board. Note the World War Two brick pill box at the entrance to the cemetery, which was used to guard the Hecla site at a time when it was heavily engaged in secret munitions work.

The cemetery was opened in 1859. Depending on your personal preference, or the weather, it

might be described as either peaceful or desolate. It is certainly a place of calm within a busy valley. Some of the headstone inscriptions reflect the harsh conditions and high infant mortality rates of the last century. Attercliffe Cemetery is quite small and, not surprisingly, a new cemetery had opened by 1882 at Tinsley Park.

The headstones, being finely carved and exposed to the elements, display the corrosive effects of acid rain which is brought about by fossil fuel burning, mainly in vehicles rather than factories nowadays. The soil here is also acidic and

NEWHALL BRIDGE IN 1961, LOOKING DOWNSTREAM FROM WHERE THE FIVE WEIRS WALK NOW RUNS. (SHEFFIELD CITY COUNCIL PLANNING.)

nutrient poor, which explains why some of the planted trees seem a little stunted. The top end of the cemetery leads into the churchyard, where the paving marks the former site of Christ Church(35). Consecrated in 1826, Christ Church replaced Hill Top Chapel as the principal Anglican place of worship in Attercliffe. It was built in response to growing non-conformism, rising population and Parliament's desire that the established church be less complacent in terms of church attendance, which was only around 10% at the time. The foundation stone was laid by the Duke of Norfolk in 1822, and James Montgomery, a radical journalist and later a hymn writer and poet, wrote a hymn to mark the occasion. He used to take long walks by the Don with the Attercliffe writer Barbara Hoole (nee Wreakes), so Five Weirs Walkers aren't the first to be inspired by the river.

Funding for Christ Church came from the 'Million Pound Act', denoting the amount voted by parliament to build Anglican churches throughout the country. Sheffield got four new churches from this act, the other three being St George's, Brook Hill (1825), St Philip's, Infirmary Road (1828) and St Mary's, Bramall Lane (1830). All were built in a similar Neo-Gothic style, so although both St Philip's and Christ Church were sadly destroyed by bombing in the Second World War, the remaining two give some idea of how Christ Church must have dominated its site on 'the cliff'.

The churchyard is within easy reach of shops, pubs and public transport on Attercliffe Road if you wish to break your journey at this point. The canal is also within ten minutes walk. (See Trails 1 and 2 on the Canal and Attercliffe Village.)

A return to the Five Weirs Walk brings you to an old lane, Liverpool Road, closed by Hadfield's for security but now reopened. Two small stone carvings can be seen here by Graeme Mitcheson and by Melanie Buckley. Just downstream is Newhall Bridge(36). The first bridge here was probably built around 1780 by Richard Swallow, resident of Attercliffe New Hall (covered in the next section) and owner of the Attercliffe Forges. At this time the bridge was named Swallow Bridge, and it acted as a link between separate parts of the New Hall grounds and Attercliffe Forge Lane as the northern part of New Hall Road was then known.

The expansion of industry and increased traffic meant that a new bridge was badly needed by the 1880s. Work commenced in 1888, at which point the design of the bridge was altered to allow for the passage of barges beneath it. This alteration was the result of a proposal for a large inland port between East Coast Road and Newhall Road, which would be the terminus of a Sheffield Ship Canal from Hull. The Ship Canal never materialised but Newhall Bridge was still built to the altered design. This explains the large iron cross members which support the road deck from above as opposed to

THE WATER POWERED FORGE AT SANDERSON'S WORKS, 1840S.

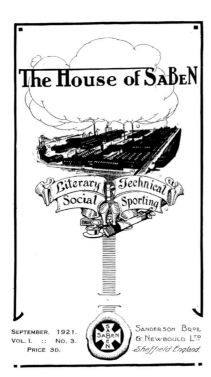

SANDERSON BROS. AND NEWBOLD STAFF MAGAZINE, 1921, SHOWING THE NEWHALL WORKS AND RIVER DON.

a more traditional arch construction. The massive stone abutments are hollow to accommodate the ends of the iron cross members. Notice the carved shields on the abutments which remain, strangely, undecorated. Perhaps they were to have carried the arms of the new canal company.

The Walk continues at the far end of the bridge on the other side of the road.

NEWHALL ROAD TO ABYSSINIA BRIDGE (NEW HALL)

This section of the walk was mainly built in 1993–94 as part of a Sheffield Development Corporation land reclamation scheme, and was officially opened in the summer of 1995. It follows the straightest stretch of river in the East End, almost completely contained within a stone and brick channel.

Attercliffe New Hall(37) once stood around 200 metres to the left of the Walk at this point, the south-west corner would have been where Castor Road runs today. The Hall was built in about 1728 by John Fell Jnr, son of the John Fell who started as a clerk at the Attercliffe Forges and eventually came to own them. It was a 40 metre long mansion with lawns sweeping down to the tree-lined riverside, presenting a somewhat different scene to that of today. It was called New Hall to distinguish it from the 'Old Hall' which stood in Attercliffe village itself (see Trail 2).

After John Fell died, in 1762, the forges were managed by Richard Swallow who later inherited New Hall. In turn, his son let it to

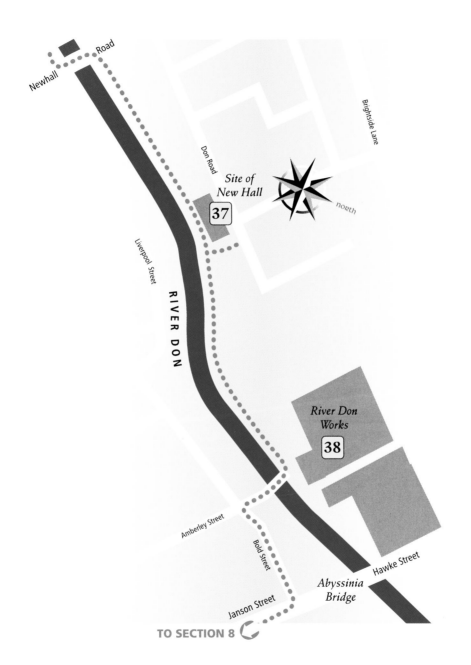

Newhall

Road

Don Road

Liverpool Street

RIVER DON

Site of
New Hall

37

north

Brightside Lane

River Don
Works

38

Amberley Street

Bold Street

Hawke Street

Abyssinia
Bridge

Janson Street

TO SECTION 8

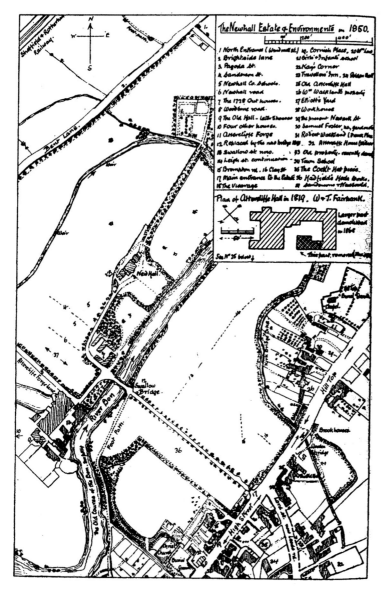

The Newhall Estate and surrounding area, c.1850. Notice the Kirk Bridge Dyke on the right of the illustration and New Hall Road shown as a tree-lined avenue up to Attercliffe Road.

John Sanderson, thus keeping the link between the hall and the forges. When Sanderson died in 1862 the estate was sold off. It became a hotel and amusement park, incorporating a cricket ground, bowling green, race course, maze, lawns and walks. Many events were hosted, including hot air ballooning, firework displays and concerts.

The Newhall pleasure grounds were also a venue for athletics, mainly running and 'ped', short for pedestrianism, a mixture of running and walking which was very popular in the 1870s–80s. Sheffield's champion athlete, George Littlewood, won his first 100 yard sprint at Newhall, aged 9, before going on to make his name as a 'ped'. Unfortunately, ped sport became associated with gambling and organised crime, and combatting this link was one factor which led to the creation of the Amateur Athletics Association.

By the 1880s the mansion had been demolished and the pleasure grounds then gave way to streets of terraced houses and the Newhall Ironworks. However, the brief existence of the grounds demonstrates that there is nothing new about sporting and leisure activity in Attercliffe.

Part of the opposite bank of the river to New Hall was occupied in the mid 1800s by Edward Rhodes' market garden, apparently famed above all for its rhubarb. One of George Littlewood's uncles was a keeper of the garden. It was eventually built over by streets of terraced houses. Another notable sight to the south of the river at this point was a windmill. Until the coming of heavy industry and the streets of houses, Attercliffe Common would have been quite open, a good site for windmills. A reminder of the mill's former presence was provided in the naming of a street off Brightside Lane to the north, but Windmill Street has also disappeared during the course of more recent redevelopments.

ABYSSINIA FOOTBRIDGE IN THE LATE 19TH CENTURY. THIS WAS THE SECOND BRIDGE ON THE SITE, REPLACED BY THE CURRENT ROAD BRIDGE IN 1908, WHICH ITSELF HAS BEEN RECENTLY WIDENED TO ACCOMMODATE THE NEW LINK ROAD. (REPRODUCED BY KIND PERMISSION OF MIKE TAYLOR.)

(TOP) THE RIVER DON IN THE EARLY 1970S. LOOKING DOWNSTREAM FROM NEW HALL BRIDGE ON THE LEFT IS NEW HALL IRONWORKS AND THE TERRACED HOUSES OF DON PLACE, ORDNANCE PLACE, AND PAGODA STREET. (BOTTOM) THE SAME VIEW TODAY. OF THE BUILDINGS, ONLY RIVER DON WORKS SURVIVES FROM THE PREVIOUS SCENE.

Vickers River Don Works(38) (later to become English, then British Steel Corporation, then Sheffield Forgemasters) used to own some 4,500 houses in the area bounded by Attercliffe Common, Weedon Street, Brightside Lane and Newhall Road. During the 1960s and 70s, the general policy was to demolish houses in the East End in order to create a purely industrial zone, the residents being dispersed to newer housing estates in the suburbs. Ironically, after the houses were cleared, much of the steel industry collapsed, leaving large areas of derelict land until the regeneration of the late '80s and the '90s. The New Hall area has now been almost entirely rebuilt for industry. Two more stone sculptures can be seen here, by Toni Whiteside and by Carol Hirsop.

In general, this isn't a section of notable value to wildlife, due mainly to the straightening and containment of the river. There is a scattering of willow, alder and sycamore, offering some cover to mallard and moorhen. Look out for a solitary fig tree on the walk side of the river opposite the path leading to Don Road (for more information on how this exotic species came to populate the Don see page 83). If you spot the fig tree, also try to spot where the Kirkbridge Dyke flows into the river on the opposite bank. The course of this small stream, which originates on the Manor Park estate and flows through Darnall, has been almost completely covered by urban developments.

A little further along, the Walk crosses the river on a specially constructed footbridge. About 200 metres downstream of the footbridge is the road bridge that carries Janson Street over the river.

This is Abyssinia Bridge, which until 1907 existed only as a small footbridge. Then Vickers Sons and Maxim, owners of the River Don Works just downstream (of which more in the next section), had the present bridge built, presumably to facilitate their expansion onto the south side of the river. The bridge has recently been widened to accommodate the new Don Valley Link Road. It is not clear why the bridge has such a strange name. In 1868 a massive expedition was launched from India, comprising 14000 troops under the command of General Napier, in order to rescue British hostages held by the Abyssinian Emperor since 1862. Although it was a complete success the cost of the expedition was huge even by Victorian standards, some £9 million, and it had a significant political impact at the time. It is interesting that Vickers moved to the River Don site in 1867, just as the Abyssinian Campaign was reaching its climax.

At the end of the footbridge turn left along the road towards Janson Street. The area between Janson Street and Amberly Street was the former site of a Naval Ordnance Depot. The presence of this depot reflected Sheffield's major role in the production of naval guns, shells and armour plate from the mid 19th century onwards. A ship's figurehead used to adorn the building's entrance, but when the depot closed the MoD moved the figurehead to Bath. The site is now occupied by new offices built for the Freemans group of companies. There are proposals to build on the south side of the river here—if this happens, you might find that a new part of the Walk follows the river bank.

Upon reaching Janson Street the route bears right and has to leave the river for a short stretch. This is because Sheffield Forgemasters occupies both banks of the river and access is not possible for safety reasons. The route is marked by painted symbols on the pavement and parts of it have a separate cycle route in red tarmac.

THE VICKERS BROTHERS - (LEFT) COLONEL TOM AND (RIGHT) 'DON ALBERTO'.

ATTERCLIFFE COMMON—100 YEARS AGO.

ATTERCLIFFE COMMON IN THE LATE 1700S, SHOWING CARBROOK HALL IN THE CENTRE BACKGROUND AND THE GIBBETED BODY OF SPENCE BROUGHTON IN THE RIGHT FOREGROUND. (REPRODUCED FROM 'SHEFFIELD ILLUSTRATED', 1886, COURTESY OF SHEFFIELD CITY MUSEUMS.)

SECTION EIGHT

ABYSSINIA BRIDGE TO WEEDON STREET (CARBROOK)

Sheffield Forgemasters(38) is a super amalgamation of great names in Sheffield steelmaking. As mentioned in the previous section, the Vickers River Don works were established by about 1867 and grew rapidly, having 300 crucible melting holes by the 1870s. Major armour plate and artillery production followed in the 1880s and, with the acquisition of the Maxim Gun Company and shipyards at Barrow, the company became one of the first 'multi-nationals'. In 1928 the steel interests of Vickers, Armstrong and Cammel Laird were amalgamated to become the English Steel Corporation. This became part of the British Steel Corporation in the late 1960s.

Following privatisation in the early 1980s amalgamation of forging interests with Firth Brown led to the creation of Sheffield Forgemasters both here, at River Don, and on Savile Street. More recently, Forgemasters

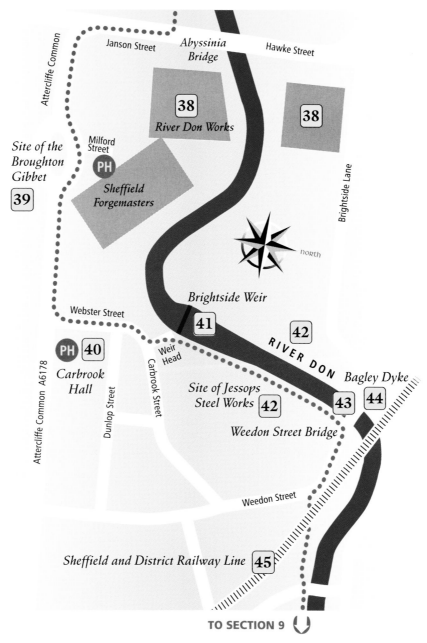

Attercliffe Common

Janson Street

Abyssinia Bridge

Hawke Street

38

River Don Works

38

Milford Street

Brightside Lane

PH

Site of the Broughton Gibbet

39

Sheffield Forgemasters

north

Brightside Weir

Webster Street

41

42

RIVER DON

Weir Head

PH 40

Carbrook Hall

Bagley Dyke

Attercliffe Common A6178

Dunlop Street

Carbrook Street

Site of Jessops Steel Works 42

43

44

Weedon Street Bridge

Weedon Street

Sheffield and District Railway Line 45

TO SECTION 9

 Brightside Weir: Portage left on private river bank, relaunching below weir.

became embroiled in the Iraqi Supergun affair. What were thought to be lengths of oil pipe for export to Iraq apparently turned out to be sections of a huge gun barrel. Quite ironic for a company whose predecessors were renowned for armaments manufacture.

gun jacket. The body of one man was apparently found in the rafters of the roof.

At the large roundabout at the end of Janson Street the Walk bears left onto Attercliffe Common. You may notice the more open feel of

CARBROOK HALL IN 1819, AN ENGRAVING BY E. BLORE SHOWING THE HALF-TIMBERED SECTION LATER DEMOLISHED. (SHEFFIELD ARTS AND MUSEUMS DEPARTMENT.)

The melting and casting of metal was a hazardous occupation and, in 1887, Vickers was the scene of one of the worst accidents in Sheffield steelmaking. Nine men died and several were seriously injured when a mould of molten metal exploded during the casting of a

the landscape here, particularly if the wind is blowing through the valley, also the effect of gaining even a small amount of altitude is appreciated if you turn to look back at the city centre. Until the late 19th century and increased urban development, Attercliffe Common was a

CARBROOK HALL IN 1910.

wide open area of common grazing through which the Car Brook flowed to the Don. This rural tradition seems to have lingered, for pig styes still existed off Milford Street until the late 1970s.

On the opposite side of the roundabout stands Carbrook School. Built in 1874, this was one of the earliest schools provided by the Sheffield Schools Board. Now it is a jazzy sports bar, called the Players Café, a transformation undreamed of by generations of teachers and children. Just behind the school is one of the East End's newer developments, the Don Valley Arena. Opened in 1991, the Arena is now established as one of the country's top concert

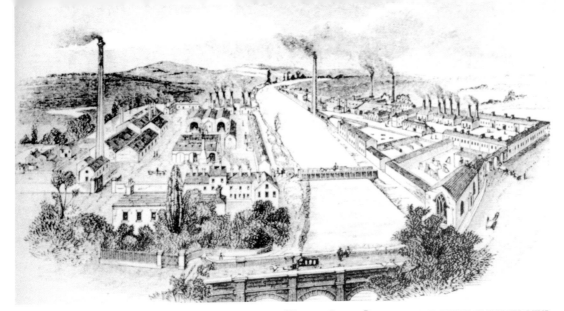

JESSOP'S BRIGHTSIDE WORKS IN 1862. IN THE FOREGROUND IS WEEDON STREET BRIDGE, BEYOND WHICH CAN BE SEEN THE MANAGER'S HOUSE AND GARDEN, AND WEIRHEAD RUNNING ALONGSIDE THE LEFT BANK OF THE DON.

venues and the home of Sheffield Steelers Ice Hockey team, representing another diversification of the sporting traditions of the valley.

A little way down Attercliffe Common is the junction with Broughton Lane, perhaps the only street in Sheffield to be named after an outlaw, Spence Broughton, whose body was hung in chains here(39) (see Trail 1).

The route continues along Attercliffe Common until it reaches the Carbrook Hall public house(40) on the left. Redevelopment along this stretch of the Don Valley Link road has incorporated space for lines of pleached lime trees, after the 17th-century fashion, which should mature into attractive avenues.

Much of the present day Carbrook Hall was built in approximately 1623 and, as such, it can claim to be the oldest surviving building in the East End. The original structure incorporated a half-timbered section, but this was replaced in the 18th century. Along with Attercliffe Old and New Halls, Carbrook was one of the valley's big manor houses. In 1623 it was in the ownership of Thomas Bright. His sons, Stephen and John, were involved in the building of Hill Top Chapel in 1629 (see Trail 1). Stephen's son, another John, took over the estate and became a leading Parliamentarian during the English Civil War of 1642–49. He was a Colonel in Cromwell's army at the decisive battle of Marston Moor in July 1644, and later that year he became Governor of Sheffield Castle following its surrender by the Royalists. Carbrook Hall had numerous owners before becoming a public house some time during the 19th century. Whether you are thirsty or not, the interior warrants examination, particularly the oak-panelled parlour dating from 1623. The Hall is now a grade II listed building. It claims to be the most haunted pub in Sheffield—though whether this is by ghosts or regulars is not certain.

The Walk turns left past Carbrook Hall along a cycleway to Carbrook Hall Road, then along Dunlop Street and immediately right onto

BRIGHTSIDE WEIR TODAY. (PHOTOGRAPH BY KEN PHILLIP.)

Carbrook Street. A little further on turn left up the walled alley called 'Weir Head'. This is the beginning of an old stretch of riverside walkway that pre-dates the enclosures and survived the industrial revolution. It was refurbished and widened by the Sheffield Development Corporation in 1997.

The Walk turns sharp right a few metres along Weir Head to emerge by the river at Brightside Weir(41). This is the fourth of the five weirs, and probably the largest. There has been a weir at this point since at least 1328, when Thomas de Furnival owned a corn mill situated just downstream on the opposite bank. This mill was joined by an adjacent cutler wheel in the late 15th century. The corn mill last appears in a lease of 1690. By 1706 two more grinding wheels had been added to the site. However, by 1789 all these wheels had been replaced by iron forges.

The Brightside Tilt, or Upper Forge, first appeared around 1738. An 80-year association with the Booths then saw major expansion of Brightside into a large works. In 1753 a head goyt was taken off the south side of the weir to supply a slitting mill which was situated adjacent to the present day Weedon Street. This later became the Lower Forge. Booths took the works freehold from the Norfolk Estate in 1814, until it was sold to Jessop and Co. in the mid 1840s. Use of water power then declined and ceased before 1900. The weir(41) and a heavy cast iron sluice visible from the viewing platform are all that visibly remains of the Brightside Forges, although one of the old Brightside tilt hammers is preserved outside Abbeydale Industrial Museum.

Further downstream you will notice vacant land on both sides of the river, which is steadily being reclaimed and redeveloped. This is the former site of Jessop's Brightside steelworks(42). The firm William Jessop and Co. originated at Blast Lane in the late 1700s, where they were one of the first crucible steel manufacturers. William himself reformed the business in around 1825 and took his two sons into partnership. One of these sons, Thomas, was instrumental in the move to Brightside and the firm's subsequent expansion, achieved partly through exports to America. By 1875 the works occupied some 30 acres and employed around a thousand people.

Thomas donated the money for the building of the Jessop Hospital for women. Costing £26,000 and opened in 1878, it still exists as a maternity hospital today (the writer of this guide was born there!).

In 1863 Thomas Jessop was both Lord Mayor and Master Cutler, a sign of his stature within the city. He died in 1887. The firm continued until 1959 when it merged with J.J. Saville and Co. to form Jessop Saville. This business was subsequently taken over by Firth Vickers before closure came in the early 1980s. For a while Jessop's distinctive office buildings on Brightside Lane survived, but even these were demolished in the late 1980s—all that remains is a decorative gateway near the junction of Brightside Lane and Weedon Street.

At the southern end of the weir a large pipe enters the river. This is the culvert carrying the

WILLIAM JESSOP & SONS. LIMITED.

BRIGHTSIDE STEEL WORKS. SHEFFIELD

Car Brook into the Don. Many of Sheffield's smaller watercourses have suffered straightening and culverting during the years of urbanisation, to a point where the course of many is now barely distinguishable. The Car Brook itself originates near Manor Top, from where it flows northwards through Woodthorpe, under the Parkway, through Darnall, under the canal and finally through the Carbrook district to the Don. It is no longer recognisable as a watercourse beyond Bowden Housteads Wood to the south of Darnall.

Upstream, the river flows through Forgemasters between concrete walls, extremely functional in appearance and contributing to what is probably the most industrial view remaining on the river. Water lilies and pondweed can occasionally be seen floating in the still waters above the weir, while downstream there is the now familiar island and stretch of shallow water, complete with crack willow, sycamore

and Japanese knotweed. Wincobank Hill provides the backdrop.

Note the crozzil-topped stone wall on the river side of the path here (see section 3 for an explanation of crozzil). There are numerous wild flowers growing between the path and the river, often obscuring the wall in summer. The established trees include sycamore, alder, willow and ash.

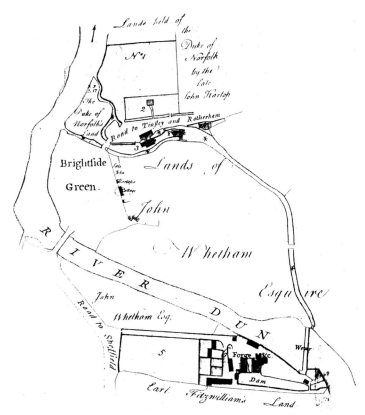

BRIGHTSIDE WEIR AND FORGES IN 1789. (BY KIND PERMISSION OF THE DUKE OF NORFOLK. FROM THE ARUNDEL CASTLE MANUSCRIPTS, SHEFFIELD ARCHIVES, COURTESY OF THE HEAD OF LEISURE SERVICES, SHEFFIELD CITY COUNCIL.)

The Walk emerges by the bridge at Weedon Street(43). There has probably been a bridge here since 1328, when Thomas de Furnival owned his corn mill opposite Weir Head. It would have been an important crossing point to reach Attercliffe Common, since the nearest bridges up and downstream for many years were Washford and Chantry (in Rotherham) respectively. The bridge, probably wooden, was completely rebuilt in 1638, and that bridge may well have survived until the present Weedon Street Bridge was built in 1904. Today's bridge is of girder construction, with three spans of latticed ironwork resting on stone piers. The latticed parapets are rivetted together, and the corrosion of the rivet heads is another indicator of atmospheric pollution within the valley.

Immediately downstream of the bridge, on the north bank, the Bagley Dyke enters the Don. This small brook originates in Longley Park, flows south past the Northern General Hospital, then veers south-east through Fir Vale before meeting the Don at this point. Like the Kirk Bridge Dyke and Car Brook its course is covered in many places.

Before commencing the next section take a look at the fig tree next to the Bridge Inn just downstream of the bridge. This is one of the largest and most impressive of the figs in the East End.

SECTION NINE

WEEDON STREET TO TINSLEY LOCKS (MEADOWHALL)

The Walk continues east along Weedon Street, away from Brightside Lane. After about 100 metres it bears left across Weedon Street and through the remains of an old railway embankment. The line carried by it was built in 1900 by the Sheffield and District Railway Company to link Treeton and Brightside junctions. Until its closure in 1939, West Tinsley Station was on this line, just off Attercliffe Common.

The Walk itself here follows the former bed of a siding which came out of Jessop's steelworks, crossed Weedon Street and into Hadfield's East Hecla steelworks. At one time the sight of railway engines trundling over public streets without formal level crossings was common in the East End. The river itself is out of sight on the left behind the now tree-lined embankment.

Passing under the Meadowhall Way road bridge, the Walk emerges by the river in the grounds of the Meadowhall retail and leisure centre(46). This section of the walk was created as part of the construction of Meadowhall in 1990. The land which the centre now occupies was the

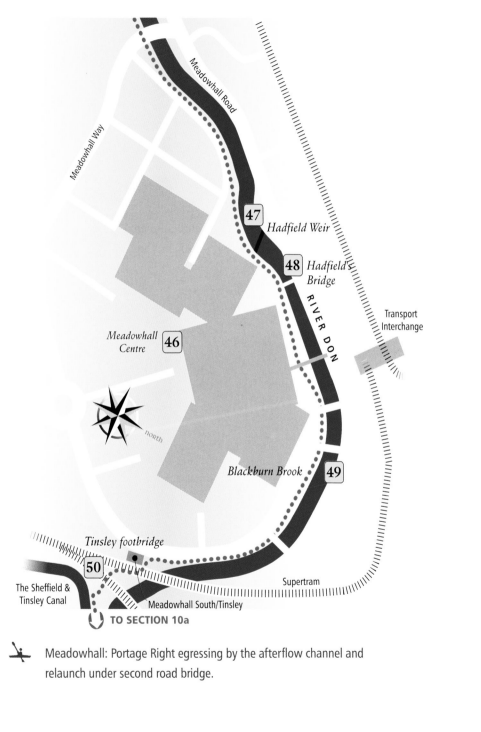

Meadowhall: Portage Right egressing by the afterflow channel and relaunch under second road bridge.

An aerial view of Hadfield's East Hecla Works in 1984, taken shortly after demolition had commenced. The site is now occupied by the Meadowhall Centre. (Sheffield City Council, Planning.)

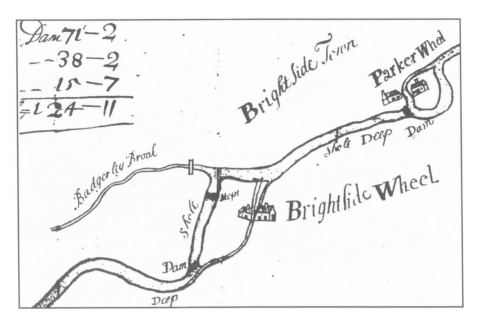

PLAN OF THE PARKER AND BRIGHTSIDE WHEELS IN THE 1720S SHOWING BOTH THE BRIGHTSIDE AND HADFIELD WEIRS, AS WELL AS THE BAGLEY DYKE, HERE SHOWN AS THE BADGERLY BROOK. (WENTWORTH WOODHOUSE MUNIMENT SHEFFIELD ARCHIVES.)

former site of Hadfield's huge East Hecla steelworks, the building of which commenced in 1897 as the company expanded from its original Hecla site upstream (see section 6). By 1914, Hadfield's employed 6,000 people, this number rising to 15,000 by the end of the First World War. After denationalisation in the 1950s it was divided in two as Dunford Hadfield and Osborn Hadfield. Dunford Hadfields closed in the early 1980s after bitter mass picketing during the 1981 Steel Strike.

By the mid 1980s much of the East End was derelict, and the strategic location of the large and vacant East Hecla site provided the opportunity to develop the Meadowhall Centre. Construction commenced in 1987 and the centre opened in 1990. It has proved to be a tremendous commercial success. As well as posessing ample free parking it is also extremely well served by public transport and attracted almost 30 million visitors in 1994. Meadowhall has its avid fans and its critics in equal measure—no doubt the debate about its merits will rage while the shopping continues.

The first part of the riverside walk at Meadowhall has a very park-like feel, consisting of neatly mown lawns, benches and herbaceous borders. The river bank is at first uncontained, with quite a dense stand of trees including birch, alder and willow. These open out opposite the entrance to the Oasis part of Meadowhall, where the focal point on the river is the last of the Five Weirs, Hadfield Weir(47).

There has been a weir at this location since about 1600. It was first used to power a cutler wheel known as the Parker Wheel. In 1738 a second cutler wheel and small tilt forge was added. These were joined in the 1750s by a paper mill which became the main user of the water supply. The paper mill carried on until a change to two corn mills and two small forges in the 1830s and a rolling mill around 1841. The corn mills were converted to steam in about 1850, followed by the rolling mill in 1870. By 1895 the corn mills were in ruins, and in 1897 Hadfield's began to build East Hecla. Despite a subsequent straightening of the river the weir has survived, and it now serves as a useful point for continuous measurement of the rate of flow in the river. Calling it Hadfield Weir seems to have been a bit of a misnomer, since it is extremely unlikely that Hadfield's would have used it, although they did rebuild it when the line of the river was altered.

THE SHELL OF THE OLD MILL BUILDING BY HADFIELD'S WEIR IN 1916. THIS PICTURE WAS TAKEN SHORTLY BEFORE HADFIELD'S DEMOLISHED THE BUILDING, STRAIGHTENED THE RIVER AND CONSTRUCTED A NEW WEIR AS PART OF THE HECTIC EXPANSION OF EAST HECLA IN THE FIRST WORLD WAR. (SHEFFIELD CITY MUSEUMS.)

HADFIELD'S WEIR WITH MEADOWHALL IN THE BACKGROUND. (PHOTOGRAPH BY KEN PHILLIP.)

Below the weir the river is contained in a straight channel between high brick walls. This provides the sheltered conditions for one of the river's most interesting alien introductions, the fig tree (see page 83 for more about how the figs got here). Several mature trees can be seen on both sides of the river between here and Tinsley viaduct.

The Walk continues in quite formal surroundings past an old footbridge(48), once a works entrance to Hadfield's, and under the new walkway from the transport interchange.

Once under the link road to Meadowhall Road, you may notice the mouth of a concrete tunnel (49) on the opposite bank where the Blackburn Brook joins the Don. This is another of Sheffield's smaller watercourses, originating to the north of High Green and flowing southward past Chapeltown and Ecclesfield. Like others it has been extensively culverted and in places its course is hard to define.

LOOKING FROM THE NORTH TOWARDS HADFIELD'S EAST HECLA WORKS IN 1966, WITH THE CONSTRUCTION OF THE TINSLEY VIADUCT IN PROGRESS AND BLACKBURN MEADOWS POWER STATION TO THE LEFT. THE LOWER DON VALLEY AT THIS TIME HAD ONE OF THE GREATEST CONCENTRATIONS OF HEAVY INDUSTRY IN EUROPE. (SHEFFIELD CITY COUNCIL PLANNING.)

The river now curves to the south-east, and the quality of Meadowhall's riverside park seems to deteriorate, perhaps because it is less in public view at this point. Over the river the scene is dominated by the Tinsley Viaduct, a mile-long span carrying the M1 across the Don Valley. The viaduct with the two cooling towers behind it is perhaps one of the most enduring modern images of Sheffield. At the time of writing there are plans to demolish the cooling towers (which are the remains of the long disused Blackburn Meadows power station), a difficult operation, which would involve closure of the motorway. In fiction, the towers were the point above which the nuclear warhead was detonated in the disturbing film of the early 1980s, 'Threads'.

In between the river and the viaduct runs the Supertram line from the city centre to Meadowhall. This was originally part of the Great Central Railway from Woodburn Junction to Meadowhall, built in 1864 to provide a direct service between Sheffield Victoria and Barnsley via the Blackburn Valley. It was closed in 1953 and reopened as Supertram in 1994. The rest of the line towards Barnsley has been earmarked as a future cycleway and footpath which will link the Five Weirs Walk to the main Trans Pennine Trail.

The Five Weirs Walk officially ends here at the Meadowhall South–Tinsley Supertram stop, where a bridge(50), long campaigned for by local residents, links to Tinsley via the canal towpath. However, a number of options are available, depending on the time and energy you have in reserve:

- Take a tram back to Sheffield city centre.
- Retrace your steps to the Meadowhall Transport Interchange for rail and bus services throughout the region.
- Go shopping!
- Cross the footbridge over the railway line to reach the towpath of the Sheffield and Tinsley Canal.

Once on the towpath you can either turn right for a 6 km walk back to the city centre via the canal (a separate guide book is available for this walk—*The Sheffield and Tinsley Canal*, Trail 1), or you can turn left for a 4 km walk to Rotherham town centre. Section 10 of this guide details the route towards Rotherham as far as the city boundary at Steel Street.

SECTION TEN

TINSLEY LOCKS TO STEEL STREET
(BLACKBURN MEADOWS)

When you reach the canal towpath, turn left towards the motorway viaduct built in 1967–68. This section of the Sheffield and South Yorkshire Navigation—which runs from Tinsley to the city centre and is called the Sheffield and Tinsley Canal—was opened in 1819 (see Trail 1 for detailed history).

Passing under the viaduct, all the different lines of transport can be seen squeezed together, canal, river, railway and supertram. Despite this confinement, the river banks are already starting to become more open, in spring and summer they are often covered in a profusion of soapwort, once commercially grown in this area for use in the textile industry for washing wool.

The Walk runs between the canal and the river past three of the eleven Tinsley Locks(51) until the two watercourses merge. (There are more locks between Sheffield and Tinsley than between Tinsley and the sea!) There is a small bridge crossing the canal just prior to the lock flight, which links to Tinsley and public transport via Wharf Road. Officially, the towpath crosses onto the other side here, but the lack of a proper bridge back over the lock means that is only fun for the agile. For the time being it is possible to stick to the unofficial path between the canal and the river.

This area is the former site of Tinsley Wharf. The river was made navigable to Tinsley in 1732 and, prior to the opening of the Sheffield

THE OLD WOODEN HALFPENNY BRIDGE, WITH THE TOLL HOUSE ON THE RIGHT. THIS BRIDGE WAS SWEPT AWAY BY FLOODS IN 1932. (REPRODUCED BY KIND PERMISSION OF MIKE TAYLOR.)

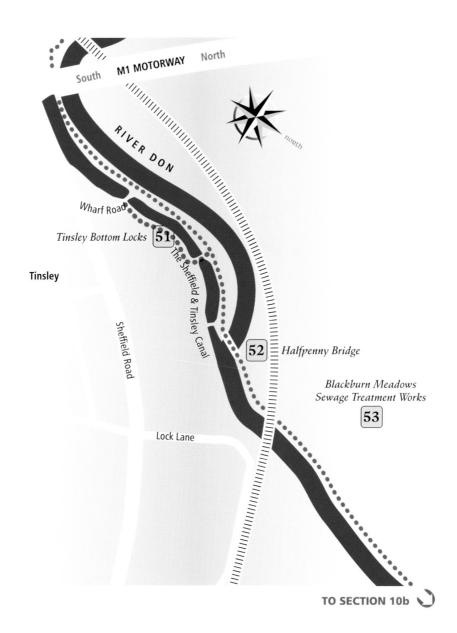

South **M1 MOTORWAY** North

R I V E R D O N

north

Wharf Road

Tinsley Bottom Locks [51]

The Sheffield & Tinsley Canal

Tinsley

Sheffield Road

[52] *Halfpenny Bridge*

Blackburn Meadows Sewage Treatment Works [53]

Lock Lane

TO SECTION 10b ↻

 Tinsley Locks: transfer to Sheffield and Tinsley Canal at Tinsley Bottom Locks through Tinsley Viaduct and Portage Right egressing via 'Giant's Steps' up to canal and return to Victoria Quays.

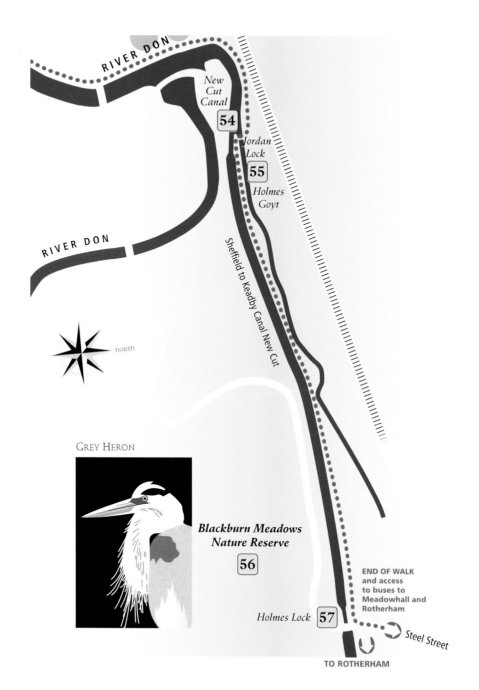

RIVER DON

New Cut Canal

54

Jordan Lock

55

Holmes Goyt

RIVER DON

north

Sheffield to Keadby Canal New Cut

GREY HERON

Blackburn Meadows Nature Reserve

56

END OF WALK and access to buses to Meadowhall and Rotherham

Holmes Lock 57

Steel Street

TO ROTHERHAM

and Tinsley Canal in 1819, the wharf served as an important inland port where virtually all Sheffield's goods were received and despatched. In the 1750s Attercliffe Road was turnpiked to provide the best possible link between Tinsley Wharf and Sheffield town centre.

Where the canal joins the river, cross over the river on Halfpenny Bridge(52). This bridge is a modern version of an old wooden one that linked Tinsley and Kimberworth (see picture on page 73). It is so called because a ha'penny was once the toll for crossing. The bridge is a good spot to look back towards the viaduct, and also downstream towards Rotherham. Note how the valley has a much more open feel. The river is slower and wider, and there are few buildings in close proximity. If there is a greenbelt between Sheffield and Rotherham then this is it.

Moving onto the riverside footpath. The land to the left was developed by Sheffield Corporation in the early 1900s to accommodate two modern municipal enterprises, the Blackburn Meadows Electric Power Station and Sewage Treatment Works(53). Only the latter survives, where sewage from some 440,000 of Sheffield's population is treated. When these works were first opened at the turn of the century they used what were then the latest techniques for treating sewage, still known as the 'Sheffield

THE WHARF WHERE COAL FOR THE POWER STATION WAS UNLOADED, 1960S. (PHOTOGRAPH BY GRAHAM HAGUE.)

System'. More recently, the works have undergone a £27 million modernisation scheme to eliminate harmful effluent and reduce smells.

Compared to upstream the river banks here feel more informal and natural, despite having much the same mix of plants and trees. It is hard to believe that only thirty years ago this section of bank was a concrete wharf for boats bringing coal to the power station and the sewage works.

Pass under the railway bridge by which sludge from the sewage treatment works used to be taken to disposal lagoons on the opposite side of the river, noting the warning signs to boats of the approaching Jordan weir.

At the weir a canal cut comes off the river to allow boat passage. This is called the New

Cut(54), made in 1835 to replace the old 1751 canal route which was bought by the Manchester, Sheffield and Lincolnshire Railway and converted to a railway line in 1868. The path follows the cut until the first of two shallow locks, known as Jordan and Holmes, is reached. These locks are needed to get boats down to the level of the river below the weir.

At the upper lock, the old Holmes Goyt(55) to the once famous Walker Ironworks at Masbrough can be seen leading off from the left of the canal cut. Walkers were one of the leading iron-masters of the 18th century who supplied cannon to Wellington's armies and cast the ironwork for Southwark Bridge. Tom Paine, the revolutionary and author of *The Rights of Man* worked for them as a designer. The firm started in Grenoside around 1741, but expansion of the works brought transport problems which precipitated the move here near the river.

The goyt was apparently used by the Walkers to transport goods to the river in special narrrow boats.

The top lock gates provide a good opportunity to cross the canal and look at the weir. Originally built in 1746 for Walkers, the weir was last rebuilt in 1980. Notice the large outfalls from the sewage treatment works to the right

Jordan Weir with Tinsley Viaduct and the soon to be demolished cooling towers in the background.(Photograph by Jonathan Ogilvie.)

HOLMES GOYT. (PHOTOGRAPH SIMON OGDEN.)

towards Rotherham; and south across Blackburn Meadows Nature Reserve towards the Templeborough Steelworks, now the proposed 'Magna' Museum of Steel. The landscape has a surprisingly pastoral feel here, with open fields and occasional grazing livestock. This recently created smallholding and the Nature Reserve both serve to emphasize that the higher ground of Sheffield is being left behind and that you are crossing into lowland England.

of the weir. Here, all the treated sewage from much of Sheffield, plus most of the surface drainage from streets and roofing, re-enters the river system. In dry weather, more water can flow out of the sewage works than actually comes down the river, so the river effectively doubles in size at this point.

The Nature Reserve(56) on the opposite bank was also once farmland. However, around 1950

BLACKBURN MEADOWS NATURE RESERVE. (PHOTOGRAPH GEOFF CARTWRIGHT.)

Cross back over the canal and continue on the towpath by the cut, which now marks the official boundary between Sheffield and Rotherham. There are good open views in most directions: upstream back towards the motorway viaduct; downstream

the area was converted into a series of lagoons into which sewage sludge from the treatment works was dumped. When this practice ceased in the mid '80s in favour of incineration, it left behind up to 15 metres of sludge loaded with toxins, most notably heavy metals. Sub-soil excavated to make way for the new Don Valley Interceptor Sewer was subsequently dumped on top of this to form a crust 2–3 metres thick. This crust was eventually colonised by rank grassland, but much further work was needed by Sheffield City Council to make the site safe. In 1989 the sludge was sealed off from the surrounding land, and pipes were installed to vent off the accumulating methane gas. Then a wetland wildlife site was created incorporating two lakes, both of which had to be lined to prevent sludge from below seeping into them. A windmill is used to pump water from the canal to supply the lakes in times of drought, and reedbeds are used to filter the incoming water. The same windmill pumps out the methane gas. All of this represents an impressive engineering operation, resulting in an important wetland habitat for wildlife amidst the surrounding urbanisation.

The junction of the towpath with Steel Street at Holmes Lock(57) marks the end of this guide. From here the wonderfully sinister Deadmans Hole Lane (part of an old route between Tinsley and Masbrough), leading over the canal to the right, provides access to Blackburn Meadows Nature Reserve (note the Heron Gates by local artist Andy Bell). The towpath continues on into Rotherham Town Centre.

For those using public transport there are three main options in terms of getting home from Steel Street:

- Retrace your steps to Meadowhall for bus, rail and supertram connections.

- Continue via the towpath to Rotherham town centre (roughly half as far as going back to Meadowhall) for bus and rail services.

- Walk the short distance up Steel Street and Psalters Lane to Meadow Bank Road. Bus services do run along Meadow Bank Road between Meadowhall and Rotherham, but it would be wise to check with operators for times and frequencies.

GENERAL INFORMATION ON THE RIVER

1. WATER POWER

Most mills in Sheffield employed what is termed the 'bypass method' of harnessing the power of flowing water. This method commonly involves the construction of a weir, head goyt, mill dam, wheel pit and tail goyt. The weir is effectively a low dam built across the river with a sloping downstream face. Water has to back up against this dam before it can overtop the weir and continue downstream. This causes an increase in the depth of water upstream of the weir, allowing a proportion of river water to be drawn off via a shuttle into a head goyt.

The head goyt, or mill race, is a channel that feeds water to the mill dam. The goyt slopes downward more gently than the bed of the river, which creates a difference in height between water in the mill dam and that in the river. It is this difference in height, or head, which determines the power output of the wheel (see diagram).

The mill dam stores the water required to turn the wheel during the working day, and also acts as a buffer against variations in river flow caused by weather or by the operation of mills further upstream. As the level of water in the dam falls, more is drawn from the river via the head goyt. It is important that the dam remains watertight, and this is usually achieved with a lining of puddled clay. To guard against excess water entering the dam and flooding the mill below it, an overflow is connected from the downstream end directly back to the river. Deep drains may be incorporated in the overflow, controlled by shuttles, to allow the dam to be drained for maintenance.

The downstream end of the dam is termed the forebay. Often massively reinforced with stone and further supported by the wall of the mill itself, it is the point where water is drawn off to turn the wheel. Water is fed into a pentrough, which is basically a wooden or cast iron box which sits over the wheel pit. From here it tumbles onto the paddles of the wheel below, causing it to turn. The rate at which water flows out of the pentrough, and thus the rate at which the wheel turns, is controlled from within the mill by means of a shuttle at the end of the pentrough called the penstock.

It is vital that the flow of spent water away from the bottom of the wheel is unimpeded, otherwise the efficiency of the wheel is reduced. Therefore, the tail goyt has to slope freely from

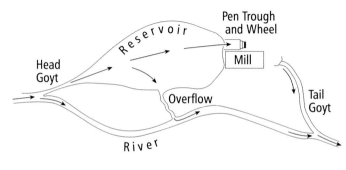

A WATER-POWERED MILL.

the wheel pit to a point where the river is low enough to enable water to be discharged back into it. The tail goyt also has to be sufficiently deep to offset the accumulation of silt and rubbish underneath the wheel, so it is often culverted underneath the mill building. Excellent working examples of this method of water power are provided at the Shepherd Wheel (OS ref. SK317854), and at Abbeydale Industrial Hamlet(OS ref. SK326819).

Variations on a theme

The system described above utilises an overshot wheel, that is water is fed onto the top of the wheel. This is fine in areas where a river slopes steeply and a sufficient head of water can be developed. However, in areas where a river slopes more gently, such as the Lower Don Valley, it was often not possible to create a sufficient head of water to utilise an overshot wheel. In this case the wheel had to be mounted at a low level in relation to the river, and a much longer tail goyt with sufficient gradient to allow a strong flow of

water underneath the wheel was constructed. Such wheels are termed undershot wheels, because the water turns them from below. An example of an undershot wheel can still be seen at Malin Bridge (OS ref. SK325894).

An intermediate system between overshot and undershot, called breast shot, can also be employed. Royds Mill had a breast shot wheel. In Sheffield the term goyt is used rather than mill race, and the word dam is generally used to describe the whole mill pond, rather than just the wall that holds back the water.

Water power has been utilised for many different industrial processes. Descriptions of the names applied to most of these processes are given below.

- Paper Mill   manufacture of paper.
- Corn Mill   grinding of corn to produce flour.
- Wheel (Cutler)   grinding of cutlery or edge tools.
- Fulling (Walk) Mill   cleansing and thickening of cloth.
- Tilt or Forge   shaping or hardening of iron and steel under heavy hammers.
- Slitting Mill   rolling of strips of steel out of large billets (bars).
- Snuff Mill   preparation of snuff powder using pestles and mortars.

2. WEIRS AND WILDLIFE

Much of the Don in Sheffield's East End is canalised, that is, the river has been contained between high walls to prevent flooding and provide space for buildings. In general, canalisation is bad news for wildlife. Firstly, building on the river's natural floodplains restricts the space available to riverside vegetation and animals. Secondly, the creation of brick or concrete lined channels speeds up the flow of water in the river and removes sheltered areas. This makes it difficult for fish to avoid being swept downstream during storms.

Although no longer used for water power, the weirs that remain in the river play a most important role in improving habitat for wildlife. The presence of a weir breaks up the uniform flow of water in

GREY WAGTAIL

MOORHEN

a lined channel. Water immediately upstream of the weir is deep and slow flowing. This provides a place where birds such as mallard and moorhen can dabble in relative safety, and it also allows the growth of pondweed and water lilies which can float in the slack water.

The tumbling of water over the weir helps to improve aeration. Oxygen is forced into the water, which encourages the breakdown of organic compounds which might be found, for example, in sewage effluent. The water downstream of the weir is shallow and turbulent. Sediment is scoured from the river bed by the plunging water, creating the clean gravelly conditions required for fish to spawn. Rocks are often exposed, providing places for grey wagtails to rest as they flit across the river in search of their favourite food, insect larvae. Under natural conditions birds such as wagtails and dippers would only be expected in shallow upland streams, but the presence of weirs creates additional habitat for them further downstream.

MALLARD

CRACK WILLOW

The sediment which is scoured from beneath the weir is often redeposited further downstream to form a long thin island in the middle of the channel. Pioneering trees like crack willow, alder and sycamore rapidly colonise these islands, while the alien species Japanese knotweed and Himalayan balsam grow quickly beneath them. The islands provide shelter and protection for a variety of birds and mammals including mallards, moorhens, little grebes, water voles and brown rats.

The only disadvantage of a large weir used for water power is to fish. Coarse fish find them too hard to ascend, so each section of river between two weirs has to be managed as a separate fishery. Game fish such as trout and salmon could probably leap the weirs in Sheffield's East End, but there are much larger obstructions on the Don further downstream that even salmon would find insurmountable.

3. OF FIG TREES, KNOTWEED & BALSAM

Drastically altered by intense human activity over the past two hundred years, the environment of the River Don corridor in Sheffield's East End is probably unique. A trip along the Five Weirs Walk will reveal wildlife communities you would never see in the countryside.

Most of the trees along the riverside are young and of even height, with very few being more than 50–60 years old. The twin effects of gross

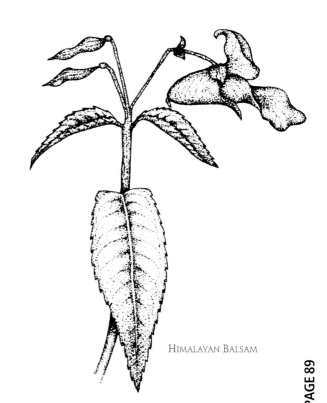

HIMALAYAN BALSAM

pollution and the occasional catastrophic flood have combined to wipe out nearly all traces of the pre-industrial tree cover, and much of what is there today has regenerated in the last 20–30 years. The main species now are crack willow, sycamore, alder and ash. If you see an oak or a wild cherry, chances are that it's been planted recently.

Beneath the trees, the ground cover is often dominated by two alien species introduced to this country by gardeners in the last century—Japanese knotweed and Himalayan balsam. Both species are remarkably tolerant to being swept downstream or having things dumped on them when the river floods. Therefore, with the improving quality of river water in the last twenty years, these two species have been the most successful in colonising the stretches of riverside laid bare by industrial pollution—but at the expense of native species.

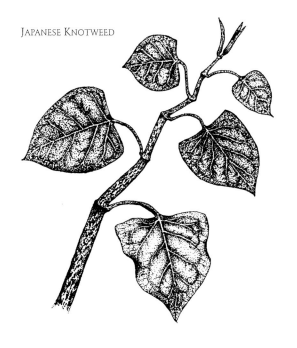

JAPANESE KNOTWEED

Japanese knotweed is a perennial that mainly spreads through root and stem fragments carried downstream by the river. It forms dense stands up to 2 metres high on woody red-brown stems, supporting large green 'spade' shaped leaves. It is almost possible to walk under its leaf canopy in some places, giving the impression of a mini woodland with its own understorey. Indeed, there is evidence that the seeds of spring flowers such as lesser celandine, wood anemone and ramsons, which are washed down river from woodlands to the west, germinate in the ground beneath where the knotweed grows. They manage to grow and flower before the

leaves of the knotweed come out in mid-May, just as if they were in an oak woodland. However, there is some debate as to whether these colonies of spring flowers are exploiting the cover of the knotweed and expanding, or whether they are remnants of former communities that are slowly being forced out by the vigorous alien. Time will tell.

Later in the season hedge bindweed climbs up the knotweed stems, using them for support. When it reaches the top it opens its white trumpet-shaped flowers, which might, from a distance, be mistaken as belonging to the knotweed. The knotweed flowers are actually more modest, stringy-looking structures, providing a rich source of nectar for bees, wasps and many other insects. After flowering the plant dies back to brittle woody stems, and new growth from the roots appears in the following spring.

In contrast to Japanese knotweed, Himalayan balsam is an annual that spreads by seed dispersal, which means that it can spread upstream from any given point just as easily as downstream. It reaches heights of 1–1.5 metres, and the shape of its showy pink flowers have earned it the alternative name of 'policeman's helmet'. Introduced to Sheffield in the 1960s, its stems and leaves have become an established source of food for a number of insects which make up that vital lower part of the food web. Balsam is a bit slower off the mark than knotweed, taking six weeks to reach its full height. A flowering period of three months then follows, after which the plants are killed off by the first hard frosts of winter.

Because Japanese knotweed and Himalayan balsam dominate long stretches of riverside at the expense of other plants, the debate rages as to whether or not they should be controlled. Perhaps the truth is that the degree of their success makes it impractical to eradicate them, and conservationists will have to work with the change they represent rather than fight against it. In the short term some clearance is essential so that access to the river can be maintained.

Possibly the most exotic of the species introduced to the East End of Sheffield is the wild fig. There are around thirty mature trees by the river, most of them towards the Meadowhall end of the Five Weirs Walk. The majority of them are over 60 years old, and they owe their origin to human appetite, imperfect sewers and the steel industry.

Each time there is a heavy storm a proportion of raw sewage overflows from the system into the rivers. This proportion was larger at the turn of the century than it is now, so considerable numbers of fig seeds found their way into the River Don. Because industry was then more widespread and much less efficient than it is now, the waters of the river in the East End ran at a constant 20°C, creating the perfect conditions for the fig seeds to germinate and grow. Nowadays the river water is much colder once more, but the shelter of the river's high retaining walls has enabled the figs to reach maturity. However, it is unlikely that new trees will establish.

The trees are characterised by multiple silver grey stems, up to 8 metres high and with a spread of 10 metres or more. Their deep green, glossy palmate leaves unfurl in late May. At the same time many small, pear shaped green figs appear. These swell slightly before falling in July. A second crop then appears but falls unripened in October with the leaves. When it comes to fruit, Meadowhall can't match the Mediterranean.

4. RIVERS AND POLLUTION

There are two types of pollution incident which can affect wildlife in a river. The first type is often described as the 'acute' or short-term incident, for example the spillage of oil from a storage tank. The second type is the slow build up of pollutants over time, known as 'chronic' pollution.

Historically, the River Don has mainly suffered from chronic pollution. The continuous inputs of industrial waste and sewage from the mid 1800s until the 1970s made the river so polluted that no one probably even noticed when acute incidents occurred. Nowadays the chronic pollution has been reduced to a level where fish populations can be returned to the river. However, with the continued presence of industry in the Don Valley there is always a chance that an acute incident might still occur. It only takes one bad acute incident to wipe out much of the wildlife recovery that has taken place over the last 10–20 years, so it is important that all of us who use the river are vigilant and prompt in reporting any pollution incident we see.

It would be wrong to say that either acute or chronic pollution of the Don in Sheffield's East End is over. Levels of pollution have been reduced considerably, but the following kinds of pollution still occur:

Eutrophication

This occurs when water becomes over-enriched with the nutrients nitrogen and phosphorus. A certain few species such as algae or sewage fungus thrive on the excess nutrients, breaking down the organic compounds in which the nitrogen and phosphorus are often contained. Unfortunately, in so doing they consume all the oxygen in the water and block out the light, killing other plants and fish and creating a 'pea soup' effect. Ironically, water polluted by eutrophication may appear to be teeming with life, but it is usually only one sort of life!

Excess nitrogen and phosphorus may come from many sources, but the main sources are nitrates from agriculture and phosphates from domestic sewage, particularly in detergents.

Oil spillages

Examine the water just above any weir on the Don and you might see that iridescent sheen that betrays a thin slick of oil. Typical sources of oil pollution are leaking storage tanks, vehicle maintenance areas and DIY car oil changes. Oil is lighter than water, and once in a river a small amount can spread very thinly over a large area—one gallon can cover an acre of water. It causes numerous pollution problems, coating bank-side vegetation and animals that come into contact with it, and blocking the contact between the water's surface and the atmosphere.

It is often assumed that anything tipped down a drain goes to the sewage works. This isn't always the case. Many sewage systems now separate surface water runoff from foul sewage, so anything tipped down a surface water drain usually goes straight to a water course. Even in the older combined systems, raw sewage will overflow to rivers during heavy rainfall to prevent the system overloading.

Heavy metals

These may often be present in industrial effluents, particularly from the steel industry and abandoned mine waters. Some metals, like mercury and cadmium, are extremely toxic to aquatic life. They may often settle and accumulate in sediment at the bottom of a river, thus posing a pollution threat for some time after their input to the river first took place. Worse still, heavy metals tend to accumulate and increase in concentration as they are passed up through the food chain. Even if heavy metals are confined to the foul sewage system, a sufficiently high dose of them at any particular time may wipe out the micro-organisms that are used at sewage treatment works to cleanse the water before it is returned to the river.

Solid waste

Sadly, the dumping of rubbish into Sheffield's rivers is a common occurrence. Volunteers who clean up stretches of the Five Weirs Walk each year have uncovered everything from crisp packets to half a Ford Fiesta! Solid waste isn't just visually unattractive. It can trap and injure animals, pollute water and even cause flooding if it blocks a water course.

Dumping rubbish is an unacceptable hangover from industrial times when the River Don was grossly polluted, out of sight and out of mind. Fortunately, as access to the city's rivers and water quality improves, people are becoming more appreciative of their rediscovered rivers and less tolerant of rubbish dumping.

Pollution cocktails

Individual toxic substances may combine to produce new types of pollution 'cocktails'. This process is often hard to predict, as two pollutants might cancel each other out, or may combine to produce an effect many times worse than either could have done in isolation.

Acknowledgements

Many thanks are due to Simon Ogden, Lisa Judson and other members of the Five Weirs Walk Trust for their valuable assistance in compiling the text and illustrations. The financial support of the National Rivers Authority (now part of the Environment Agency) is also gratefully acknowledged.

Thanks must go to all the staff of the Sheffield City Council's Local History Library for their invaluable service to local historians. All illustrations are from this collection unless otherwise stated.

Staff at Sheffield City Museum also rendered valuable assistance in locating several books and other information relating to the East End of Sheffield.

Design and maps by Jonathan Ogilvie, SCC Department of Environment and Leisure Presentation Team.

Wildlife drawings are by Caroline Hobson.

Bibliography and Further Reading

Sheffield in Tudor and Stuart Times, **D. Bostwick** (Sheffield City Museums, 1985) ISBN 0-86321-031-7.

The Great Sheffield Picture Show, **D. Bostwick** (RLP (Sheffield) Ltd, 1989) ISBN 0-86321-096-1.

Water Power on the Sheffield Rivers, **D. Crossley (Ed)** (Sheffield Trades Historical Society, and University of Sheffield Division of Continuing Education, 1989) ISBN 0-950660-12-4.

Crossin' o'er: About Our Bridges - Past and Present, **S.R. Davey** (Parker Press, Sheffield, 1984) Out of print.

Where T'watter Runs O'er T'weir, **S.R. Davey** (Parker Press, Sheffield, 1984) Out of print.

Sheffield's East Enders, **K. Farnsworth** (Sheffield City Libraries, 1987) 107pp. ISBN 0-86321-073-2.

The History of the River Don Fishery, **C. Firth** (Environment Agency, 1997).

'**The Ecology of an Urban River**', **O.L. Gilbert** (*British Wildlife*, 1992).

The Attercliffe Village Trail, **R. Harman & S.N. Ogden** (The Hallamshire Press, 1997) ISBN 1-874718-31-8.

'The Distribution of Water-Powered Sites in Sheffield', **R. Hawkins** (*Sheffield City Museums Information Sheet* 4. Third Edition, 1976).

'The Distribution of Crucible Steel Furnaces in Sheffield', **R. Hawkins** (*Sheffield City Museums Information Sheet* 1. Second Edition, 1981).

***The Sheffield and Tinsley Canal*, S.N. Ogden** (The Hallamshire Press, 1997) ISBN 1-874718-26-1.

***A Railway Chronology of the Sheffield Area*, R.V. Proctor, (Ed)** (Sheffield City Libraries Local Studies Leaflet, 1975) ISBN 0-900660-25-2.

***The Complete Guide to the Sheffield and South Yorkshire Navigation*, C. Richardson & J. Lower** (The Hallamshire Press, 1995) ISBN 1-874718-07-5.

Buildings and Sites of Historic Importance in the Lower Don Valley (Sheffield City Council, 1986) Unpublished report from Department of Land and Planning.

***Sheffield: Road Travel and Transport Before the Railway Age*, H. Smith** (Sheffield City Libraries Local Studies Leaflet, 1980) ISBN 0-9006-6058-9.

'The River Don on Old Picture Postcards', **M. Taylor** (*Yesterday's Yorkshire* series no. 3. Reflections of a Bygone Age, 1995). ISBN 1-900138-00-X.

***A Popular History of Sheffield*, J.E Vickers** (Applebaum Bookshop, Sheffield, 1992). ISBN 0-906787-04-1.

***The Story of Old Attercliffe*, G.R. Vine** (Ward Bros, Attercliffe, 1936) Out of print.

***Sheffield - its Story and its Achievements*, M. Walton** (Amethyst Press, Fifth Edition, 1984) Out of print.

Five Weirs Walk Trust
c/o Keeble, Hawson, Moorhouse
Old Cathedral Vicarage
St James' Row
Sheffield S1 1XA

Author's royalties from this book will go to the *Five Weirs Walk Trust* for the furtherance of its work.

BEANS & PULSES
—— COOKERY ——

Sue and Bill Deeming
BEANS & PULSES
— COOKERY —

Hamlyn
London · New York · Sydney · Toronto

Originally published under the title
Bean Cookery
by H.P. Books, P.O. Box 5367, Tucson, AZ 85703

This edition published in 1983 by
The Hamlyn Publishing Group Limited
London · New York · Sydney · Toronto
Astronaut House, Feltham, Middlesex, England

ISBN 0 600 322333 1

Cover photograph by Martin Brigdale
Illustrations by the Hayward Art Group

Filmset in 11 on 12pt Monophoto Garamond by
Servis Filmsetting Limited, Manchester
Printed in Denmark

Contents

Useful Facts and Figures

Notes on metrication

In this book quantities are given in metric and Imperial measures. Exact conversion from Imperial to metric measures does not usually give very convenient working quantities and so the metric measures have been rounded off into units of 25 grams. The table below shows the recommended equivalents.

Ounces	Approx g to nearest whole figure	Recommended conversion nearest unit of 25
1	28	25
2	57	50
3	85	75
4	113	100
5	142	150
6	170	175
7	198	200
8	227	225
9	255	250
10	283	275
11	312	300
12	340	350
13	368	375
14	396	400
15	425	425
16 (1 lb)	454	450
17	482	475
18	510	500
19	539	550
20 (1¼ lb)	567	575

Note: When converting quantities over 20 oz first add the appropriate figures in the centre column, then adjust to the nearest unit of 25. As a general guide, 1 kg (1000 g) equals 2.2 lb or about 2 lb 3 oz. This method of conversion gives good results in nearly all cases, although in certain pastry and cake recipes a more accurate conversion is necessary to produce a balanced recipe.

Liquid measures   The millilitre has been used in this book and the following table gives a few examples.

Imperial	Approx ml to nearest whole figure	Recommended ml
¼ pint	142	150 ml
½ pint	283	300 ml
¾ pint	425	450 ml
1 pint	567	600 ml
1½ pints	851	900 ml
1¾ pints	992	1000 ml (1 litre)

Spoon measures   All spoon measures given in this book are level unless otherwise stated.

Can sizes   At present, cans are marked with the exact (usually to the nearest whole number) metric equivalent of the Imperial weight of the contents, so we have followed this practice when giving can sizes.

Oven temperatures

The table below gives recommended equivalents.

	°C	°F	Gas Mark
Very cool	110	225	¼
	120	250	½
Cool	140	275	1
	150	300	2
Moderate	160	325	3
	180	350	4
Moderately hot	190	375	5
	200	400	6
Hot	220	425	7
	230	450	8
Very hot	240	475	9

Notes for American and Australian users

In America the 8-oz measuring cup is used. In Australia metric measures are now used in conjunction with the standard 250-ml measuring cup. The Imperial pint, used in Britain and Australia, is 20 fl oz, while the American pint is 16 fl oz. It is important to remember that the Australian tablespoon differs from both the British and American tablespoons; the table below gives a comparison. The British standard tablespoon, which has been used throughout this book, holds 17.7 ml, the American 14.2 ml, and the Australian 20 ml. A teaspoon holds approximately 5 ml in all three countries.

British	American	Australian
1 teaspoon	1 teaspoon	1 teaspoon
1 tablespoon	1 tablespoon	1 tablespoon
2 tablespoons	3 tablespoons	2 tablespoons
3½ tablespoons	4 tablespoons	3 tablespoons
4 tablespoons	5 tablespoons	3½ tablespoons

An Imperial/American guide to solid and liquid measures.

Imperial	American
Solid measure	
1 lb butter or margarine	2 cups
1 lb flour	4 cups
1 lb granulated or castor sugar	2 cups
1 lb icing sugar	3 cups
8 oz rice	1 cup
Liquid measures	
¼ pint liquid	⅔ cup liquid
½ pint	1¼ cups
¾ pint	2 cups
1 pint	2½ cups
1½ pints	3¾ cups
2 pints	5 cups (2½ pints)

NOTE: When making any of the recipes in this book, only follow one set of measures as they are not interchangeable.

Introduction

Beans, lentils and peas are classified as legumes: plants with seed-filled pods. They may all be dried and stored for long periods or used at different stages in their life cycles: for example bean sprouts are the roots of bean seeds and green beans are the tender, immature pods enclosing the seeds. *Beans and Pulses Cookery* includes recipes which use both fresh and dried beans as well as bean sprouts, lentils and dried peas.

Buying and storing beans

Health food and wholefood shops sell a wide variety of beans and pulses; they are usually packeted but are sometimes sold loose. You will find that many super-markets or small specialist stores also stock a range of dried or canned beans. When you buy dried beans, look carefully at the packet to make sure that they are in good condition. There should be very few broken or wrinkled beans and they should be fairly uniform in size and colour. It is particularly important to check beans which are sold loose.

Dried beans can be stored for a relatively long period of time, but not forever! With correct storage their quality can be maintained for six months to a year. If kept too long they will lose too much moisture and will not cook satisfactorily. If stored incorrectly, the beans may absorb water and spoil before you have a chance to use them. Airtight plastic bags will keep the beans fresh and once opened the bag must be reclosed with a wire twist tie. For the longest storage life, keep your beans in a glass or plastic container with a tight-fitting lid. Always keep the packet or jar in a cool, dry place.

Preparing dried beans and pulses

Dried beans go through a series of thrashing and sifting processes to remove pods, foreign material and under-sized beans before packaging. However, this mechanical process does not remove all the small stones, soil and dust, so it is necessary to sort and rinse the beans at home.

Sorting means picking over the beans before cooking them. Remove any grit, pieces of dirt and beans which have holes or are badly misshapen and wrinkled. If any beans look discoloured or undersized they should also be discarded.

When the beans are sorted they should be rinsed and soaked if necessary, but do not rinse them until you are ready to soak or cook them. Soaking is not an essential step in bean preparation: it simply shortens the cooking time by starting the softening process. Unsoaked beans take longer to cook and require more attention during cooking so that they don't dry up and burn.

During soaking the water lost in drying is re-absorbed and the beans or pulses double in size. Enough water must be used to keep the beans covered while they are soaking and this is usually discarded and replaced by fresh, measured cooking liquid. There are two methods of soaking – long soaking or quick soaking. Both work well and once soaked, the beans will cook in 1–3 hours depending on type.

When sorting beans, remove those that have holes, or are broken or very small.

Long soaking takes some advance planning but needs little effort. First cover the beans with water at room temperature, then soak them overnight for about 8–10 hours. If the water is hot it may cause the beans to turn sour. Beans which are allowed to soak for much longer than 12 hours can absorb too much water and lose their characteristic texture and flavour.

Quick soaking, on the other hand, reconstitutes dried beans in little more than an hour. Bring the beans and water for soaking to the boil, boil for 2 minutes, then cover the pan and remove it from the heat. Allow the beans to soak in the cooking water for 1 hour. At the end of the soaking time pour off the water and sort through the beans, discarding any which have not absorbed the water and are small and shrivelled. Do not leave the beans to stand in the soaking water for more than 2–3 hours.

Cooking beans and pulses

Cooking unsoaked beans When you are cooking unsoaked beans, use twice the amount of cooking water than is specified in the recipe. Rinse and sort the beans, add them to the water in a large saucepan and bring them to the boil. Cover the pan and reduce the heat to maintain a simmer. The beans will absorb the water while they are cooking so you will have to watch them carefully and add more water whenever necessary to keep them covered. The cooking time for unsoaked beans can vary by up to 2 hours but most beans will be tender in 2–3 hours.

All cooking times given in this book apply to soaked beans unless otherwise stated.

Cooking soaked beans The dried, soaked beans can be cooked in a saucepan, slow cooker or in the oven. The water or other cooking liquid is required only for softening the beans as they cook. There must be enough liquid to keep the beans covered while they are cooking as any which are left out of the liquid will dry up and become inedible.

Oil or fat may be used in cooking to lessen the possibility of the cooking water boiling over and to improve the flavour. Salt should also be added to bring out the flavour of the beans, but there is some controversy as to when is the best time to do so. Some cooks add salt only after the beans have softened in cooking; others prefer to add it to the cooking water with the beans. In our experience adding the salt at the beginning of cooking gives a better flavour and does not significantly influence the cooking time or tenderness of the beans. Acidic ingredients, such as tomatoes,

vinegar, ketchup, chilli sauce or lemon juice can retard the cooking and softening of the beans, so always follow the recipe when adding these ingredients.

When dried beans boil a foam forms on the top of the cooking liquid. There is no need to remove this since it will be absorbed back into the liquid.

Check the beans during cooking to make sure that they are covered with water. Any saucepan used to cook beans should have a tight-fitting lid to prevent steam from escaping while the beans simmer. To test if the beans are cooked, pinch or bite a few after the minimum time suggested in the recipe, and then again after every 10–15 minutes until tender.

As a general guide, allow 750 ml/1$\frac{1}{4}$ pints water to each 225 g/8 oz beans, add 1 teaspoon salt and 1 tablespoon oil. The following table gives a guide to the cooking times of some commonly used beans and pulses.

Beans (soaked)	Cooking time
Black beans	1–1$\frac{1}{4}$ hours
Borlotti beans	1–1$\frac{1}{2}$ hours
Butter beans	1–1$\frac{1}{2}$ hours
Chick peas	1–1$\frac{1}{2}$ hours
Haricot beans	1–1$\frac{1}{4}$ hours
Red kidney beans	1–1$\frac{1}{4}$ hours
Soya beans	2$\frac{1}{2}$–3 hours
Beans (unsoaked)	
Black-eye beans	1–1$\frac{1}{2}$ hours
Lentils	30–40 minutes
Split peas	30–40 minutes

The dried weight of beans will usually double during the cooking process; for example 225 g/8 oz dried beans will yield 450 g/1 lb cooked beans.

Pressure cooking If you have a pressure cooker, take advantage of this speedy cooking method to prepare the beans. Follow the manufacturer's instructions for quantities and timing.

Oven cooking Baking in the hot, dry air of the oven is a slow process but it's the only way to create the glazed, crusty top characteristic of baked bean casseroles. Generally, oven baking is used in combination with boiling. Be sure that the beans are not overcooked before baking or they will be mushy. Large earthenware pots are traditionally used for baking beans but you can also use ordinary ovenproof casseroles.

Electric slow cookers The advantage of using a slow cooker is that you can put the food in it, turn it on and forget it, then several hours later the dish is ready to eat.

Always remember that red kidney beans must first be *boiled* for 3–5 minutes to eliminate dangerous toxins. Slow cookers can also be used to reheat pre-cooked beans and they are useful for keeping bean soups and stews hot while you finish preparing the rest of the meal.

Freezing

Freeze the cooked beans or bean dishes in portions of a size that you will find most useful. Freezer containers should be airtight and moisture-proof and allow enough room for the beans to expand as they freeze. The cooked beans and bean dishes will keep in the freezer for 2–3 months, but after that time their flavour and texture will begin to deteriorate. You will find that the beans maintain their shape better if they are thawed slowly. Defrost them overnight in the refrigerator, or for several hours at room temperature, or for about an hour in their container standing in a bowl of hot water. When the beans can be removed from their container put them into a saucepan to reheat and finish cooking if necessary.

Bean Sprouts

Bean sprouts are usually sprouted mung beans and they are sold fresh or canned in many supermarkets. Fresh bean sprouts spoil very quickly, losing their bright white colour and crispness, so avoid any that are brownish or damp and store them for a day or two. Canned bean sprouts keep indefinitely until the can is opened, but they lack the crunchiness and flavour of fresh sprouts. Although lentil sprouts are not grown commercially, packaged dried lentils from the supermarket or health food shop can be sprouted at home.

With a little planning you can easily have freshly sprouted beans whenever you want them. You don't need expensive equipment – just a large, clean, wide-necked jar. Cover the mouth of the jar with cheesecloth or nylon mesh, such as a clean stocking, and secure it with a rubber band. This mesh-like cover will make rinsing and draining easier.

Think ahead and start sprouting mung beans 3–5 days before you need them so the sprouts will have time to grow. Lentils need only 3 days. First, remove all foreign material and broken seeds. Pour enough water into the jar to cover the mung beans or lentils by 3–4 times their depth, then let them stand at room temperature for about 8 hours or overnight. Drain the beans or lentils thoroughly. Place the jar on its side and cover it with a dry tea-towel to protect the growing sprouts from too much light which may make them bitter. Do not cover the top of the jar or hide it in a cupboard as the growing sprouts need air. The ideal temperature for sprouting is 20–25 C/65–75 F. The sprouts need to be rinsed in water at room temperature three times a day until they are completely sprouted. Drain them thoroughly after each rinsing. During the last two days of sprouting many of the mung bean seed coats will come loose and can be washed away during rinsing. They are not harmful but some people don't like their bitter taste.

Mung bean sprouts are ready to eat when they are 2.5–5 cm/1–2 in long. To remove any remaining seed coats from the beans, place them in a large bowl of cool water, then skim the green coats off as they rise to the surface. Shake the sprouts by the handful in the water to loosen more of the seed coats, but it's not necessary to remove them all. Drain the bean sprouts and pat them dry with paper towels. Lentil sprouts are ready when they are 1–1.5 cm/½–1 in long and their seed coats do not need to be removed. If you refrigerate the young sprouts in an airtight container, they will keep for up to 7 days.

The bean or lentil sprouts can be stir-fried in butter or oil for a few minutes, sprinkled with soy sauce and served as a crunchy side dish. For variety mix bean sprouts with lentil sprouts or alfalfa sprouts as well as other sprouted grains. Home grown sprouts are delicious in salads, soups and sandwiches and you will find many interesting ways of using them among the recipes in this book.

1 Put the sorted mung beans or lentils and water in a large jar. Cover the jar with cheesecloth, secure it with a rubber band and leave to soak overnight. Drain the beans through the cheesecloth, rinse and drain again. Place the jar on its side, leaving the top covered with cheesecloth for ventilation, and cover with a tea-towel.

2 The seeds will begin to germinate – or sprout – after 24 hours. Rinse and drain the sprouts three times a day. The sprouts in the above picture have been removed from the jar to show them more clearly : they should be left in the jar to grow.

3 Mung bean sprouts are ready when they are 2.5–5 cm/1–2 in long and lentil sprouts grow to 1–1.5/$\frac{1}{2}$–$\frac{3}{4}$ in. in length.

4 Gently agitate the sprouts in a bowl of cold water. The seed coats will float to the surface of the water and can be removed. Thoroughly drain and refrigerate the sprouts as directed.

Glossary of Beans and Pulses

Aduki beans Small, round, red beans with a sweet, nutty taste.

Black beans Small, oval beans with shiny black skins and creamy flesh. They are interchangeable with red kidney beans in some recipes.

Black-eye beans White beans with a characteristic black mark which resembles an eye.

Borlotti beans Mottled, oval beans which are quite flat. They are similar to pinto beans which are also mottled, but they are pink in colour.

Butter beans Either small or large, these are flat, white beans which are traditionally served as a vegetable with boiled or roast meats.

Cannellini beans Plump, white Italian haricot beans.

Chick peas Nutty-flavoured, creamy-coloured beans which are similar, both in size and shape, to hazelnuts.

Green split peas Interchangeable with yellow split peas, these are a useful ingredient for soups and hotpots.

Haricot beans Oval, white beans which may be very small or medium-sized. A traditional and useful ingredient for casseroles and stews.

Lentils Small, quick-cooking pulses which are most commonly red, but are also available with either green or brown skins.

Mung beans Very small, round green beans which are also commercially sprouted and sold as bean sprouts.

Red kidney beans These are plump, red, kidney-shaped beans which are widely available both dried and canned.

Soya beans Small, round, honey-coloured beans which are rich in protein, fat, minerals and vitamins.

Yellow split peas A common ingredient, sold in most supermarkets and used in soups and hotpots.

Key to Illustration on Endpapers

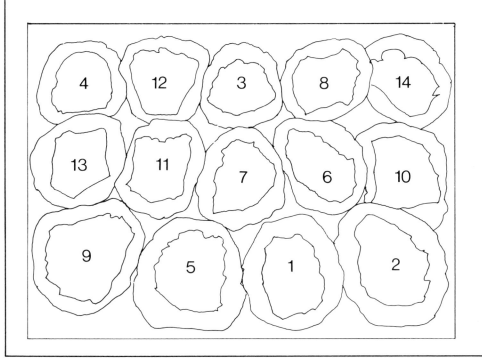

1 Lentils
2 Mung beans
3 Large haricot or cannellini beans
4 Black beans
5 Green split peas
6 Aduki beans
7 Black-eye beans
8 Borlotti beans
9 Yellow split peas
10 Soya beans
11 Chick peas
12 Red kidney beans
13 Small haricot beans
14 Butter beans

Soups and Starters

The first course to any winter meal should warm your family or guests as well as stimulate their appetites for the dishes to come. Bearing this in mind, next time you're planning a menu, instead of the familiar dips and crisps you serve so often try preparing a warming bean soup or Black-eye Bean Fritters with some crunchy roasted chick peas.

The variety of flavours and textures in bean soups is endless: the soups can be thick or thin with whole or puréed beans and meat, poultry or vegetables added. The cooked soup can be thinned down with extra stock or milk, or thickened by reducing some of the beans to a purée and stirring it into the pan. During cooking the beans will readily absorb the flavour of the other ingredients, and they will also add texture to the soup.

Serve only small bowls of the more filling soups as a starter or, for a hearty lunch or supper, ladle generous portions into warmed bowls and have hot French bread or granary bread as an accompaniment. A wedge of mature Cheddar cheese or some well-flavoured smoked cheese always tastes excellent with steaming hot soup. In fact, you will probably find that many of these soups are quite substantial and nutritious enough to form the main dish.

Bean and Shrimp Chowder

25 g/1 oz butter
1 small onion, finely chopped
3 tablespoons plain flour
¼ teaspoon dry mustard
300 ml/½ pint chicken stock
450 ml/¾ pint milk
1 (425-g/15-oz) can creamy-style corn
1 (425-g/15-oz) can butter beans
¼ teaspoon salt
white pepper
350 g/12 oz peeled shrimps
4 tablespoons dry white wine
1 egg, hard boiled and sieved

Melt the butter in a large saucepan, add the onion and cook, stirring continuously, until soft but not browned. Add the flour and mustard, mixing well, then slowly pour in the chicken stock and milk, stirring constantly to prevent lumps from forming. Bring to the boil and stir in the corn, butter beans, salt, white pepper to taste and shrimps. Cover and simmer for 10 minutes, stirring frequently. Stir in the wine and cook for a minute before serving. Garnish each serving with a little sieved egg. **Serves 6–8**

Spanish Chicken Soup

2 chicken portions
1 litre/1¾ pints water
2 chicken stock cubes
1 (425-g/15-oz) can chick peas, drained
1 (397-g/14-oz) can chopped tomatoes
3 tablespoons concentrated tomato purée
2 tablespoons oil
1 clove garlic, crushed
1 onion, chopped
1 green pepper, chopped
salt and freshly ground black pepper
pinch of saffron
croûtons to garnish (see below)

Place the chicken, water and stock cubes in a saucepan, bring to the boil and reduce the heat. Cover the pan and simmer until the chicken is cooked and tender – about 40 minutes.

Remove the chicken from the pan and cut the meat off the bones. Discard the bones and dice and reserve the meat. Add the chick peas to the chicken stock. Stir in the tomatoes, tomato purée and reserved chicken. Heat the oil in a small frying pan, add the garlic, onion and green pepper and cook until the onion is soft but not browned.

Add the sautéed vegetables to the soup together with the salt and pepper to taste and saffron. Heat through, then serve individual bowls of soup garnished with croûtons. **Serves 4–6**

Note To make croûtons, fry small cubes of day-old bread in butter, or a mixture of butter and oil, turning frequently until golden brown.

Corn Bean Chowder

350 g/12 oz haricot beans
1.4 litres/2½ pints water
1 meaty bacon hock
1 onion, chopped
1 teaspoon salt
25 g/1 oz butter
1 green pepper, chopped
1 (340-g/12-oz) can sweet corn, drained
about 300 ml/½ pint milk

Soak the beans overnight, then drain them and discard any that have not absorbed the water. Place them in a large saucepan and pour in the measured water. Add the bacon hock, onion and salt and bring to the boil. Reduce the heat, cover the pan and simmer until the beans are tender – about 1–1½ hours.

Remove the bacon, cut the meat from the bones and dice it. Mash the beans lightly with a potato masher. Melt the butter in a frying pan, add the green pepper and cook until softened. Add the pepper to the chowder together with the bacon, sweet corn and enough milk to thin down the soup to the required consistency. Heat gently but do not allow the soup to boil. Serve immediately. **Serves 6–8**

Beer Soup with Sausage

350 g/12 oz lentils
1.4 litres/2½ pints water
2 tablespoons oil
1 onion, chopped
1 clove garlic, crushed
2 large parsnips or 1 small turnip, cut into chunks
300 ml/½ pint beer
½ teaspoon dried marjoram
1 teaspoon salt
225 g/8 oz knackwurst or Polish sausage, cut into
2.5-cm/1-in thick slices

Place the lentils in a large saucepan and add the water. Heat the oil in a frying pan, add the onion, garlic and parsnips or turnip and cook until the onion is soft but not browned. Add the onion mixture to the lentils, then stir in the beer, marjoram, salt and sliced sausage. Bring to the boil, reduce the heat and cover the pan. Simmer for about 45 minutes or until the lentils are tender. **Serves 6–8**

Chick Pea and Sausage Soup

350 g/12 oz chick peas
1.75 litres/3 pints water
3 chicken stock cubes
bay leaf
10 peppercorns
25 g/1 oz butter
1 onion, chopped
1 small green pepper, chopped
1 clove garlic, crushed
225 g/8 oz Italian salami or garlic sausage, cubed
or 450 g/1 lb pork sausages with herbs, cooked
and thickly sliced
½ teaspoon Worcestershire sauce
½ teaspoon paprika
1 medium potato, diced
½ teaspoon salt

Soak the chick peas overnight, then drain them and place them in a saucepan with the water, stock cubes, bay leaf and peppercorns. Bring to the boil and reduce the heat, then cover the pan and simmer until the beans are tender – about 1–1½ hours. Remove and discard the bay leaf and peppercorns.

Melt the butter in a frying pan, add the onion, green pepper and garlic and cook until the onion is softened. Add the salami or sausage and mix well, then stir the mixture into the chick peas together with the Worcestershire sauce, paprika, potato and salt. Cover the pan and simmer for a further 30 minutes or until the potato is tender.

Ladle the soup into large mugs or bowls and serve immediately. **Serves 4–6**

Note Canned chick peas can be used instead of the dried ones in this recipe. Use 2 (425-g/15-oz) cans, drained, and half the quantity of water given in the above recipe. Add the chick peas 5 minutes before the end of the cooking time.

Chick Pea and Sausage Soup

Hungarian Bean Soup

175 g/6 oz borlotti beans
2 rashers rindless streaky bacon
225 g/8 oz lean pork, cubed
1 large onion, chopped
1 clove garlic, crushed
450 g/1 lb beef or pork bones
3 tablespoons concentrated tomato purée
2.25 litres/4 pints water
½ teaspoon dry mustard
1 tablespoon paprika
1½ teaspoon salt
1 teaspoon Worcestershire sauce
2 teaspoons cider vinegar
¼ teaspoon hot paprika (optional)
150 ml/¼ pint soured cream

Soak the beans overnight in cold water. Drain and discard any that have not absorbed the water. Dry-fry the bacon until it is crisp, then drain it on absorbent kitchen paper. Brown the pork cubes in the bacon drippings, then use a slotted spoon to remove them from the pan. Sauté the onion and garlic in the remaining drippings until the onion is soft but not browned.

Place the soaked beans, bones, browned pork, sautéed onion mixture, tomato purée and water in a saucepan and mix well. Stir in the mustard, paprika, salt, Worcestershire sauce, vinegar and hot paprika, if used. Crumble the cooked bacon over the soup, bring to the boil and reduce the heat. Cover the pan and simmer until the beans and pork are tender – about 1½ hours. Remove the bones and top each individual serving of the soup with a little soured cream. **Serves 8**

Cheese Soup

450 g/1 lb borlotti beans
1.4 litres/2½ pints water
2 rashers lean rindless bacon, chopped
1 onion, chopped
1½ teaspoons salt
1 (397-g/14-oz) can chopped tomatoes
2 teaspoons chilli powder (optional)
½ teaspoon ground cumin
¼ teaspoon dried oregano
175 g/6 oz Cheddar cheese, grated

Soak the beans overnight, then drain them and discard any that have not absorbed the water. Place them in a large saucepan with the measured water, bacon, onion and salt. Bring to the boil, reduce the heat and cover the pan. Simmer until the beans are tender – about 1–1½ hours.

Drain the beans, reserving the cooking liquid. Purée the beans, a few at a time in a liquidiser, adding the reserved cooking liquid as needed. Mix the remaining cooking liquid with the bean purée, tomatoes, chilli powder (if used), cumin, and oregano adding a little extra water (if necessary) to give the required consistency. Heat the soup gently in a saucepan, then cover the pan and simmer for 20 minutes. Add the cheese and stir constantly over medium heat until it melts. Serve immediately. **Serves 4–6**

Serving Suggestion For a warming winter lunch, serve this soup with thick slices of toasted French bread and mustard butter. Cut 8–12 thick slices of French bread. Cream 75 g/3 oz butter with 1 tablespoon mild wholegrain mustard. Toast the slices of bread on one side, then spread the untoasted sides with the mustard butter. Place under the hot grill, buttered side up, and cook until golden. Float 2 slices of bread, buttered side up, in each portion of the soup and serve immediately.

Bean Medley

100 g/4 oz borlotti beans
100 g/4 oz haricot beans
2 tablespoons oil
225 g/8 oz meaty beef bones
1 onion, chopped
1 carrot, sliced
1.5 litres/2¾ pints water
4 beef stock cubes
40 g/1½ oz pearl barley
¼ teaspoon dry mustard
2 tablespoons chopped fresh parsley
50 g/2 oz green or yellow split peas
50 g/2 oz lentils

Soak the borlotti and haricot beans overnight, then drain them and discard any that have not absorbed the water. Heat the oil in a heavy-based saucepan, add the beef bones and fry them until well browned. Add the onion and carrot and cook, stirring continuously, until the onion is soft but not browned. Add the soaked beans, measured water, stock cubes, pearl barley, mustard and parsley. Bring to the boil, reduce the heat and cover the pan, then simmer the soup for 45 minutes.

Add the split peas and lentils to the soup, then cover the pan and simmer for a further 30–45 minutes until both beans and split peas are tender. Remove the bones from the soup and cut the meat off them. Dice the meat and return it to the soup before serving. **Serves 4–6**

Brazilian Bean Soup

450 g/1 lb black beans
2 beef stock cubes
1.75 litres/3 pints water
100 g/4 oz pepperoni, thinly sliced
½ teaspoon salt
3 rashers rindless streaky bacon
1 medium onion, sliced
150 ml/¼ pint red wine
2 medium oranges
pared rind of 1 orange, finely shredded (optional)

Soak the beans overnight, then drain them and discard any that have not absorbed the water. Place the beans, stock cubes, water, pepperoni and salt in a saucepan.

Dry-fry the bacon until it is crisp, then drain it on absorbent kitchen paper. Sauté the onion in the fat remaining in the pan until soft but not browned, then add it to the beans. Bring the bean mixture to the boil, reduce the heat and cover the pan. Simmer until the beans are tender – about 1–1½ hours. Stir in the red wine and simmer for a further 30 minutes. Remove a few beans from the pan with a slotted spoon and mash them until smooth. Return the mashed beans to the soup.

Peel the oranges, taking care to remove all the pith. Cut between the membranes to remove the segments and add these to the soup. Heat through for 5 minutes then serve immediately. The soup may be garnished with thin shreds of orange rind. **Serves 6–8**

Mixed Bean Chowder

350 g/12 oz butter beans
100 g/4 oz borlotti beans
1.15 litres/2 pints water
1½ teaspoons salt
25 g/1 oz butter
1 onion, chopped
1 clove garlic, crushed
1 medium potato, diced
1 small green pepper, diced
about 300 ml/½ pint milk

Soak the beans overnight. Drain them and discard any that have not absorbed the water, then place them in a large saucepan with the water and salt. Melt the butter in a frying pan, add the onion and garlic and cook until the onion is soft but not browned. Add the cooked onion to the beans, bring to the boil and reduce the heat. Cover the pan and simmer until the beans are almost tender – about 1 hour – adding more hot water as required.

Stir the potato into the chowder and simmer for a further 30 minutes. Remove about 150 ml/¼ pint of the bean mixture from the pan and mash it to a smooth paste. Return the mashed mixture to the soup and stir well. Add the green pepper and enough milk to give the desired consistency for the soup. Heat through over low heat for about 10 minutes, stirring occasionally to prevent the soup burning on the base of the pan. **Serves 4–6**

Variations

Seafood Bean Chowder Cook the beans as above. Add 450 g/1 lb skinned haddock or cod fillets, cut into chunks, and 225 g/8 oz peeled prawns to the soup with the potatoes. Continue as above.

Bean Chowder with Frankfurters Prepare the soup as above. Add 225 g/8 oz thickly sliced frankfurters to the soup with the green pepper and continue as above.

Bean Soup with Bacon

350 g/12 oz haricot beans
1.75 litres/3 pints water
2 teaspoons salt
bay leaf
6 rashers rindless streaky bacon
1 onion, chopped
2 carrots, diced
leaves trimmed from 1 head celery, chopped
about 150 ml/¼ pint tomato juice

Soak the beans overnight then drain them, discarding any that have not absorbed the water. Place them in a large saucepan and add the measured water, salt and bay leaf. Dry-fry the bacon until it is crisp, then drain it on absorbent kitchen paper. Sauté the onion, carrot and celery leaves in the bacon fat remaining in the pan until the onion is soft but not browned.

Stir the sautéed vegetables into the beans and bring to the boil. Reduce the heat, cover the pan and simmer until the beans are tender – about 1–1½ hours. Remove and discard the bay leaf. Remove about 8 tablespoons of the beans from the pan and set aside. Drain the remaining beans, reserving the cooking liquid, and purée them in a liquidiser, adding the cooking liquid as necessary. Combine the bean purée and reserved beans in a saucepan. Stir in the tomato juice, adding enough to give the required consistency. Heat through for 10 minutes before serving. **Serves 4–6**

Serving suggestions For a light lunch or supper dish, try serving this soup with a variety of accompaniments which may be sprinkled over individual portions as required. For example, serve bowls of diced cooked ham or garlic sausage, grated Gruyère cheese or crumbled Stilton cheese, peeled prawns and croûtons – small, crisp-fried cubes of bread.

Pease Soup with Meatballs

450 g/1 lb green split peas
1.75 litres/3 pints water
4 beef stock cubes
1 onion, chopped
1 teaspoon salt
$\frac{1}{2}$ teaspoon dried basil
$\frac{1}{2}$ teaspoon dried marjoram
freshly ground black pepper
5 stalks celery with leaves, chopped
225 g/8 oz fresh spinach, chopped
MEATBALLS
450 g/1 lb minced beef
1 egg
50 g/2 oz fresh fine breadcrumbs
1 teaspoon salt
$\frac{1}{2}$ teaspoon dried basil
2 tablespoons oil

Place the peas in a large saucepan with the water. Crumble the stock cubes into the pan and add the onion, salt, basil, marjoram, pepper to taste and celery.

Bring to the boil, reduce the heat, then cover the pan and simmer until the peas are tender – about 45 minutes. Remove about 300 ml/$\frac{1}{2}$ pint of the soup from the pan and purée it in a liquidiser. Return the puréed soup to the pan and add the spinach.

Meanwhile make the meatballs, mix the beef with the egg, breadcrumbs, salt and basil until thoroughly combined. Dampen your hands and shape walnut-sized portions of the meat into neat balls. Heat the oil in a frying pan, add the meatballs and cook, turning continuously, until evenly browned. Add them to the soup and simmer for 15 minutes. **Serves 6–8**

Pease Soup with Meatballs

1 Roll walnut-sized pieces (small spoonfuls) of the meat mixture into balls. Shape all the meat mixture before frying any of the meatballs.

2 When all the meatballs are browned and removed from the pan, lower them into the soup and simmer gently.

Black-eye Bean Soup

50 g/2 oz butter
2 onions, chopped
450 g/1 lb black-eye beans
3 chicken stock cubes
1.4 litres/2½ pints water
bay leaf
¼ teaspoon dried thyme
2 teaspoons salt
1 (397-g/14-oz) can chopped tomatoes
8 frankfurters, sliced
2 tablespoons dry sherry

Melt the butter in a large saucepan, add the onions and cook, stirring, until soft but not browned. Meanwhile rinse the beans and add them to the pan with the stock cubes, water, bay leaf, thyme and salt. Bring to the boil, reduce the heat and cover the pan. Simmer for about 1–1½ hours until the beans are tender.

Add the tomatoes and stir in the frankfurters, cover the pan and simmer for a further 30 minutes. Add about 1 teaspoon sherry to each bowl of soup before it is served. **Serves 6–8**

Variations

Sliced cabanos, or garlic sausage or salami, cut into chunks, may be substituted for the frankfurters in this soup. Add a wedge of white cabbage, finely shredded, with the tomatoes and continue as above. Serve the soup with hot rye bread.

Black Bean Soup

450 g/1 lb black beans
25 g/1 oz butter
1 onion, chopped
1 clove garlic, crushed
1 stalk celery, chopped
½ lemon
4 cloves
1 meaty bacon hock
1 (435-g/14¾-oz) can consommé
1.75 litres/3 pints water
bay leaf
sprig of thyme
3 tablespoons dry sherry
2 hard-boiled eggs, sieved
2 tablespoons chopped parsley

Soak the beans overnight, then drain them and discard any that have not absorbed the water. Melt the butter in a frying pan, add the onion, garlic and celery and cook until the onion is soft but not browned.

Cut the lemon half into quarters and stick a clove into each quarter. In a large saucepan mix the lemon pieces, soaked beans, sautéed vegetables, bacon hock, consommé, water, bay leaf and thyme. Bring to the boil, reduce the heat, then cover the pan and simmer until the beans are tender – about 1–1½ hours.

Remove the hock and bay leaf from the soup. Reserve the meat from the hock for salads or sandwiches. Reduce the soup to a purée in a liquidiser, then press it through a fine sieve and return it to the pan. Stir in the sherry and reheat gently. Garnish each serving with sieved egg and a little chopped parsley. **Serves 4–6**

Creamed Butter Bean Soup

1 (425-g/15-oz) can butter beans
1 medium potato, diced
1 chicken stock cube
900 ml/1½ pints water
25 g/1 oz butter
1 small green pepper, chopped
1 small onion, chopped
1 clove garlic, crushed
2 tablespoons chopped fresh parsley
¼ teaspoon dried thyme
½ teaspoon dried basil
½ teaspoon salt
225 g/8 oz cream cheese
6 tablespoons milk

Place the butter beans, potato, stock cube and water in a large saucepan. Melt the butter in a frying pan, add the pepper, onion and garlic and cook until the onion is soft but not browned. Add this sautéed mixture to the butter beans and stir in the parsley, thyme, basil and salt. Bring to the boil, reduce the heat, then cover the pan and simmer for 30 minutes.

Stir in the cream cheese and milk. Heat the soup gently for 10 minutes, stirring occasionally, until the cheese melts. Serve immediately. **Serves 4**

Peanut Soup

225 g/8 oz butter beans
225 g/8 oz haricot beans
225 g/8 oz black-eye beans
1.75 litres/3 pints water
3 tablespoons oil
2 carrots, sliced
2 stalks celery, sliced
1 onion, chopped
1 green pepper, chopped
1 teaspoon salt
cayenne pepper to taste
1½ teaspoons dried basil
½ teaspoon ground coriander
100 g/4 oz salted peanuts, roughly chopped

Soak the butter, haricot and black-eye beans overnight, then drain them and discard any that have not absorbed the water. Place the soaked beans in a large saucepan with the water.

Heat the oil in a frying pan, add the carrots, celery, onion and green pepper and cook, stirring, until the onion is soft but not browned. Add the sautéed vegetables to the beans, stir in the salt, cayenne, basil and coriander. Bring to the boil, then reduce the heat and cover the pan. Simmer until the beans are tender – about 1–1½ hours. Add the peanuts and simmer for a further 10 minutes. **Serves 6–8**

Ginger Soup

1 To finely grate fresh root ginger, first use a sharp knife to cut away the tough skin.

2 Once the ginger is peeled, it can be finely grated.

Ginger Soup

350 g/12 oz butter beans
1.75 litres/3 pints water
1 meaty beef bone
2 beef stock cubes
2 tablespoons oil
1 medium onion, sliced
1 tablespoon grated fresh root ginger
1 teaspoon salt
1 tablespoon soy sauce
2 tablespoons cornflour
3 tablespoons water
1 medium green pepper
175 g/6 oz thin egg noodles

Soak the beans overnight, then drain them and discard any that have not absorbed the water. Mix the soaked beans with the measured water, beef bone and stock cubes in a large saucepan.

Heat the oil in a frying pan, add the onion and ginger and cook until the onion is soft but not browned. Add this fried mixture to the beans together with the salt and soy sauce. Bring to the boil, reduce the heat, then cover the pan and simmer until the beans are tender – about 1–1½ hours.

Mix the cornflour to a smooth cream with the water, then add it to soup, stirring constantly. Bring to the boil. Cut the green pepper in half lengthwise, remove the seeds, pith and stalk and cut the flesh first into fine strips and then into 5-cm/2-in lengths. Finally, stir the green pepper and noodles into the soup and cook for 10 minutes before serving. **Serves 6–8**

Variations

Lemon Ginger Soup Add the grated rind and juice of 1 lemon to the soup with the cornflour mixture, then continue as above.

Gingered Chicken and Sweet Corn Soup Omit the beef bone and beef stock cubes. Use chicken stock instead of the water and add 450 g/1 lb diced cooked chicken to the soup with the green pepper. Add 1 (340-g/12-oz) can sweet corn instead of the noodles.

Lentil Soup with Dumplings

450 g/1 lb lentils
1.15 litres/2 pints water
½ teaspoon salt
2 chicken stock cubes
2 tablespoons oil
2 large carrots, sliced
1 small head celery, finely sliced
1 medium onion, sliced
300 ml/½ pint milk
75 g/3 oz butter
75 g/3 oz Gruyère cheese, grated
50 g/2 oz cooked ham, chopped
100 g/4 oz self-raising flour
1 egg
½ teaspoon dry mustard

Mix the lentils, water, salt and stock cubes in a large saucepan. Bring to the boil and cook for 2 minutes, stirring occasionally, then remove the pan from the heat.

Heat the oil in a frying pan, add the carrot, celery and onion and cook until the onion is soft but not browned. Stir the sautéed vegetables into the lentils. Bring to the boil, reduce the heat, then cover the pan and simmer until the lentils are tender – about 45 minutes. Stir in the milk and heat through until the soup is hot but not boiling.

Meanwhile, prepare the dumplings. Cream the butter with the cheese and ham until soft. Stir in the flour, egg and mustard. Dust your hands with flour and shape generous teaspoons of the dumpling mixture into small balls – it should make about 24 dumplings. Drop the dumplings into the soup, cover the pan and simmer the soup gently until the dumplings are cooked – about 15 minutes. **Serves 6–8**

Lentil Soup with Dumplings

1 Drop the small dumplings into the simmering soup, then cover the pan and simmer for about 15 minutes. Do not stir the soup while the dumplings are cooking.

2 During cooking the dumplings will become soft and light. Ladle them carefully into the serving bowls.

Lentil Soup

4 rashers rindless streaky bacon, diced
1 medium onion, chopped
2 medium carrots, sliced
1 large stalk celery, sliced
450 g/1 lb lentils
2.25 litres/4 pints water
2 teaspoons salt
$\frac{1}{2}$ teaspoon pepper
$\frac{1}{2}$ teaspoon dried thyme
2 bay leaves
1 large potato, diced
1 meaty bacon hock

Dry-fry the bacon in a saucepan over low heat until crisp, then drain it on absorbent kitchen paper. Add the onion, carrots and celery to the fat remaining in the pan and cook until the onion is soft but not browned. Return the bacon to the pan, add the lentils, water, salt, pepper, thyme, bay leaves, potato and bacon hock.

Bring to the boil and reduce the heat, then cover the pan and simmer until the lentils are tender – about 45 minutes. Remove the hock and bay leaves from the pan and cut the meat off the bones. Dice the meat and add it to the soup, then heat through and serve immediately. **Serves 4–6**

Note When you boil a bacon or gammon joint reserve or freeze the stock to make soup. Dice any small amounts of leftover meat to add to the soup at the end of the cooking time, or add diced smoked sausage instead of the bacon hock.

Lentil Tomato Soup

350 g/12 oz lentils
1.15 litres/2 pints water
25 g/1 oz butter or margarine
1 onion, chopped
1 clove garlic, crushed
2 teaspoons salt
generous pinch of pepper
2 teaspoons sugar
$\frac{1}{4}$ teaspoon dried oregano
$\frac{1}{4}$ teaspoon dried basil
1 tablespoon chopped fresh parsley
1 (397-g/14-oz) can chopped tomatoes
3 tablespoons concentrated tomato purée

Mix the lentils and water in a large saucepan. Melt the butter or margarine in a frying pan, add the onion and garlic and cook until the onion is soft but not browned. Add the onion to the lentils, then stir in the salt, pepper, sugar, oregano, basil and parsley.

Bring to the boil and reduce the heat. Cover the pan and simmer until the lentils are tender – about 45 minutes. Add the tomatoes and tomato purée, stir well and simmer for a further 15 minutes. **Serves 4**

Variation

Try adding the grated rind and juice of 1 orange to this soup with the tomatoes and tomato purée. Swirl a little soured cream into each portion and garnish with chopped chives.

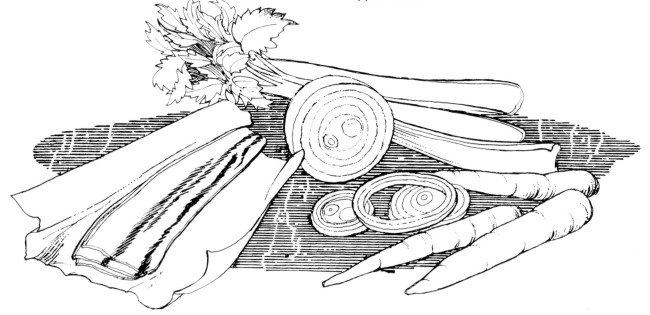

Haricot Bacon Soup

350 g/12 oz haricot beans
1.5 litres/2¾ pints water
1 meaty smoked bacon hock
25 g/1 oz butter
1 clove garlic, crushed
1 onion, chopped
1 teaspoon salt
freshly ground black pepper
2 bay leaves

Soak the beans overnight. Drain and discard any that have not absorbed the water. Place the soaked beans, measured water and hock in a saucepan.

Melt the butter in a frying pan, add the garlic and onion and cook until the onion is soft but not browned. Add this sautéed mixture to the beans. Stir in the salt, pepper to taste and bay leaves, then bring to the boil and reduce the heat. Cover the pan and simmer the soup until the beans are tender; about 1–1½ hours.

Remove the bacon hock and bay leaves from the pan. Cut the meat off the hock and discard the bones. Dice the meat, and return it to the soup. Heat through for 10 minutes before ladling into large soup bowls. **Serves 4–6**

Haricot Herb Soup

450 g/1 lb haricot beans
4 rashers rindless streaky bacon, diced
1 small onion, chopped
1 clove garlic, crushed
2 stalks celery, chopped
2.25 litres/4 pints water
2 teaspoons salt
freshly ground black pepper
½ teaspoon dried basil
¼ teaspoon dried oregano
450 g/1 lb pumpkin or marrow flesh

Soak the beans overnight, then drain them and discard any that have not absorbed the water. Dry-fry the bacon until crisp, then drain it on absorbent kitchen paper. Sauté the onion, garlic and celery in the fat remaining in the pan until the onion is soft but not browned. Transfer the vegetables to a large saucepan and add the bacon, beans, water, salt, pepper to taste, basil and oregano. Bring to the boil, reduce the heat and cover the pan. Simmer for 1 hour.

Cut the pumpkin or marrow into 2.5-cm/1-in cubes and add to the beans. Cook for a further 30 minutes. Remove a few of the beans from soup and mash them to a smooth paste. Stir the mashed bean paste into the soup to thicken it slightly and continue to cook for a further 10 minutes, stirring occasionally. **Serves 6–8**

Split Pea and Bacon Soup

2 tablespoons oil
1 medium potato, diced
2 stalks celery, chopped
1 small onion, chopped
1 clove garlic, crushed
450 g/1 lb green split peas
1 meaty bacon hock
freshly ground black pepper
2.25 litres/4 pints water
2 chicken stock cubes
bay leaf
150 ml/¼ pint milk

Heat the oil in a saucepan, add the potato, celery, onion and garlic and cook until the onion is soft but not browned. Add the split peas, bacon hock, pepper to taste, water, stock cubes and bay leaf. Bring to the boil, reduce the heat and cover the pan, then simmer until the split peas are tender – about 45 minutes.

Remove and discard the bay leaf. Lift the hock out of the soup and cut the meat from the bones. Dice and reserve the meat. Purée the soup in a liquidiser and return it to the pan. Stir in the diced meat and milk. Cook over medium heat for 10 minutes, stirring frequently, then serve steaming hot in large soup bowls. **Serves 6–8**

Split Pea and Mushroom Soup

450 g / 1 lb yellow split peas
2.25 litres / 4 pints water
3 chicken stock cubes
1 tomato, peeled and chopped
50 g / 2 oz butter
2 carrots, sliced
3 stalks celery, chopped
1 onion, chopped
225 g / 8 oz mushrooms, sliced
2 tablespoons chopped fresh parsley
bay leaf
$\frac{1}{2}$ teaspoon salt
$\frac{1}{2}$ teaspoon dried marjoram

Place the split peas, water, stock cubes and tomato in a large saucepan. Melt half the butter in a frying pan, add the carrot, celery, onion and half the mushrooms, then cook, stirring, until the onion is soft but not browned.

Add the vegetable mixture to the split peas and stir in the parsley, bay leaf, salt and marjoram. Bring to the boil, reduce the heat and cover the pan. Simmer until the peas are tender – about 45 minutes.

Melt the remaining butter in a small frying pan or saucepan, add the remaining mushrooms and stir them until the butter is absorbed. Add them to the soup and serve immediately. **Serves 6–8**

Vegetable Beef Soup

225 g / 8 oz butter beans
450 g / 1 lb meaty beef bones
2 litres / $3\frac{1}{2}$ pints water
2 beef stock cubes
1 teaspoon salt
6 peppercorns
1 stalk celery with leaves, chopped
bay leaf
1 medium onion, sliced
40 g / $1\frac{1}{2}$ oz pearl barley
2 carrots, sliced
about 75 g / 3 oz white cabbage (a medium wedge)
1 large tomato, peeled and diced
225 g / 8 oz French or runner beans, trimmed and cut into 2.5-cm / 1-in lengths
1 turnip or swede, diced
1 parsnip, diced

Soak the beans overnight, then drain them and discard any that have not absorbed the water. To prepare the stock place the beef bones, water, stock cubes, salt, peppercorns, celery, bay leaf and onion in a large saucepan. Bring to the boil, then reduce the heat and cover the pan. Simmer for 2 hours, then remove the bones and cut any meat off them. Dice the meat and set it aside.

Strain the stock through a fine sieve and return it to the pan. Add the soaked beans and pearl barley to the stock and bring to the boil. Reduce the heat, cover the pan and simmer the soup until the beans are tender – about 1 hour. Add the carrots, cabbage, tomato, French beans, turnip or swede and parsnip. Stir in the diced beef and simmer the soup for a further 30 minutes. **Serves 8**

Vegetable Beef Soup

Vegetable Soup

1 stalk celery including the leaves
1 carrot
50 g/2 oz butter
1 bunch spring onions, chopped
100 g/4 oz button mushrooms, thinly sliced
900 ml/1½ pints water
2 chicken stock cubes
½ teaspoon dried basil
salt and freshly ground black pepper
225 g/8 oz French beans, sliced diagonally
225 g/8 oz fresh spinach, finely shredded

Cut the celery and carrot into julienne strips. Melt the butter in a saucepan, add the spring onions, mushrooms, celery and carrot and cook until the onion is soft but not browned. Stir in the water, stock cubes, basil and seasoning to taste. Bring to the boil, then reduce the heat and cover the pan. Simmer for 10 minutes before adding the beans. Simmer for a further 15 minutes, then stir in the spinach and cook for 3 minutes. Serve immediately. **Serves 6–8**

Variation

To accentuate the oriental flavour of this soup, add sliced canned water chestnuts and canned whole baby sweet corn with the beans. Stir in 1 tablespoon light soy sauce and 2 tablespoons dry sherry before serving the soup.
For a low-calorie meal, serve a portion of this soup with a couple of slices of crispbread topped with cottage cheese and a sliced tomato. Follow up with a natural yogurt and fresh fruit for dessert.

Mixed Vegetable and Bean Soup

175 g/6 oz soya beans
1 thick gammon steak
1 tablespoon oil
1 small onion, chopped
1.15 litres/2 pints water
1 clove garlic, crushed
bay leaf
25 g/1 oz butter
2 stalks celery, chopped
2 carrots, chopped
1 (425-g/15-oz) can tomatoes
salt and freshly ground black pepper
2 chicken stock cubes

Soak the beans overnight, then drain them and discard any that have not absorbed the water. Trim the rind off the gammon and cut the meat into small dice. Heat the oil in a frying pan, add the gammon and onion and cook until the onion is soft but not browned.

Mix the soya beans, cooked onion and gammon, water, garlic and bay leaf in a large saucepan. Bring to the boil, reduce the heat, then cover the pan and simmer until the beans are tender – about 3 hours. Add a little extra water during cooking to keep the beans covered.

Remove the bay leaf, drain the beans and measure the cooking liquid. Add more water if necessary to make it up to 600 ml/1 pint. Reduce the beans to a smooth purée in a liquidiser, adding the reserved cooking liquid as needed.

Melt the butter in a frying pan, add the celery and carrots and cook for a few minutes. Add the tomatoes, stirring continuously to break them up, and season to taste. Mix the bean purée, any remaining cooking liquid and the sautéed vegetables in a large saucepan. Add the stock cubes and heat through, stirring until they have dissolved. Cover the pan and simmer for 15 minutes, then taste and adjust the seasoning before serving. **Serves 4–6**

Spinach and Bean Soup

225 g/8 oz butter beans
600 ml/1 pint water
¾ teaspoon salt
¼ teaspoon pepper
bay leaf
25 g/1 oz butter
1 onion, chopped
1 clove garlic, crushed
900 ml/1½ pints chicken stock
450 g/1 lb fresh spinach leaves, shredded
4 tablespoons grated Parmesan cheese

Soak the beans overnight, then drain them and discard any that have not absorbed the water. Transfer the beans to a medium saucepan and pour in the measured water. Add the salt, pepper and bay leaf, bring to the boil and reduce the heat. Cover the pan and simmer until the beans are tender – about 1–1½ hours.

Melt the butter in a small frying pan, add the onion and garlic and cook until the onion is soft but not browned. Add the onion mixture and chicken stock to the beans. Cover and simmer for a further 10 minutes before adding the spinach to the soup. Cook for a further 5 minutes, then remove and discard the bay leaf. Ladle the soup into individual bowls and sprinkle each with Parmesan cheese. **Serves 4**

Spanish Soup

450 g/1 lb butter beans
1.75 litres/3 pints water
4 chicken stock cubes
1 bacon hock
1 chicken joint
2 cloves garlic, crushed
1 onion, chopped
1 large tomato, peeled and quartered
2 medium potatoes, peeled and cubed
½ cabbage, shredded
salt and freshly ground black pepper

Soak the butter beans overnight, then drain them and discard any that have not absorbed the water. Place the beans in a large saucepan, then add the water and stock cubes. Bring to the boil, stirring until the stock cubes dissolve. Add the bacon, chicken, garlic and onion. Bring back to the boil, reduce the heat, then cover the pan and simmer until the beans are tender about 1–1½ hours.

Add the tomato and potatoes to the pan and cook for a further 30 minutes. Remove the bacon and chicken from the pan and cut the meat off the bones. Dice the meat and return it to the pan with the cabbage, then simmer for 10 minutes. Taste and adjust the seasoning if necessary. **Serves 6–8**

Minestrone

450 g/1 lb haricot beans
2 chicken stock cubes
1.4 litres/2½ pints water
1 teaspoon salt
2 tablespoons olive oil
25 g/1 oz butter
1 medium onion, halved and sliced
2 cloves garlic, crushed
2 carrots, cut into 5-mm/¼-in slices
1 stalk celery, sliced
1 leek, sliced
1 (425-g/15-oz) can tomatoes
1 tablespoon chopped fresh parsley
2 teaspoons dried basil
½ teaspoon dried oregano
salt and freshly ground black pepper
1 medium courgette, cut into 5-mm/¼-in thick slices
1 tomato, peeled and diced
½ small cabbage, shredded
50 g/2 oz elbow macaroni
freshly grated Parmesan cheese

Soak the beans overnight, then drain them discarding any that have not absorbed the water. Place the soaked beans in a large saucepan with the stock cubes and water. Add the salt and bring to the boil. Cover the pan and reduce the heat, then cook the haricot beans until they are tender – about 1–1½ hours.

Mix the olive oil with the butter in a large frying pan and heat slowly until the butter melts. Add the onion, garlic, carrot, celery and leek and cook, stirring, until the onion is soft but not browned. Stir in the tomatoes, parsley, basil, oregano and seasoning to taste.

Stir this cooked vegetable mixture into the beans and simmer for 20 minutes. Add the courgette, tomato, cabbage and macaroni and continue cooking for a further 15–20 minutes, until the macaroni is tender. Serve the soup in large bowls and sprinkle each serving with a little Parmesan cheese. **Serves 6–8**

Antipasto Platter

450 ml/¾ pint chicken stock
250 ml/8 fl oz dry white wine
4 tablespoons oil
2 tablespoons olive oil
6 tablespoons vinegar
6 sprigs fresh parsley
2 cloves garlic, crushed
1 teaspoon dried oregano
1 teaspoon salt
6 whole black peppercorns
2 small onions, quartered
1 small cauliflower, separated into florets
3 carrots, cut into 5-mm/¼-in slices
1 green pepper, cut into strips
1 large courgette, cut into 5-mm/¼-in slices
100 g/4 oz button mushrooms
1 (425-g/15-oz) can chick peas, drained
1 (425-g/15-oz) can cannellini beans
175 g/6 oz salami sliced
175 g/6 oz, Provolone or Gruyère cheese, sliced
½ quantity Vinaigrette Dressing (page 104)
12 to 16 black olives

To make the marinade, mix the first ten ingredients in a saucepan and bring to the boil. Reduce the heat, cover the pan and simmer for 10 minutes.

Add the onions, cauliflower and carrots to the pan, bring back to the boil and simmer for 3 minutes. Stir in the green pepper and courgettes, bring back to the boil, then drain the vegetables and reserve the marinade.

Place the blanched vegetables in a bowl, add the mushrooms and mix well. Mix the chick peas with the cannellini beans in a bowl. Pour some of the marinade over both the vegetables and the beans and chill both for at least 6 hours or overnight.

To serve, drain the beans and vegetables and arrange them in two neat piles on a large platter. Lay the salami and cheese around the edge of the platter and pour a little Vinaigrette Dressing over. Garnish with the olives. **Serves 4–6**

Miniature Croquettes

350 g/12 oz cooked black beans
25 g/1 oz butter
2 small onions, chopped
1 teaspoon salt
¼ teaspoon dried oregano
5 tablespoons grated Parmesan cheese
225 g/8 oz Cheddar cheese
1 egg
1 tablespoon water
50 g/2 oz dry white breadcrumbs
oil for deep frying

Roughly mash the beans. Melt the butter in a small frying pan, add the onion and cook until it is soft but not browned. Add the cooked onion, salt, oregano and 2 tablespoons of the Parmesan cheese to the beans and mix well. Cut the Cheddar cheese into 1-cm/½-in cubes.

Lightly whisk the egg with the water. Mix the breadcrumbs and remaining Parmesan cheese together on a plate. Take a generous tablespoon of the bean mixture and press a cube of cheese into it. Shape the bean mixture into a ball around the cheese, making sure that the cheese is completely covered. Continue until all the mixture is used.

Roll the croquettes first in the egg mixture and then in the breadcrumbs and Parmesan. Heat the oil to 180 C/350 F, then fry the croquettes until golden. Drain them on absorbent kitchen paper and serve hot or warm. **Makes 32**

Serving suggestion Arrange the croquettes on simple green salads in 4–6 individual dishes and pour a little Marinara Sauce (page 108) over each portion before serving.

Alternatively, for an informal start to a meal, pile the croquettes in a dish or on a platter and serve them with bowls of Creole Dipping Sauce (page 108) and Green Mayonnaise (page 106). Offer the croquettes and dips to your guests with their drinks before the main course.

Miniature Croquettes

1 Shape generous tablespoons of the bean mixture around the cheese cubes. Roll into neat balls, making sure the cheese is completely covered with the bean mixture.

2 Roll the croquettes first in the egg mixture, then in the breadcrumbs and Parmesan cheese.

Stuffed Avocado

1 (425-g/15-oz) can cannellini beans
2 tablespoons oil
1 teaspoon dried basil
100 g/4 oz peeled prawns
2 teaspoons chilli sauce (optional)
2 tablespoons tomato ketchup
2 teaspoons vinegar
2 drops Tabasco sauce
2 tablespoons diced celery
2 tablespoons chopped onion
2 ripe avocado pears

Mix the drained beans with the oil and basil, stirring well to coat the beans thoroughly with the oil. Stir the prawns into the bean mixture. Mix the chilli sauce (if used) with the ketchup, vinegar, Tabasco sauce, celery and onion. Pour this sauce over the bean mixture and stir to coat the beans and prawns. Halve and stone the avocados. Pile the bean and prawn mixture into them and serve immediately. **Serves 4**

Tangy Butter Bean Appetizer

225 g/8 oz butter beans
600 ml/1 pint water
1 teaspoon salt
3 tablespoons oil
2 cloves garlic, crushed
1 carrot, sliced
$\frac{1}{2}$ green pepper, diced
2 tablespoons chopped fresh parsley
pinch of dried dill weed
225 g/8 oz fresh young spinach leaves, washed and trimmed
1 lemon, cut in wedges

Soak the beans overnight. Drain them and discard the soaking water. Mix the beans, measured water and salt in a saucepan, bring to the boil, then reduce the heat and cover the pan. Simmer until the beans are tender – about 45 minutes.

Meanwhile, heat the oil in a frying pan, add the garlic, carrot and pepper and cook, stirring, for 2 minutes. Stir in the parsley and dill weed and cook for a further 3 minutes. Stir this vegetable mixture into the beans 15 minutes before the end of the cooking time. Remove the cooked beans from the heat and allow to cool.

Shred the spinach leaves and arrange them on six individual plates. Spoon the bean mixture over the spinach and garnish each portion with a wedge of lemon. **Serves 6**

Black-eye Bean Fritters

350 g/12 oz cooked black-eye beans
2 rashers rindless streaky bacon
2 small onions, finely chopped
1 clove garlic, crushed
1 egg, beaten
25–50 g/1–2 oz plain flour
$\frac{1}{4}$ teaspoon salt
freshly ground black pepper
pinch of dried thyme
oil for deep frying
1 quantity Creole Dipping Sauce (page 108)

Coarsely mash the beans. Dry-fry the bacon in a small frying pan until it is crisp. Drain it on absorbent kitchen paper and sauté the onion and garlic in the fat remaining in the pan. The onion should be soft but not browned. Add the sautéed onion mixture to the black-eye beans and stir in the egg. Add enough flour to give a stiff mixture and season it with salt, pepper and thyme. Mix thoroughly to combine all the ingredients.

Heat the oil for deep frying to 180 C/350 F or until a cube of day-old bread turns golden in 1 minute. Drop teaspoonsful of the fritter mixture into the oil and cook until golden brown – about 3–5 minutes. Drain the fritters on absorbent kitchen paper and serve hot or warm with Creole Dripping Sauce. **Serves 4**

Hummus

1 (425-g/15-oz) can chick peas
2 tablespoons lemon juice
½ teaspoon salt
2 tablespoons olive oil
50 g/2 oz cottage cheese
1 clove garlic, crushed
1 small onion, finely chopped
2 tablespoons sesame seeds
2 tablespoons chopped fresh parsley

Place the chick peas, lemon juice, salt, half the oil, cottage cheese and garlic in a liquidiser. Blend to a smooth purée. Heat the remaining oil in a frying pan, add the onion and cook until soft but not browned.

Carefully roast the sesame seeds over low heat in a heavy-based frying pan until golden, stirring continuously without allowing them to burn. Add the sesame seeds, parsley and fried onion to the chick pea purée. Serve immediately. Alternatively, chill thoroughly before serving with wedges of warm pitta bread and slices of cucumber to dip. **Serves 4**

Tofu and Avocado Dip

(illustrated on page 111)

225 g/8 oz tofu
1 ripe avocado pear
2 tablespoons soured cream or mayonnaise
½ teaspoon salt
1 teaspoon lemon juice
2 teaspoons finely chopped or grated onion
4 drops Tabasco sauce
cayenne pepper to taste

Break up the tofu with a fork. Halve the avocado, remove the stone and scoop out all the flesh. Mash it thoroughly and add it to the tofu together with all the remaining ingredients. Mix well and chill the dip for at least an hour before serving with crisps or small savoury biscuits to dip. **Serves 2–4**

Spicy Dip

25 g/1 oz butter
1 small onion, chopped
1 clove garlic, crushed
½ quantity Bean Purée (page 116)
100 g/4 oz tomatoes, peeled and chopped
freshly ground black pepper
1 teaspoon chilli powder
450 g/1 lb cocktail sausages, cooked *or* 1 quantity
Meatballs (Pease Soup with Meatballs page 23)

Melt the butter in a small saucepan, add the onion and garlic and cook until the onion is soft but not browned. Add the bean purée, tomatoes, pepper to taste and chilli powder. Mix well and bring to the boil, then serve hot with cocktail sausages or meatballs for dipping. **Serves 2–4**

Hot Bean and Cheese Dip

25 g/1 oz butter
1 large onion, finely chopped
3 green chillies, chopped
1 quantity Creamed Beans (page 74)
225 g/8 oz mature Cheddar cheese, grated

Melt the butter in a saucepan, add the onion and chillies and cook over a low heat until the onion is soft but not browned. Add the beans and heat through, stirring frequently over low heat until the mixture boils. Stir in the cheese and heat the mixture gently until it melts. Serve the dip immediately with bowls of crisps, savoury crackers and crispbread to dip. **Serves 6**

Main Dishes

You need add only small quantities of meat or poultry to bean dishes to create substantial main dishes, reducing both the cost and the effort involved in preparing a steak or roast beef dinner. The less expensive cuts of meat can be cooked for the same long periods that are needed to soften the beans, with tender, juicy results. Many of the bean stews in this chapter are complete meals: serve them with crusty bread and, if you like, a light salad to add variety to the meal.

There is, however, absolutely no need to set aside your favourite bean casserole for a mid-week family meal – a perfectly cooked, steaming hot casserole will often provide an interesting dish for an informal dinner party. You will be able to relax with your friends while the main course simmers away gently in the oven. Serve a simple starter, then accompany the casserole with a sophisticated salad – Iceberg lettuce with sliced avocado pear, perhaps, or a simple combination of cucumber

with fresh herbs – and a basket of sliced pumpernickel or rye bread.

One of the main advantages of bean casseroles and bakes is their excellent freezing properties. Spend a free afternoon preparing some of your favourite bean pots, bakes and stews (best not to finish cooking them completely) then pack them away in the freezer for your next supper party or busy family weekend. Remember to defrost the dish in advance so that it can be quickly reheated before serving.

With a little forethought, many of the dishes in this chapter can be adapted to feed a vegetarian friend – simply replace the meat and meat stock with vegetable stock and add some chopped nuts or cheese before serving. You are sure to find a main dish for almost every occasion in this chapter – the problem will be in deciding which one to cook.

Brunswick Stew (page 57)

Pot Roast of Beef

2 teaspoons salt
$\frac{1}{4}$ teaspoon pepper
$\frac{1}{2}$ teaspoon paprika
1.5 kg/3 lb boned and rolled brisket of beef
100 g/4 oz butter beans
100 g/4 oz borlotti beans
1.15 litres/2 pints water
2 beef stock cubes
2 tablespoons oil
1 onion, chopped
1 clove garlic, crushed
3 carrots, cut into 2.5-cm/1-in pieces

Mix the salt with the pepper and paprika and rub this seasoning all over the meat. Leave to stand overnight. Soak the beans overnight, then drain them discarding any that have not absorbed the water. Place the soaked beans in a large pan with the water and stock cubes.

Heat the oil in a large frying pan and brown the joint of brisket on all sides. Stand it on top of the beans in the saucepan. Sauté the onion and garlic in the fat remaining in the pan and add them to the meat in the saucepan with any juices from the frying pan.

Bring to the boil, cover the pan and reduce the heat, then simmer gently for 2 hours. Add the carrots and cook for a further 1 hour. Serve the meat on a large, deep, warmed platter surrounded by the beans, carrots and cooking juices. **Serves 6–8**

Variation

This recipe can also be made using a boiling chicken. Substitute chicken stock cubes for the beef stock cubes and do not brown the chicken before cooking. Cook for the same length of time as above, then remove the chicken from the pan, cut the meat off the bones and return to the pan to serve.

Cholent

225 g/8 oz haricot beans
2 tablespoons oil
1 onion, chopped
1 kg/2 lb boned and rolled brisket of beef
1 kg/2 lb potatoes, halved
salt and freshly ground black pepper
2 teaspoons paprika
2 beef stock cubes
1.15 litres/2 pints water

Soak the beans overnight, then drain them discarding any that have not absorbed the water. Heat the oil in a frying pan, add the onion and cook until soft but not browned. Add the brisket and brown it on all sides. Place the meat, onion, beans and potatoes in a large saucepan and sprinkle generously with salt and pepper. Add the paprika, crumbled stock cubes and pour in the water. Bring to the boil, cover the pan and reduce the heat, then simmer for 2 hours. **Serves 6**

Texas Chilli with Beans

1 tablespoon chilli powder
2 teaspoons ground cumin
3 tablespoons plain flour
1 teaspoon salt
1 kg/2 lb stewing steak
2 tablespoons oil
2 cloves garlic, crushed
900 ml/1$\frac{1}{2}$ pints beef stock
$\frac{1}{2}$ teaspoon dried oregano
1 quantity Western Beans (page 79)

Mix the chilli powder with the cumin, flour and salt. Cut the meat into bite-sized cubes and coat them in the seasoned flour. Heat the oil in a heavy-based flameproof casserole or saucepan, add the meat and garlic and cook, turning frequently, until evenly browned. Pour in the stock, add the oregano and heat gently to simmering point, stirring continuously. Cover the pan and cook the stew very gently for at least 2 hours or until the meat is tender.

Add the beans with their cooking liquid and bring back to simmering point. Simmer, uncovered, for 30 minutes. Serve piping hot. **Serves 4–6**

Spicy Beans with Beef

350 g/12 oz red kidney beans
1 litre/1¾ pints water
4 rashers rindless streaky bacon, diced
450 g/1 lb braising steak, trimmed and cut into cubes
2 onions, chopped
2 cloves garlic, crushed
1–2 tablespoons chilli powder
2 tablespoons cider vinegar
1 beef stock cube
1 tablespoon brown sugar
450 ml/¾ pint tomato juice
generous pinch of cayenne pepper (optional)
1 teaspoon salt

Soak the beans overnight, then drain them and discard any that have not absorbed the water. Transfer the beans to a large pan and pour in the measured water. Dry-fry the bacon until the fat runs leaving the pieces crisp. Stir the bacon into the beans. Add the beef to the fat remaining in the pan and fry it quickly until browned. Transfer the meat to the bean and bacon mixture. Quickly sauté the onions in the pan with the garlic and chilli powder, then add them to the beef mixture. Add the cider vinegar, stock cube, sugar and tomato juice, then stir in the cayenne (if used) and salt. Bring to the boil, boil for 3 minutes, then reduce the heat, cover the pan and simmer for 1–1½ hours until the beans and meat are tender. **Serves 4–6**

Ginger Steak

675 g/1½ lb braising steak, in one large slice
2 tablespoons plain flour
1 tablespoon oil
1 tablespoon grated fresh ginger root
600 ml/1 pint water
1 beef stock cube
2 tablespoons soy sauce
2 stalks celery, sliced
1 small onion, sliced
1 green pepper, chopped
225 g/8 oz mung bean sprouts
1 tablespoon cornflour

Dust the steak with the flour and pound it thoroughly on both sides with a meat mallet. Heat the oil in a large frying pan, add the steak and brown it on both sides. Add the ginger, water, stock cube and soy sauce. Bring to the boil, then cover the pan and simmer gently for about an hour until the meat is tender.

Remove the meat from the pan, place it on a warmed serving platter and keep hot. Add the celery, onion, green pepper and bean sprouts to the pan, cover and cook for 10 minutes. Remove the vegetables from the pan with a slotted spoon and arrange them over the meat. Blend the cornflour with a little water to give a smooth cream, gradually pour this into the pan and bring to the boil, stirring continuously. Simmer for a minute then pour this sauce over the vegetables and serve immediately. **Serves 4**

Beef and Bean Cobbler

450 g/1 lb minced beef
2 stalks celery, chopped
1 onion, chopped
1 green pepper, chopped
1 clove garlic, crushed
½ teaspoon salt
1 teaspoon paprika
1 (425-g/15-oz) can borlotti beans
350 g/12 oz cooked black-eye beans
4 tablespoons concentrated tomato purée
450 ml/¾ pint beef stock
225 g/8 oz plain flour
2 teaspoons baking powder
1 teaspoon salt
50 g/2 oz butter or margarine
150 ml/¼ pint milk

Fry the mince in a large heavy-based frying pan until evenly browned, add the celery, onion, green pepper and garlic and continue cooking until the onion is softened, then stir in the salt and paprika. Drain the borlotti beans and add them to the beef mixture together with the black-eye beans. Stir in the tomato purée and stock. Bring to the boil, reduce the heat and simmer for 30 minutes. Remove about an eighth of the meat mixture from the pan and allow it to cool.

To make the scone topping, sift the flour, baking powder and salt into a bowl, add the butter or margarine and rub it into the flour until the mixture resembles fine breadcrumbs. Stir in the milk to make a soft dough. Roll out the dough into a 30 × 20-cm/12 × 8-in rectangle. Spread the cooled mince mixture over this and roll up the dough from the long side. Cut 1-cm/½-in slices off the roll.

Transfer the beef mixture to an ovenproof dish and top with the neatly arranged scone pinwheels. Bake in a hot oven (220 C, 425 F, gas 7) for about 7–10 minutes or until the topping is cooked. Serve immediately.
Serves 4–6

Beef and Bean Cobbler

1 Roll out the scone dough to a 30 × 20-cm/12 × 8-in rectangle – the edges do not have to be perfectly straight as the dough will rise during cooking. Spread the cool mince mixture over and roll up.

2 Cut 1-cm/½-in thick slices off the roll and arrange them on top of the remaining mince mixture in an ovenproof dish.

Pozole

225 g/8 oz borlotti beans
2 rashers rindless streaky bacon
1 kg/2 lb stewing beef, trimmed and cubed
1 onion, chopped
1 clove garlic, crushed
750 ml/1¼ pints water
2 beef stock cubes
1 teaspoon dried oregano
2 stalks celery with their leaves, chopped
salt and pepper

Soak the beans overnight, then drain them discarding any that have not absorbed the water. Dry-fry the bacon until the fat runs, then remove it from the pan and drain it on absorbent kitchen paper. Add the beef to the pan and fry it, turning continuously, until browned on all sides. Add the onion and garlic and cook until the onion is softened.

Place the soaked beans in a large saucepan, crumble the bacon over them and add the beef and onion mixture. Pour in the water, then stir in the stock cubes, oregano and chopped celery. Bring to the boil, reduce the heat and simmer gently, in a covered pan, for 2½ hours. Taste and adjust the seasoning before serving.
Serves 4–6

Variation

This recipe makes an excellent pie filling: turn the cooked Pozole into a pie dish and top with Shortcrust Pastry (page 116). Brush with beaten egg or milk to glaze and bake in a moderately hot oven (200 C, 400 F, gas 6) for 30–40 minutes, until golden brown.

Mixed Meat and Haricot Stew

350 g/12 oz haricot beans
1.15 litres/2 pints water
1 chicken portion
1 chicken stock cube
1 teaspoon salt
225 g/8 oz stewing steak, cut into strips
225 g/8 oz carrots, sliced
1 medium onion, sliced
¼ teaspoon dried thyme
¼ teaspoon dried oregano
1 medium potato, diced

Soak the beans overnight, then drain them discarding any that have not absorbed the water. Transfer them to a saucepan, pour in the measured water, then add the chicken, crumbled stock cube, salt, stewing steak, carrots, onion, thyme and oregano. Bring to the boil, reduce the heat and cover the pan, then simmer for 30 minutes.

Remove the chicken portion from the pan and cut the meat from the bones. Add the potato to the beans and continue simmering for 1 hour. Meanwhile dice the chicken meat, add it to the pan and cook for a further 15 minutes. Serve immediately. **Serves 4–6**

Serving suggestion Serve this stew with thickly sliced hot granary bread or hot French bread and a crisp green salad.

Winter Hotpot

2 tablespoons oil
450 g/1 lb braising steak, cut into 2.5-cm/1-in cubes
450 g/1 lb lean boneless pork, cut into 2.5-cm/1-in cubes
1 onion, chopped
2 cloves garlic, crushed
1 (425-g/15-oz) can tomatoes
1.15 litres/2 pints water
3 beef stock cubes
1 teaspoon cumin seeds
1 (425-g/15-oz) can borlotti beans
2 medium potatoes, cubed
225 g/8 oz frozen cut French beans
salt and freshly ground black pepper

Heat the oil in a large frying pan, add the beef and pork and stir over medium heat until the meat is browned. Stir in the onion and garlic and cook for 2 minutes or until the onion is soft. Transfer the browned meat mixture to a large heavy-based saucepan and add the tomatoes, water, stock cubes and cumin seeds. Break up the tomatoes with a fork and bring the mixture to the boil, then reduce the heat. Cover and simmer until the meat is tender – about 1–1½ hours.

Add the borlotti beans, potatoes, French beans and seasoning to taste, then simmer for a further 30 minutes before serving. **Serves 6–8**

Variation

This hotpot tastes delicious made with lamb. Substitute 1 kg/2 lb stewing lamb for the braising steak and pork and continue as above. Alternatively use a boned breast of lamb cut into strips: omit the oil and dry-fry the lamb in a heavy-based pan until golden. Drain thoroughly and retain about 2 tablespoons of the dripping to cook the onion. Continue as above.

Puchero

450 g/1 lb chick peas
2 tablespoons oil
225 g/8 oz stewing beef, cut into 1-cm/½-in cubes
225 g/8 oz boneless pork, cut into 1-cm/½-in cubes
1 onion, chopped
2 cloves garlic, crushed
1.75 litres/3 pints water
4 chicken stock cubes
¼ teaspoon cumin seeds or ground cumin
1 dried red chilli *or* pinch of cayenne pepper
1 medium potato, cubed
1 medium tomato, peeled and diced
1 small green pepper, sliced into rings
275 g/10 oz frozen sweet corn
1 teaspoon salt

Soak the chick peas overnight, then drain them and discard any that have not absorbed the water. Heat the oil in a large frying pan, add the beef and pork and cook, stirring, until evenly browned. Remove the meat from the pan, place it in a large saucepan and add the soaked chick peas.

Add the onion and garlic to the frying pan and cook until soft but not browned. Stir the onion mixture, water, stock cubes, cumin, red chilli or cayenne into the beans. Bring to the boil, reduce the heat, then cover the pan and simmer for 1–1½ hours until the beans are tender.

Add the potato, tomato and green pepper to the pan. Stir in the sweet corn and salt and simmer for 30 minutes before serving. **Serves 4–6**

Beefy Burgundy Beans

1 quantity Western Beans (page 79)
450 g/1 lb lean minced beef
1 teaspoon salt
freshly ground black pepper
1 onion, chopped
1 clove garlic, crushed
3 tablespoons plain flour
300 ml/½ pint beef stock
300 ml/½ pint dry red wine
1 tablespoon concentrated tomato purée
½ teaspoon dried thyme
bay leaf
225 g/8 oz ribbon noodles

Prepare the Western Beans according to the recipe instructions, then drain them. Brown the beef in a heavy-based frying pan, seasoning it with the salt and pepper. Add the onion and garlic and cook, stirring, until the onion is soft. Sprinkle the flour over the meat mixture and stir to mix. Stir in the stock, wine and tomato purée, add the drained beans, thyme and bay leaf and mix well. Cover the pan and simmer for 30 minutes.

Cook the noodles in plenty of boiling salted water, then drain and transfer them to a warmed serving dish. Arrange the bean mixture on top and serve immediately. **Serves 6**

Note Beer can be substituted for the wine and stock in this recipe, but add 1 beef stock cube with the liquid.

Chilli Con Carne

450 g/1 lb minced beef
1 onion, chopped
2 stalks celery, chopped
2 cloves garlic, crushed
2 (397-g/14-oz) cans chopped tomatoes
150 ml/¼ pint tomato juice
300 ml/½ pint beef stock
2 teaspoons salt
generous pinch of cayenne pepper
2 (425-g/15-oz) cans red kidney beans
1–2 tablespoons chilli powder

Cook the beef in a large frying pan over low heat until well browned. Push the beef to one side of the pan and sauté the onion, celery and garlic on the other side until the onion is soft but not browned. Stir the beef and onion mixture together, then add the tomatoes, tomato juice, beef stock, salt, cayenne pepper and drained beans.

Stir in the chilli powder to taste. If you are not familiar with chilli dishes add it by the teaspoonful, tasting after each addition. Bring to the boil, then cover the pan and reduce the heat. Simmer for 45 minutes, then serve piping hot. **Serves 6**

Serving suggestion Serve Chilli con Carne with boiled rice and a cucumber or mixed green salad.

Meatballs with Beans

450 g/1 lb lean minced beef
100 g/4 oz minced pork
50 g/2 oz fine fresh breadcrumbs
1 egg
1 teaspoon salt
¼ teaspoon pepper
½ teaspoon ground cumin
20 stuffed olives
3 tablespoons oil
1 (425-g/15-oz) can red kidney beans, drained
1 (425-g/15-oz) can borlotti beans, drained
300 ml/½ pint beef stock

Combine the minced meats with the breadcrumbs, egg, salt, pepper and cumin. Mix thoroughly to bind the ingredients. Using wet hands, shape spoonfuls of the mince mixture into small meatballs around each of the olives.

Heat the oil and fry the meatballs, turning carefully until browned all over. Mix the beans with the stock in a saucepan and bring to the boil. Lower the meatballs into the pan, cover and reduce the heat. Simmer the beans and meatballs for about 30–40 minutes until the meat is cooked through and the sauce slightly thickened. Serve immediately. **Serves 4–6**

Beef-Topped Scone

225 g/8 oz minced beef
1 onion, chopped
1 (425-g/15-oz) can red kidney beans, drained
100 g/4 oz frozen sweet corn
1 (425-g/15-oz) can tomatoes, drained and chopped
2 tablespoons concentrated tomato purée
½ teaspoon ground cumin
salt and freshly ground black pepper
225 g/8 oz plain flour
1 teaspoon salt
4 teaspoons baking powder
¼ teaspoon turmeric
50 g/2 oz butter or margarine
150 ml/¼ pint milk
100 g/4 oz mature Cheddar cheese, grated

Fry the beef in a large, heavy-based frying pan over medium heat until evenly browned. Add the onion and cook until softened. Stir in the beans, sweet corn, tomatoes, tomato purée, cumin and seasoning to taste.

Prepare the spiced scone dough. Sift the flour, salt, baking powder and turmeric into a bowl, add the butter and rub it in until the mixture resembles fine breadcrumbs. Stir in the milk to form a soft dough. Knead lightly on a floured surface, then roll out into a 23-cm/9-in round and place it on a baking tray. Spread the beef mixture on top and sprinkle the cheese over. Bake in a hot oven (220 C, 425 F, gas 7) for 15–20 minutes until the dough is risen and cooked. Serve immediately. **Serves 6**

Beef-Topped Scone

Braised Spareribs

1.5 kg/3 lb pork spareribs
2 teaspoons salt
$\frac{1}{2}$ teaspoon pepper
$\frac{1}{2}$ teaspoon dried oregano
$\frac{1}{2}$ teaspoon dried basil
2 teaspoons chilli powder
2–4 tablespoons oil
1 large onion, sliced
2 cloves garlic, crushed
450 ml/$\frac{3}{4}$ pint dry red wine
2 (425-g/15-oz) cans red kidney beans, drained

Trim the spareribs of any excess fat and separate them into individual ribs. Mix the salt, pepper, oregano, basil and chilli powder, then rub these seasonings over the meat.

Heat the oil in a large frying pan, add the pork and cook, turning frequently, until the ribs are browned on all sides. Remove them from the pan and set aside. Add the onion and garlic to the oil in the pan and cook until the onion is soft. Transfer the onion to an ovenproof casserole and arrange the ribs on top. Pour the wine over the meat, cover the casserole and cook in a moderate oven (180 C, 350 F, gas 4) for $1\frac{1}{2}$–2 hours until the ribs are tender.

Remove the ribs from the casserole, arrange them on a warmed platter and keep hot. Stir the beans into the juices and heat for a further 5 minutes, then spoon them around the ribs and serve immediately. **Serves 6**

Chalupa

450 g/1 lb borlotti beans
1 tablespoon oil
450 g/1 lb boneless pork, shredded
2 cloves garlic, crushed
1 tablespoon ground cumin
1 teaspoon dried oregano
2 tablespoons chilli powder
2 teaspoons salt
1.15 litres/2 pints water
1 lettuce, shredded
1 large tomato, chopped
50 g/2 oz Cheddar cheese, grated
25 g/1 oz black olives, stoned and sliced
150 ml/$\frac{1}{4}$ pint soured cream

Soak the beans overnight, then drain them and discard any that have not absorbed the water. Heat the oil in a frying pan, add the pork and cook, stirring, until evenly browned. Place the beans, pork, garlic, cumin and oregano in a large saucepan. Stir in the chilli powder, salt and water and bring to the boil. Reduce the heat, cover the pan and simmer for $1\frac{1}{2}$–2 hours until the beans are tender. Arrange the lettuce in a ring on a large platter and top with the chopped tomato. Fill the middle of the lettuce with the bean mixture, sprinkle the cheese on top and add the sliced olives. Serve with soured cream. **Serves 4–6**

Black Beans and Rice

450 g/1 lb black beans
35 g/1 oz butter
1 onion, chopped
1.5 litres/2¾ pints water
1 beef stock cube
1 bacon hock
2 bay leaves
½ teaspoon dried thyme
½ teaspoon dried oregano
½ teaspoon salt
1 dried red chilli *or* generous pinch of cayenne pepper
225 g/8 oz long-grain rice
¼ teaspoon salt
1 green pepper, chopped
4 tablespoons dark rum (optional)
150 ml/¼ pint soured cream

Soak the beans overnight, then drain them and discard any that have not absorbed the water. Melt the butter in a large saucepan and sauté the onion in it until soft but not browned. Add the soaked beans, 1 litre/1¾ pints of the measured water, stock cube, bacon hock, bay leaves, thyme, oregano, salt and chilli or cayenne pepper. Bring to the boil, reduce the heat and cover the pan. Simmer until the beans are tender – about 1–1½ hours.

Meanwhile cook the rice in the remaining water and salt for about 15–20 minutes. Remove 4 tablespoons of the beans from the stew and mash them in a small bowl. Return the mashed beans to the stew and stir well. Remove the bacon hock and cut the meat from the bones. Dice the meat and return it to the pot with the green pepper and rum. Cover the pan and simmer for a further 15 minutes. Serve the beans on a bed of the drained rice and top with soured cream. **Serves 4–6**

Aduki Bean Stew

450 g/1 lb aduki beans
1 tablespoon oil
2 spring onions, chopped
1 onion, chopped
2 stalks celery with their leaves, chopped
2 cloves garlic, crushed
1.15 litres/2 pints water
1 teaspoon salt
¼ teaspoon pepper
dash of Tabasco sauce
1 (675-g/1½-lb) boneless bacon joint, cubed

Soak the beans overnight, then drain them and discard any that have not absorbed the water. Heat the oil in a heavy-based saucepan. Add the spring onions, and chopped onion, celery and garlic, then cook until the onion is soft but not browned. Add the beans, measured water, salt, pepper, Tabasco sauce and bacon to the pan and stir well. Bring to the boil, reduce the heat, cover the pan and simmer until the beans are tender – about 1–1½ hours.

Remove a few spoonfuls of the beans from the pan and mash them to a smooth paste, then return it to the pan and heat through thoroughly. Serve with boiled rice. **Serves 4–6**

Note For a simple vegetarian dish, omit the bacon from this recipe. Add 225 g/8 oz diced carrots and 2 sliced leeks halfway through the cooking time. Sprinkle the cooked beans with a mixture of chopped walnuts and finely grated cheese, garnish with chopped parsley and serve with cooked brown rice.

Old-fashioned Beans and Ham

1 You can use a bacon knuckle joint for this dish. Remove the bacon from the pan and carefully cut the meat off the bones.

2 Trim and discard any excess fat off the meat, then cut it into bite-sized pieces and stir it back into the beans.

Old-fashioned Beans and Ham

450 g/1 lb butter beans
4 rashers rindless bacon, diced
1 onion, chopped
3 bay leaves
1-kg/2-lb bacon joint
about 1.15 litres/2 pints water

Soak the beans overnight, then drain them and discard any that have not absorbed the water. Transfer them to a large saucepan. Dry-fry the bacon until it is crisp, add the onion and continue cooking until it is soft but not browned. Stir the bacon mixture into the beans. Add the bay leaves and bacon joint, then pour in just enough water to cover the meat. Bring to the boil, reduce the heat and cover the pan. Simmer for about 1 hour, until the beans are tender, then remove from the heat and allow to cool for at least an hour.

Lift out the bacon, cut off the fat and rind and cut the meat into bite-sized cubes. Return the meat to the pan and bring back to the boil. Reduce the heat and simmer, uncovered, for a further 30 minutes. Remove and discard the bay leaves, then serve on deep plates or in soup bowls. **Serves 4–6**

Variation

To make a wholesome winter hotpot, add a selection of prepared vegetables to the beans with the trimmed pieces of bacon. For example, add diced carrots, swedes, turnips or parsnips, sliced leeks and coarsely shredded cabbage. Stir in 4 tablespoons chopped fresh parsley, then serve with thickly sliced granary bread and wedges of mature Cheddar cheese.

To make a particularly filling meal, prepare herb dumplings to cook in this traditional winter dish. Sift 225 g/8 oz self-raising flour with a generous sprinkling of salt. Add 2 teaspoons dried mixed herbs and stir in 100 g/4 oz shredded suet. Add enough cold water to mix the dry ingredients to a soft dough, then shape the mixture into 8 dumplings. Add them to the pan 20 minutes before the end of the cooking time and continue to cook in the covered pan.

Lamb Stew

175 g/6 oz chick peas
1 tablespoon oil
1 kg/2 lb neck of lamb, cut into pieces
1 medium onion, sliced
1 carrot, sliced
2 cloves garlic, crushed
2 stalks celery, sliced
600 ml/1 pint beef stock
bay leaf
$\frac{1}{2}$ teaspoon dried thyme
1 teaspoon salt
$\frac{1}{2}$ teaspoon pepper
2 medium courgettes, thinly sliced
12 small (cherry) tomatoes, peeled

Soak the chick peas overnight, then drain them and discard any that have not absorbed the water. Heat the oil in a frying pan, add the lamb and cook, turning frequently, until browned all over. Remove from the pan and set aside. Sauté the onion, carrot, garlic and celery in the fat remaining in the pan until the onion is soft but not browned.

Transfer the sautéed vegetables to a large, heavy-based saucepan and add the soaked chick peas, browned lamb, stock, bay leaf, thyme, salt and pepper. Bring to the boil, reduce the heat, then cover the pan and simmer until the beans and lamb are tender – about 1–1$\frac{1}{2}$ hours.

At the end of the cooking time stir in the courgettes and cook for a further 5 minutes. Finally, stir in the tomatoes and simmer for 5 minutes before serving. **Serves 4**

Note Canned chick peas can be used for this recipe, in which case they should be drained and added to the casserole with the courgettes.

Peeling Tomatoes

1 Put the tomatoes in a colander and place it in a bowl. Pour boiling water over the tomatoes and leave to stand for $\frac{1}{2}$ minute.

2 Lift the colander from the bowl and discard the hot water. Place the tomatoes in the bowl and pour cold water over them. Use a small pointed knife to peel the tomatoes.

Lamb with Lentils

1 tablespoon oil
8 lamb chump end chops
2 cloves garlic, crushed
2 carrots, chopped
2 stalks celery, chopped
bay leaf
½ teaspoon dried thyme
900 ml/1½ pints water
salt and freshly ground black pepper
225 g/8 oz lentils
1 medium onion, peeled and quartered
pared rind from ½ lemon
1 teaspoon salt
GARNISH
sprigs of parsley
pared rind of 1 lemon

Heat the oil in a large frying pan or heavy-based saucepan. Add the chops and brown them on both sides. Add the garlic, carrot, celery, bay leaf, thyme, half the water, and seasoning to taste. Cover and simmer until the lamb is tender – about 1 hour.

While the lamb is cooking rinse the lentils and place them in a medium saucepan. Add the onion, lemon peel, remaining water and salt. Bring to the boil, reduce the heat and cover the pan. Simmer until the lentils are tender – about 45 minutes.

Remove the chops from their cooking liquid and stir the cooked lentils into it. Pour this mixture into an ovenproof dish and lay the chops on top. Dot each chop with a little butter and bake, uncovered, in a moderate oven (180 C, 350 F, gas 4) for 30 minutes. Garnish with sprigs of parsley and twists of pared lemon rind before serving. **Serves 4**

Cassoulet

(Illustrated on cover)

450 g/1 lb haricot beans
1.75 litres/3 pints chicken stock
2 tablespoons oil
1 duck
225 g/8 oz pickling onions
2 cloves garlic, crushed
100 g/4 oz rindless streaky bacon, chopped
450 g/1 lb Toulouse sausage, cut into chunks
few sprigs each of parsley and marjoram
2 bay leaves
½ teaspoon black peppercorns
1 (425-g/15-oz) can chopped tomatoes
3 tablespoons concentrated tomato purée

Soak the haricot beans overnight, then drain them and discard any that have not absorbed the water. Place the beans in a large saucepan and pour in the stock. Bring to the boil, then cover the pan and simmer gently for an hour.

Heat the oil in a large frying pan, add the duck and cook it, turning frequently, until evenly browned. Remove the duck from the pan and drain it on absorbent kitchen paper. Add the onions and garlic to the pan and cook, stirring continuously, for 5 minutes. Transfer the onions to a large ovenproof casserole and pour in the beans together with all the stock. Add the bacon and sausage to the frying pan, cook for a few minutes, then stir both into the beans.

Chop the duck into eight or ten pieces and add them to the pan. Tie the herbs and peppercorns up in a small piece of muslin or cheesecloth and add this bouquet garni to the casserole with the tomatoes and tomato purée. Cover the casserole and cook in a moderate oven (180 C, 350 F, gas 4) for 1½ hours or until the beans are tender, adding more water if necessary. Remove the bouquet garni before serving. **Serves 8**

Chicken and Okra Stew

1 (1.5-kg/3-lb) chicken
1 meaty bacon hock
1 litre/1¾ pints water
225 g/8 oz carrots, sliced
2 onions, chopped
1 green pepper, diced
2 stalks celery, chopped
2 teaspoons Worcestershire sauce
1 teaspoon salt
dash of Tabasco sauce
225 g/8 oz okra, trimmed and sliced
1 (425-g/15-oz) can butter beans, drained

Place the chicken in a large pan with the hock, water, carrots, onions, green pepper and celery. Add the Worcestershire sauce, salt and Tabasco sauce. Bring to the boil, reduce the heat and cover the pan, then simmer for 1 hour.

Remove the chicken and bacon hock and cut all the meat from the bones. Dice the meat and return it to the stew. Cook for a further 30 minutes, then stir in the okra and butter beans. Simmer for about 10 minutes, until the okra are tender, before serving in large soup bowls. **Serves 4-6**

Pioneer Stew

175 g/6 oz red kidney beans
175 g/6 oz chick peas
1 (1.5-kg/3-lb) chicken
1.5 litres/2¾ pints water
2 chicken stock cubes
1 dried red chilli
bay leaf
1 large onion, chopped
¾ teaspoon dried oregano
½ teaspoon dried basil
pinch of dried thyme
1 teaspoon salt
1 tablespoon chopped fresh parsley
2 tablespoons long-grain rice

Soak the beans and chick peas together overnight, then drain them and discard any that have not absorbed the water. Place the chicken in a large, heavy-based pan, add the water, stock cubes, chilli, bay leaf, drained beans, onion, oregano, basil, thyme, salt and parsley. Bring to the boil, boil for 3 minutes, then cover the pan and simmer gently until the chicken is tender – about 1 hour.

Remove the chicken from the pan and cut the meat from the bones. Dice the meat, return it to the pan and continue simmering until the beans are almost tender – about 15 minutes. Add the rice and simmer for a final 20 minutes. Serve immediately. **Serves 6-8**

Savoury Chicken

1.15 litres/2 pints water
3 chicken stock cubes
275 g/10 oz black-eye beans
5-cm/2-in piece thinly pared lemon rind
1 onion, finely chopped
1 carrot, grated
salt
150 ml/¼ pint natural yogurt
3 tablespoons lemon juice
2 cloves garlic, crushed
1 teaspoon ginger
¼ teaspoon ground cumin
¼ teaspoon turmeric
2 drops Tabasco sauce
6 chicken portions
2 tablespoons oil

Bring the water to the boil, add the stock cubes, beans, lemon peel, onion, carrot and salt. Return to the boil, cover the pan and reduce the heat. Simmer until the beans are tender – about 1–1½ hours.

Meanwhile mix the yogurt, lemon juice, garlic, 1 teaspoon salt, ginger, cumin, turmeric and Tabasco sauce. Pour this mixture over the chicken pieces and turn them in it to coat all sides. Allow to marinate while the beans are cooking.

Drain the beans, reserving 150 ml/¼ pint of the cooking liquid. Remove and discard the lemon peel. Heat the oil in a large frying pan, add the chicken pieces, remove them from the marinade and cook, turning until evenly browned. Place the drained beans with the measured, reserved cooking liquid in an ovenproof casserole. Pour in the marinade from the chicken and stir well. Lay the browned chicken portions on top, cover and cook in a moderate oven (180 C, 350 F, gas 4) for 45–50 minutes or until the chicken is cooked. **Serves 6**

Thrifty Chicken with Split Peas

1 litre/1¾ pints water
450 g/1 lb split peas
1 clove garlic, crushed
1 teaspoon salt
25 g/1 oz butter
1 bunch spring onions, chopped
225 g/8 oz button mushrooms, sliced
1 tablespoon oil
6 chicken portions
1 (283-g/10-oz) can cream of chicken soup
150 ml/¼ pint chicken stock
½ teaspoon dried basil
2 tablespoons chopped fresh parsley

Bring the water to the boil in a medium-sized saucepan. Add the split peas, garlic and salt, bring to the boil and boil for 2 minutes. Remove from heat, cover the pan and allow to stand for 30 minutes, then drain the peas and discard the liquid.

Melt the butter in a frying pan, add the spring onions and mushrooms and sauté them for a few minutes. Remove from the pan and place in an ovenproof casserole. Pour the oil into the frying pan, heat it gently, then add the chicken pieces and fry them, turning frequently until they are browned all over. Place the chicken in the casserole with the spring onion mixture and add the split peas.

Mix the soup with the stock and basil and pour this into the casserole. Stir lightly, then bake in a moderate oven (180 C, 350 F, gas 4) for 45–60 minutes. Keep the casserole covered for the first 30 minutes, then remove the lid and allow the top of the chicken pieces to brown. Sprinkle with chopped parsley and serve immediately. **Serves 6**

Curried Chicken with Beans

double quantity Savoury White Beans (page 74)
300 ml/½ pint chicken stock
2 boneless chicken breasts, skinned
1 tablespoon oil
25 g/1 oz butter
1 medium onion, chopped
1 clove garlic, crushed
3 medium carrots, sliced
1 small green pepper, diced
2 teaspoons curry powder
2 tablespoons plain flour
1 teaspoon salt

Prepare the Savoury White Beans according to the recipe instructions and drain them, reserving the cooking liquid. Add enough chicken stock to the cooking liquid to make it up to 300 ml/½ pint. Reserve any remaining chicken stock. Use a steak mallet or rolling pin to flatten the chicken breasts between two sheets of greaseproof paper, then cut each one in half lengthwise. Roll up each piece, starting at the short side, and secure with wooden cocktail sticks.

Heat the oil in a frying pan, add the chicken rolls and brown them on all sides. Add the reserved chicken stock and simmer until the chicken is tender – about 20 minutes. Remove the chicken from the cooking liquid and take out the cocktail sticks. Set aside.

Melt the butter in a saucepan, add the onion, garlic, carrot, green pepper and curry powder and cook until the onion is softened. Stir in the flour and salt and cook for a minute. Gradually pour in the cooking liquid from the chicken and the beans. Bring to the boil, then stir in the beans. Arrange the chicken rolls in an ovenproof casserole and pour in the beans. Cover and cook in a moderate oven (180 C, 350 F, gas 4) for 30 minutes. Serve immediately. **Serves 4**

To Skin and Bone Chicken Breasts

1 First remove the skin from the chicken. Lift the edge of the skin and cut it away from the flesh with a sharp, pointed knife.

2 Remove the bones from the chicken breast using a sharp, pointed knife. Carefully cut between the flesh and the bone, working along the length of the bones and cutting off as much of the meat as possible.

Spanish Rice

450 ml/¾ pint water
2 chicken stock cubes
¼ teaspoon saffron strands
2 tablespoons oil
6 chicken drumsticks
1 onion, chopped
1 clove garlic, crushed
225 g/8 oz long-grain rice
2 tomatoes, peeled and diced
salt and freshly ground black pepper
1 (425-g/15-oz) can chick peas, drained
100 g/4 oz pepperoni, sliced

Bring the water to the boil with the stock cubes. Stir in the saffron, then remove from the heat and allow to stand.

Heat the oil in a large frying pan, add the drumsticks and fry them, turning frequently, until golden brown. Remove from the pan and keep warm. Sauté the onion and garlic in the fat in the pan until the onion is softened, then add the rice. Cook, stirring continuously, until the rice is golden. Add the tomatoes and remove the pan from the heat.

Carefully strain the stock into the pan and season to taste. Stir in the chick peas and bring to the boil. Place the chicken drumsticks on top and cover the pan. Simmer gently for 20–30 minutes, adding the pepperoni for the last 5 minutes. Serve the dish, either from the cooking pan or on individual plates. **Serves 4–6**

Chicken Paprika

350 g/12 oz cooked butter beans
25 g/1 oz plain flour
1 teaspoon salt
3 teaspoons paprika
4 chicken portions
2 tablespoons oil
1 medium onion, sliced
225 g/8 oz frozen cut French beans, thawed
1 (425-g/15-oz) can chopped tomatoes
300 ml/½ pint chicken stock

Drain the butter beans. Mix the flour with the salt and 1 teaspoon of the paprika on a plate, then coat the chicken pieces in it. Heat the oil in a large frying pan and brown the chicken in it until golden. Remove from the pan and set aside. Sauté the onion in the oil remaining in the pan until soft but not browned.

Place the chicken portions in an ovenproof casserole. Add the fried onion, butter beans and French beans. Sprinkle over the remaining paprika and pour in the canned tomatoes and stock. Cover the casserole and cook for 45–60 minutes in a moderate oven (180 C, 350 F, gas 4) or until the chicken is cooked. Serve immediately. **Serves 4**

Variation

Pork Paprika Substitute pork chops for the chicken and add 1 large red or green pepper, sliced, instead of the French beans. Continue as above.

Brunswick Stew

(Illustrated on page 38)

4 chicken or rabbit portions
900 ml/1½ pints water
1 large onion, sliced
2 chicken stock cubes
pinch of cayenne pepper
2 teaspoons Worcestershire sauce
¼ teaspoon dried thyme
½ teaspoon dried oregano
225 g/8 oz shelled broad beans
2 medium potatoes, diced
1 (425-g/15-oz) can chopped tomatoes
275 g/10 oz frozen sweet corn
1 teaspoon salt
2 slices white bread

Place the chicken or rabbit portions in a large saucepan, then pour in the water and add the onion, stock cubes, cayenne pepper, Worcestershire sauce, thyme and oregano. Bring to the boil, reduce the heat and cover the pan. Simmer until the chicken or rabbit is tender and cooked – about 1 hour.

Remove the meat from the pan, then add the broad beans and potatoes to the boiling broth. Cover the pan and simmer until the potatoes are tender – about 20 minutes. Add the tomatoes, corn and salt and return the chicken or rabbit to the pot. Cover and simmer for a further 10 minutes. Break the bread into small cubes and add it to the stew, then cook for a minute stirring constantly, until thickened slightly. Serve the chicken or rabbit portions in large soup bowls and surround them with the cooking juices. **Serves 4**

Curried Chicken and Noodles

225 g/8 oz egg noodles
salt
50 g/2 oz butter
25 g/1 oz plain flour
½ teaspoon curry powder
300 ml/½ pint chicken stock
300 ml/½ pint dry white wine
¾ teaspoon dried dill weed
freshly ground black pepper
225 g/8 oz frozen French beans
350 g/12 oz cooked chicken, diced
4 tablespoons fine breadcrumbs

Cook the noodles in boiling salted water until tender – about 6–8 minutes. Meanwhile, melt half the butter in a small saucepan, add the flour and curry powder and cook, stirring continuously, for 2 minutes. Gradually stir in the stock and wine, then bring the sauce to the boil. Stir in the dill weed and seasoning to taste. Add the French beans and cook for 2 minutes before stirring in the chicken. Cook for a further 5 minutes.

Arrange the drained noodles in an even layer in the base of a serving dish. Pour in the sauce and keep hot. Melt the remaining butter in a frying pan, add the breadcrumbs and stir them over medium heat until golden brown. Sprinkle the crumbs over the sauce and serve immediately. **Serves 4**

Lunch and Supper Dishes

It is as important to consider the nutritional value of food when you are preparing a light lunch or supper as it is when you are thinking up the menu for the main meal of the day. So often a quickly snatched lunch or suppertime snack consists of little more than carbohydrate and fat. Beans and pulses, however, are an excellent source of protein as well as being quite filling, an advantage which makes them ideal for serving to a hungry, growing family.

This combination of bulk and high nutritional value means that beans and pulses can form the basis of a dish which can be served as a meal in itself, and which is particularly suitable for lunch or supper. Why not try, for example, making a Fiesta Casserole, Lentil Burgers or Italian Beans with Macaroni – these are all dishes that could easily become family favourites.

Many of the recipes in this chapter make use of the wide variety of canned beans which are available. Several types of canned beans are in no way inferior to those that are dried. The time saved in preparation makes canned beans one of the most valuable convenience foods. And don't forget that you can freeze many of the ready-prepared dishes in advance for heating up in a hurry.

Fiesta Casserole (page 60)

Fiesta Casserole

(Illustrated on page 58)

225 g/8 oz minced beef
1 onion, chopped
1 teaspoon salt
¼ teaspoon pepper
1 (425-g/15-oz) can borlotti beans, drained
2 (425-g/15-oz) cans chopped tomatoes
1 clove garlic, crushed
½ teaspoon ground cumin
2 teaspoons chilli powder
½ teaspoon dried oregano
4 tablespoons concentrated tomato purée
8 pancakes (page 69)
175 g/6 oz Cheddar cheese, grated
150 ml/¼ pint soured cream
parsley sprig to garnish

Brown the beef in a large frying pan, stirring continuously to prevent it from sticking to the base. Add the onion and cook until soft but not browned. Season generously with the salt and pepper, then add the beans and stir well. Combine the tomatoes, garlic, cumin, chilli powder, oregano and tomato purée in a saucepan. Bring to the boil, reduce the heat, then cover the pan and simmer for 10 minutes.

Layer the beef mixture with the pancakes and tomato sauce in an ovenproof dish, ending with a layer of sauce. Sprinkle the grated cheese on top and bake in a moderately hot oven (200 c, 400 f, gas 6) for about 30–40 minutes until golden brown and bubbling. Serve immediately and top with soured cream. Garnish with a sprig of parsley. **Serves 4–6**

Minced Beef Bake

225 g/8 oz lean minced beef
1 medium onion, sliced
salt and freshly ground black pepper
1 (425-g/15-oz) can red kidney beans
25 g/1 oz butter or margarine
2 tablespoons plain flour
600 ml/1 pint milk, warmed
3 medium potatoes, thinly sliced

Brown the beef in a heavy-based frying pan, stirring continuously. Add the onion and cook, stirring, until soft but not browned. Season with salt and plenty of pepper. Stir in the drained beans and set aside.

Melt the butter or margarine in a saucepan, stir in the flour and gradually add the warm milk, stirring continuously until smooth. Stir constantly over medium heat until the mixture boils and thickens. Season lightly. Layer the potatoes with the meat mixture, ending with the potatoes. Pour the sauce over and bake in a moderate oven (180 c, 350 f, gas 4) for an hour, until lightly browned and bubbling hot. **Serves 4**

Variations

Pork and Spinach Bake Substitute minced pork for the beef. Add 225 g/8 oz finely chopped fresh spinach and a pinch of dried sage with the beans. Continue as above.

Spicy Lamb Bake Substitute minced lamb for the beef. Cook 1 clove garlic, crushed, with the onion and stir in ¼ teaspoon mixed spice with the beans.

Ham and Cheese Bake Use 225 g/8 oz chopped cooked ham instead of the beef. Fry the onion in 25 g/1 oz butter, add the ham and continue as above. Top the bake with 100 g/4 oz grated mature Cheddar cheese before cooking.

Chilli Hamburgers

1 quantity Chilli Beans (page 80)
450 g/1 lb lean minced beef
50 g/2 oz fresh white breadcrumbs
1 egg, lightly beaten
1 teaspoon salt
freshly ground black pepper
$\frac{1}{4}$ teaspoon ground cumin
3–4 tablespoons oil
4 hamburger buns
50 g/2 oz butter
50 g/2 oz Cheddar cheese, grated

Prepare the Chilli Beans according to the recipe instructions and keep hot. Mix the minced beef, breadcrumbs, egg, salt, pepper and cumin together until thoroughly combined. Shape this meat mixture into four hamburgers.

Heat the oil in a large frying pan and fry the hamburgers over medium-high heat until browned on both sides and barely pink in the middle. Split the buns and butter both halves of each. Toast them, buttered side up, under a hot grill until golden. Place a hamburger on the base of each bun and top with the beans. Sprinkle the cheese over and place the second half of the bun on top. Serve immediately. **Serves 4**

Variations

Pork Burgers Substitute minced pork for the beef, omit the cumin and continue as above.

Sausage Burgers Use pork sausagemeat with herbs instead of the minced beef. Omit the cumin and continue as above.

Lentil Burgers

175 g/6 oz lentils
600 ml/1 pint water
1 teaspoon salt
50 g/2 oz brown rice
50 g/2 oz fresh breadcrumbs
50 g/2 oz walnuts, chopped
1 onion, finely chopped
freshly ground black pepper
$\frac{1}{4}$ teaspoon dried basil
50 g/2 oz wheatgerm
2 tablespoons oil
4 pieces pitta bread
1 small lettuce, shredded
2 tomatoes, sliced
150 ml/$\frac{1}{4}$ pint mayonnaise

Rinse the lentils and put them into a saucepan with the water and salt. Bring to the boil, then stir in the rice and reduce the heat. Cover the pan and simmer for 45 minutes. Stir the mixture occasionally to prevent it sticking to the pan. Mash the lentils and rice together, then stir in the breadcrumbs, walnuts, onion, pepper and basil. Allow to cool completely.

Shape the lentil mixture into four burgers and coat them in the wheatgerm. Heat the oil in a large frying pan and fry the burgers until they are browned, turning them once to brown both sides. Slit each piece of pitta bread horizontally and carefully separate the sides of bread to make a pocket. Place a cooked burger, with some of the lettuce and some tomato in each piece of bread. Serve immediately topped with mayonnaise. **Serves 4**

Sausage and Sauerkraut Bake

350 g/12 oz borlotti beans
25 g/1 oz butter
1 clove garlic, crushed
1.15 litres/2 pints water
1½ teaspoons salt
225 g/8 oz pork sausagemeat
1 onion, chopped
1 (450-g/1-lb) jar sauerkraut, drained
salt and freshly ground black pepper
1 (350-g/12-oz) smoked sausage, cut into 2.5-cm/1-in pieces

Soak the beans overnight, then drain them discarding any that have not absorbed the water. Transfer them to a large saucepan and add the butter, garlic, water and salt. Bring to the boil, reduce the heat and cover the pan, then simmer the beans for about 1–1½ hours until they are tender.

Meanwhile, dry-fry the sausagemeat in a heavy-based frying pan, breaking it up, until lightly browned. Add the onion and cook for a further 2–3 minutes. Drain the beans and layer them in an ovenproof casserole with the sausagemeat mixture and sauerkraut. Sprinkle each layer with a little seasoning. Top the casserole with the smoked sausage and pour in the stock. Bake, uncovered, in a moderate oven (180 C, 350 F, gas 4) for an hour. Serve immediately with a fresh spinach salad and thickly sliced black or light rye bread. **Serves 4 6**

Black Beans with Sausage

450 g/1 lb sausagemeat
1 tablespoon dried mixed herbs
1 clove garlic, crushed
1 large onion, chopped
1 green pepper, diced
3 large yellow or green courgettes
450 g/1 lb small (cherry) tomatoes
salt and freshly ground black pepper
½ teaspoon dried oregano
350 g/12 oz cooked black beans

Mix the sausagemeat with the dried mixed herbs and garlic. Cook in a large heavy-based frying pan, breaking it up into chunks. Carefully remove the sausagemeat and sauté the onion and green pepper in the fat remaining in the pan until the onion is soft but not browned.

Cut the courgettes lengthwise into quarters and then into 2.5-cm/1-in pieces. Peel the tomatoes and cut them in half. Add the courgettes, tomatoes, salt and pepper to taste and the oregano to the onion mixture. Stir in the black beans and the sausagemeat and cook over medium heat for about 15 minutes or until the courgettes are cooked. Serve immediately with boiled rice. **Serves 4-6**

Black Beans with Sausage

Bean and Sausage Stew

1 (425-g/15-oz) can red kidney beans
1 (425-g/15-oz) can borlotti beans
1 (425-g/15-oz) can chick peas
225 g/8 oz Italian salami
100 g/4 oz garlic sausage
1 onion, chopped
1 green pepper, chopped
1 (425-g/15-oz) can tomatoes
4 tablespoons concentrated tomato purée
1 teaspoon sugar
$\frac{1}{2}$ teaspoon dried basil
150 ml/$\frac{1}{4}$ pint chicken stock

Drain both cans of beans and the chick peas. Remove the skin from the salami and garlic sausage and cut both into chunks. Cook the salami with the garlic sausage, onion and pepper in a frying pan until the onion is soft but not browned.

Combine the kidney and borlotti beans in a saucepan. Add the chick peas and fried mixture, then pour in the tomatoes, tomato purée, add the sugar, basil and stock. Bring to the boil, then reduce the heat, cover the pan and simmer for 30 minutes. Serve with a fresh green salad and hot crusty bread. **Serves 4–6**

Variations

You can use smoked Dutch sausage, frankfurters or cabanos instead of the salami and garlic sausage in this recipe. Alternatively, use cooked ham or skinless chipolata sausages. The cooked mixture can be turned into an ovenproof dish, topped with 2 tablespoons breadcrumbs mixed with 2 tablespoons grated Parmesan cheese and browned under a hot grill before serving.

Frankfurter Casserole

25 g/1 oz butter
1 large onion, chopped
1 (425-g/15-oz) can butter beans, drained
1 (425-g/15-oz) can baked beans
1 (425-g/15-oz) can red kidney beans, drained
225 g/8 oz frankfurters, cut in 2.5-cm/1-in slices
3 tablespoons tomato ketchup
2 tablespoons brown sugar
1 teaspoon Worcestershire sauce
1 tablespoon prepared mustard
1 beef stock cube
300 ml/$\frac{1}{2}$ pint boiling water

Melt the butter in a heavy-based saucepan. Add the onion and cook until soft but not browned. Stir the butter beans, baked beans and kidney beans into the pan. Add the frankfurters, ketchup, sugar, Worcestershire sauce and mustard. Dissolve the stock cube in the boiling water and pour into the pan. Mix well, bring to the boil and simmer for 30 minutes before serving. **Serves 6**

Savoury Baked Beans

4 rashers rindless streaky bacon
1 onion, chopped
1 (425-g/15-oz) can baked beans
2 tablespoons chilli sauce
1 tablespoon brown sugar
1 teaspoon Worcestershire sauce
$\frac{1}{2}$ teaspoon prepared mustard

Dry-fry the bacon until crisp, then drain it on absorbent kitchen paper. Sauté the onion in the bacon fat remaining in the pan until soft but not browned. Add the beans and stir in the chilli sauce, brown sugar, Worcestershire sauce and mustard. Heat gently to boiling point, then crumble the bacon over the beans and serve immediately. **Serves 2**

Mixed Bean Bake

3 rashers rindless streaky bacon
1 medium onion, sliced
1 clove garlic, crushed
2 tablespoons brown sugar
2 tablespoons cider vinegar
2 teaspoons prepared mustard
1 (425-g/15-oz) can borlotti beans, drained
1 (425-g/15-oz) can baked beans
1 (425-g/15-oz) can red kidney beans, drained

Dry-fry the bacon over low heat until crisp, then drain it on absorbent kitchen paper. Sauté the onion and garlic in the fat remaining in the pan until the onion is softened – about 1 minute. Add the brown sugar, vinegar and mustard to the onion mixture and stir well.

Combine the borlotti beans, baked beans, kidney beans and onion mixture in an ovenproof casserole. Crumble the bacon over the top and stir to combine all the ingredients. Cover the casserole and bake in a cool oven (150 C, 300 F, gas 2) for 1 hour. Check the beans during cooking and add a little water if necessary to prevent them from drying up. **Serves 6**

Tomato Bean Bake

double quantity Savoury White Beans (page 74)
1 (425-g/15-oz) can chopped tomatoes
4 tablespoons concentrated tomato purée
½ teaspoon dried basil
salt and freshly ground black pepper
1 green pepper, diced
100 g/4 oz Emmental cheese, diced

Prepare the Savoury White Beans according to the recipe instructions. Drain the beans and place them in an ovenproof casserole. Add the tomatoes, tomato purée, basil, salt and pepper and stir well. Finally mix in the green pepper and cheese and bake in a moderate oven (180 C, 350 F, gas 4) for about 45 minutes. **Serves 4–6**

Mixed Chilli Fondue

(Illustrated on page 111)

450 g/1 lb mature Cheddar cheese, grated
225 g/8 oz minced beef
1 large onion, chopped
½ quantity Green Chilli Sauce (page 108)
1 teaspoon salt
2 (425-g/15-oz) cans red kidney or borlotti beans
1 French loaf, cut into cubes

Melt the cheese in a double saucepan or basin over a pan of hot water, stirring occasionally. Cook the mince in a frying pan with the onion until the meat is browned and the onion is softened. There should be enough fat from the meat to cook both it and the onion. Add the Green Chilli Sauce, salt and beans to the meat mixture and stir well. Cover the pan and cook over low heat for about 10 minutes until the mixture is cooked.

Stir the bean mixture into the melted cheese and transfer it to a fondue pan. Keep hot but do not allow the sauce to stick to the bottom of the pan. Dip the pieces of bread into the sauce. Sprigs of cauliflower, slices of eating apple and chunks of celery also taste good with the fondue. **Serves 4**

Boston Baked Beans

450 g/1 lb haricot beans
1.4 litres/3 pints water
1 medium onion, halved and sliced
100 g/4 oz belly of pork rashers, sliced
4 tablespoons molasses
3 tablespoons sugar
1 teaspoon dry mustard
1½ teaspoons salt
¼ teaspoon pepper

Soak the beans overnight, then drain them and discard the water. Mix the soaked beans and water in a saucepan. Bring to the boil, reduce the heat, then cover the pan and simmer for 10 minutes. Drain the beans in a colander over a large bowl, reserving the cooking liquid. Layer the beans, onion and pork in a large ovenproof casserole.

Mix the molasses, sugar, mustard, salt and pepper with a little of the reserved cooking liquid. Pour this mixture over the beans, then add more of the reserved cooking liquid to cover the beans. Cover the casserole and bake in a cool oven (150 C, 300 F, gas 2) for 4–6 hours until the beans are tender. Check the beans several times during cooking, stirring in more of the cooking liquid if necessary to keep the beans just covered while they are cooking. **Serves 6–8**

Note This is, perhaps, one of the best known and most widely imitated traditional bean dishes. The familiar baked beans that you buy in cans are, in fact, based on this old American bean pot recipe.

When you take the trouble to prepare this dish, it is worth spending a little time planning the rest of the meal to suit it. You will find that, for a nourishing lunch or supper, you need only serve as accompaniments a crisp mixed salad with either a Creamy Spinach Dressing (page 107) or a Thousand Island Dressing (page 106). Alternatively, for a more substantial meal, crisp grilled or barbecued chicken, hamburgers, sausages, chops or gammon steaks are all complemented by Boston Baked Beans.

Boston Baked Beans

1 Layer the beans, onion and pork in an ovenproof casserole.

2 Mix the molasses, sugar, mustard, salt and pepper together with a little of the reserved cooking liquid and pour this mixture over the beans.

Spanish Rice and Bean Pie

1 Use the back of a metal spoon to press the rice mixture around the sides of a shallow pie dish.

2 Spread the cottage cheese over the rice, then top with the cooked beans.

Spanish Rice and Bean Pie

1 quantity Western Beans (page 79)
1 teaspoon ground cumin
250 ml/8 fl oz water
1 chicken stock cube
100 g/4 oz long-grain rice
25 g/1 oz butter
1 onion, chopped
1 green pepper, chopped
2 tablespoons chopped canned pimiento
100 g/4 oz cottage cheese
100 g/4 oz Cheddar cheese, coarsely grated

Prepare the Western Beans according to the recipe instructions. Drain the beans and reserve about 150 ml/¼ pint of the cooking liquid. Stir the cumin into the beans and set aside. Bring the water and stock cube to the boil, stirring to dissolve the cube. Add the rice and bring back to the boil. Reduce the heat to the lowest setting, cover the pan and simmer for 20 minutes until the stock is absorbed.

Melt the butter in a frying pan, add the onion and green pepper and cook until the onion is soft but not browned. Stir in the pimiento and add this mixture to the rice. Stir well, then press the rice around the base and sides of a shallow 23-cm/9-in pie dish to line it completely. Fill the rice shell with the cottage cheese and top with the cooked beans. Sprinkle the Cheddar evenly over the top and bake in a moderate oven (180 C, 350 F, gas 4) for about 30–40 minutes until the cheese has melted and lightly browned. Allow to stand for 10 minutes before serving. **Serves 4–6**

Swiss Beans

450 g/1 lb French beans
150 ml/¼ pint water
½ teaspoon salt
25 g/1 oz butter
1 small onion, finely chopped
1 tablespoon plain flour
1 teaspoon salt
white pepper
150 ml/¼ pint soured cream
100 g/4 oz Emmental cheese, grated

Trim the French beans and cut them into 2.5-cm/1-in pieces. Bring the water and salt to the boil, add the beans, reduce the heat and cover the pan. Simmer for 10–15 minutes until just tender and drain well.

Melt the butter, add the onion and cook until soft but not browned, then stir in the flour, salt and pepper. Cook, stirring continuously, for about 3 minutes. Add the soured cream and stir over low heat until thickened. Stir in the French beans and transfer to an ovenproof casserole. Sprinkle the cheese on top and bake in a moderate oven (180 C, 350 F, gas 4) for 20 minutes. Serve immediately. **Serves 4–6**

Beans with Cheese

1 quantity Savoury White Beans (page 74)
25 g/1 oz butter
1 tablespoon plain flour
450 ml/¾ pint milk
225 g/8 oz mature Cheddar cheese, grated
salt and freshly ground black pepper

Prepare the Savoury White Beans according to the recipe instructions, then drain off the cooking liquid.

While the beans are cooking make the cheese sauce. Melt the butter in a saucepan, add the flour and cook, stirring continuously, for 2 minutes. Gradually add the milk and bring to the boil stirring all the time. Stir in most of the grated cheese and seasoning to taste. Heat gently until the cheese has melted.

Place the beans in an ovenproof dish. Pour over the cheese sauce and sprinkle the remaining cheese on top. Brown under a hot grill and serve immediately. **Serves 3–4**

Italian Beans with Macaroni

225 g/8 oz elbow macaroni
2 tablespoons olive oil
1 onion, chopped
2 cloves garlic, crushed
2 large tomatoes, peeled and chopped
4 tablespoons concentrated tomato purée
300 ml/½ pint chicken stock
1 tablespoon chopped fresh parsley
pinch of dried basil
½ teaspoon dried oregano
freshly ground black pepper
1 (425-g/15-oz) can cannellini beans
4 slices Mozzarella cheese

Cook the macaroni in plenty of boiling salted water until just tender – about 10 minutes. Drain and set aside. Heat the oil in a frying pan and sauté the onion and garlic until the onion is soft but not browned. Stir in the tomatoes, tomato purée, stock, parsley, basil, oregano and pepper. Cover and simmer for 5 minutes.

Add the beans with their liquid and macaroni to the sauce and mix well. Arrange the cheese slices over the mixture, cover the pan and simmer over very low heat for 15 minutes. Serve straight from the pan. **Serves 4**

Celery and Cheese Casserole

25 g/1 oz butter
4 stalks celery, sliced diagonally
225 g/8 oz frozen cut French beans, thawed
225 g/8 oz frozen asparagus, thawed and cut up
225 g/8 oz frozen broccoli, thawed
1 (283-g/10-oz) can cream of celery soup
100 g/4 oz Cheddar cheese, grated

Melt the butter in a frying pan, add the celery and cook until it is softened but not browned. Transfer the celery to an ovenproof dish, add the French beans, asparagus and broccoli and stir in the soup. Cover the dish and bake in a moderate oven (180 C, 350 F, gas 4) for 40 minutes. Uncover the dish, sprinkle the cheese over the bean mixture and cook for a further 15 minutes. Serve immediately. **Serves 4–6**

Stuffed Pancakes

25 g / 1 oz butter
2 spring onions, sliced
1 small green pepper, chopped
1 quantity Creamed Beans (page 74)
100 g / 4 oz Cheddar cheese, grated
4 large pancakes (see next recipe)
3 tablespoons oil
4 eggs
½ quantity Green Chilli Sauce (page 108)
2 medium tomatoes, diced
1 small lettuce, shredded

Melt the butter in a saucepan, add the spring onions and green pepper and cook until soft but not browned. Add the beans and warm them through over medium heat for 10 minutes, stirring frequently. Stir in half the cheese, cover and cook gently until the cheese melts.

Heat the pancakes in a large frying pan and keep hot. Heat the oil in the pan and fry the eggs in it until the whites are set. Divide the bean mixture between the pancakes, spreading it over one half of each. Place a fried egg on top of the beans and sprinkle with some of the Chilli Sauce. Finally top each with the diced tomato and remaining cheese. Fold up the pancake in the shape of an envelope to enclose the filling completely.

Transfer to warmed serving plates and garnish each with a generous quantity of shredded lettuce. Top with more Chilli Sauce and serve immediately. **Serves 4**

Variations

There are many recipes which are suitable for stuffing pancakes: for example try pancakes with Bean and Sausage Stew (page 64), Black Beans with Sausage (page 62) or Celery and Cheese Casserole (opposite).

Pancakes

50 g / 2 oz plain flour
pinch of salt
1 large egg
150 ml / ¼ pint milk
oil or butter for frying

Sift the flour and salt into a bowl and make a well in the centre. Crack the egg into the hollow and add a little of the milk. Gradually beat the egg and milk into the dry ingredients, adding more of the milk to make a smooth batter. Leave the batter to stand for 30 minutes if possible.

Heat a large frying pan and grease it with a little oil or butter. Pour in enough of the batter to form a thin layer over the base of the pan. Cook over fairly high heat until the pancake is set and golden underneath, then turn it over and cook until browned on the second side. **Makes 4 large pancakes**

Taco Beans

1 quantity Creamed Beans (page 74)
450 g / 1 lb lean minced beef
1 teaspoon chilli powder
½ teaspoon ground cumin
1 teaspoon salt
1 teaspoon plain flour
6 tablespoons beef stock
8 taco shells
1 lettuce, shredded
2 tomatoes, diced
100 g / 4 oz Gouda cheese, grated
1 (300-g / 10.6-oz) can taco or tomato sauce, heated

Prepare the Creamed Beans according to the recipe instructions and keep hot. Brown the mince in a frying pan, stirring continuously until evenly cooked. Add the chilli powder, cumin, salt and flour, then stir in the stock, cover the pan and cook for 10 minutes.

Fill the taco shells first with the beans, then with the mince and top with shredded lettuce and diced tomato. Sprinkle the cheese over and drizzle the taco or tomato sauce on top. Serve immediately. **Serves 4**

Aubergine Rolls

1 Cut the tops off the aubergines and peel them. Cut the aubergines lengthwise into slices.

2 Brush both sides of the aubergine slices with oil before cooking them for about 3 minutes on each side.

3 Place a little of the filling on each slice of aubergine and roll up, securing with a wooden cocktail stick if necessary. Arrange the rolls in an ovenproof dish.

Aubergine Rolls

2 large aubergines
6 tablespoons oil
1 (425-g/15-oz) can chick peas
100 g/4 oz cottage cheese
1 egg yolk
225 g/8 oz fresh spinach, chopped, cooked and thoroughly drained
1 tablespoon chopped fresh parsley
2 spring onions, chopped
1 teaspoon salt
1 quantity Marinara Sauce (page 108)
100 g/4 oz Mozzarella cheese, grated

Trim and peel the aubergines, then cut them lengthwise into thin slices. Brush both sides of the slices with a little oil and cook them gently in a frying pan until soft. Mix the chick peas with the cottage cheese, egg yolk, spinach and parsley. Stir in the spring onions and salt, mix well and place a little of this filling on each slice of aubergine. Roll up and secure with wooden cocktail sticks.

Place the rolls in an ovenproof dish and pour the sauce over them. Sprinkle the cheese on top and bake in a moderate oven (180 C, 350 F, gas 4) for 30 minutes. Serve immediately. **Serves 4–6**

Ham and Bean Sprout Omelette

50 g/2 oz butter
50 g/2 oz cooked ham, diced
2 tablespoons chopped chives
1 tablespoon chopped parsley
100 g/4 oz mung bean sprouts or lentil sprouts
2 tablespoons cottage or cream cheese
3 eggs
2 tablespoons milk
salt and freshly ground black pepper

Warm a serving plate. First prepare the filling: melt half the butter in a saucepan, add the ham, chives, parsley and bean or lentil sprouts. Toss well then stir in the cheese and allow to heat slowly as you cook the omelette.

Beat the eggs lightly with the milk and seasoning. Melt the remaining butter in a large frying pan. When it is very hot pour in the eggs and cook quickly, lifting the sides of the omelette as it sets to let the uncooked egg run on to the pan. When the underneath is golden brown spoon the filling into the middle of the omelette. Roll one side of the set egg mixture over the filling, then roll the middle of the filled omelette over the third portion and on to the warmed plate. Cut the omelette in half and serve immediately. **Serves 2**

Egg Foo Yung

1 tablespoon cornflour
2 tablespoons water
300 ml/½ pint chicken stock
salt and freshly ground black pepper
1 tablespoon soy sauce
4 eggs
350 g/12 oz fresh mung bean sprouts
4 mushrooms, sliced
6 water chestnuts, diced
2 spring onions, chopped
½ teaspoon salt
3 tablespoons oil

Blend the cornflour with the water. Heat the chicken stock with seasoning to taste and the soy sauce. Stir in the cornflour mixture and bring to the boil. Cover the pan and leave the sauce over very low heat.

Beat the eggs and stir in the bean sprouts, mushrooms, water chestnuts, spring onions and salt. Heat the oil in a wok or frying pan and add about a quarter of the egg mixture. Cook until set and brown on the underneath, then turn over and cook until brown on the second side. Transfer to a warmed serving plate and serve immediately with the sauce. Repeat with the remaining mixture. **Serves 4**

Savoury Bean Pizza

1 quantity Savoury White Beans (page 74)
¼ teaspoon dried oregano
1 tablespoon chopped fresh parsley
pinch of dried thyme
¼ teaspoon dried basil
1 quantity Marinara Sauce (page 108)
1 (275-g/10-oz) packet white bread mix
100 g/4 oz Italian salami, sliced
100 g/4 oz pepperoni, sliced
1 medium onion, sliced and separated in rings
50 g/2 oz black olives, stoned and sliced
1 medium green pepper, cut into rings
175 g/6 oz Mozzarella cheese

Prepare the Savoury White Beans according to the recipe instructions, then drain and mash them reserving a little of the cooking liquid. Add enough of the cooking liquid to make a spreading consistency. Stir in the oregano, parsley, thyme and basil. Prepare the Marinara Sauce according to the recipe instructions.

Make up the bread mix according to the packet instructions and roll it out into a circle 35 cm/14 in. in diameter. Place the circle of dough on a baking tray or pizza plate and spread the bean mixture over it. Top with the Marinara Sauce and layers of the salami, pepperoni, onion, olives and pepper. Slice the Mozzarella and lay it on top of the pizza. Bake in a moderately hot oven (200 C, 400 F, gas 6) for 40 minutes. Serve bubbling hot. **Serves 4**

Baked Chilli Sandwiches

10 thick slices bread
50 g/2 oz butter
1 quantity Texas Chilli with Beans (page 40)
100 g/4 oz Cheddar cheese, grated
2 eggs
150 ml/¼ pint milk
½ teaspoon salt

Spread one side of each of 6 slices of the bread with the butter and arrange them, buttered side down, in a large ovenproof dish. Spoon the chilli mixture on top and sprinkle the cheese over. Cut the remaining slices of bread in half diagonally and arrange them on top. Beat the eggs with the milk and salt and pour this mixture over the bread, allowing it to soak in. Bake in a moderate oven (180 C, 350 F, gas 4) until risen and golden brown – about 45–60 minutes. Serve immediately. **Serves 4–6**

Stuffed Pitta Bread

1 (425-g/15-oz) can chick peas
1 ripe avocado, peeled, stoned and diced
50 g/2 oz stuffed olives, sliced
100 g/4 oz fresh young spinach leaves, washed and trimmed
3–4 tablespoons Sesame Seed Dressing (page 107)
4 pieces pitta bread

Combine the drained chick peas, avocado, olives, spinach and Sesame Seed Dressing and toss gently. Make a horizontal slit into each piece of pitta bread to make a pocket and stuff each with some of the chick pea mixture. Serve immediately. **Serves 4**

Oriental Pocket Sandwiches

50 g/2 oz mung bean sprouts
2 tablespoons light sesame oil
1 boneless chicken breast, skinned and shredded
1 stalk celery, diced
1 small onion, finely chopped
100 g/4 oz mangetouts, cut into thirds
50 g/2 oz water chestnuts, sliced
½ teaspoon salt
2 tablespoons chicken stock
1 tablespoon dry white wine
2 teaspoons soy sauce
¼ teaspoon sugar
generous pinch of ginger
1 teaspoon cornflour
1 tablespoon water
4 pieces pitta bread
2 tablespoons flaked almonds, toasted

Rinse and dry the bean sprouts. Heat the oil in a wok or large frying pan. Add the chicken, celery and onion. Stir-fry until the chicken is cooked, then add the mangetouts, water chestnuts and salt. Stir in the chicken stock, wine, soy sauce, sugar and ginger, simmer gently for 5 minutes, then stir in the bean sprouts. Mix the cornflour to a smooth cream with the water and stir into the chicken mixture. Stir constantly over medium heat until the liquid thickens and boils.

Make a slit in each piece of pitta bread to form a pocket and carefully separate the sides of the bread. Fill the bread with the chicken mixture and top with flaked almonds. Serve immediately. **Serves 4**

Hearty Accompaniments

There are times when we all tire of the same old potato ideas, boiled rice or buttered pasta. So, for a change, why not try one of the recipes in this chapter as an accompaniment to your main dish? You will find a whole variety of sweet and spicy bean pots and cooked beans to complement all manner of fish or meat dishes.

If you're planning a barbecue or quick grill meal, you can have the accompanying bean dish prepared in advance ready to reheat and serve at the last minute. Most cooked bean dishes will keep quite well for a few days in a covered dish in the refrigerator. It is also worth remembering the wide range of canned beans which can be found in most good supermarkets: they are already cooked and are very quickly prepared.

Try and use your imagination in your presentation of the bean dishes – you could serve them on a platter as a base on which to arrange a colourful casserole, kebabs or some crisp grilled chicken portions. Make sure that beans which are meant to be served hot are, indeed, piping hot; and remember that bean dishes are quite filling. Encourage people to help themselves – that way they will be able to take as much or as little as they want.

Creamed Beans

1 quantity Western Beans (page 79)
50 g/2 oz butter
50 g/2 oz Cheddar cheese, grated
150 ml/¼ pint soured cream

Drain and reserve the cooking liquid from the beans. Melt the butter in a large frying pan, add the beans and mash them with a potato masher as they cook. Continue cooking, stirring continuously, until all the fat is absorbed. Stir in some of the reserved cooking liquid, a little at a time, for a thinner consistency. Add the cheese and cook, stirring continuously, until it melts. Serve immediately, topped with soured cream. **Serves 4**

Savoury White Beans

225 g/8 oz large or small butter beans
900 ml/1½ pints water
2 chicken stock cubes
1 tablespoon oil
2 tablespoons chopped onion
1 clove garlic, crushed
¼ teaspoon salt

Soak the beans overnight. Drain them, discarding any which have not absorbed the water and place them in a medium saucepan. Add the water and stock cubes. Heat the oil in a small frying pan and sauté the onion and garlic in it until soft but not browned.

Stir this onion mixture into the beans with the salt. Bring to the boil, reduce the heat and cover the pan. Simmer for about an hour or until the beans are tender. **Serves 4**

Country-Style Butter Beans

350 g/12 oz butter beans
1.95 litres/3¼ pints water
100 g/4 oz lean rindless bacon, chopped
1 medium onion, quartered
2 teaspoons salt
1 teaspoon Worcestershire sauce
1 tablespoon vinegar
¼ teaspoon dry mustard
4 tablespoons molasses
dash of chilli sauce

Rinse the beans, then place them in a pan with the water, bacon, onion and salt. Bring to the boil, reduce the heat and cover the pan. Simmer until the beans are almost tender – about 1–1½ hours. Add hot water as needed to keep the beans just covered while they are cooking.

Drain the beans reserving 300 ml/½ pint of the cooking liquid. Stir the beans and reserved cooking liquid, Worcestershire sauce, vinegar, dry mustard, molasses and chilli sauce together in a casserole. Cover and bake in a cool oven (150 C, 300 F, gas 2) for a further 30 minutes. **Serves 6–8**

Lemon Butter Beans

1 (425-g/15-oz) can butter beans, drained
2 carrots, coarsely grated
4 spring onions, chopped
2 tablespoons chopped fresh parsley
grated rind of 1 large lemon
2 tablespoons lemon juice
3 tablespoons salad oil
freshly ground black pepper
1 clove garlic, crushed

Mix the drained beans with the carrots, spring onions and parsley. In a small container with a tight-fitting lid, combine the lemon rind and juice, oil, a generous sprinkling of pepper and garlic. Shake vigorously for about a minute, then pour this dressing over the salad and stir gently. Chill for several hours or overnight if possible. **Serves 4**

Butter-baked Beans

450 g / 1 lb butter beans
2 litres / 3½ pints water
1 tablespoon oil
2 teaspoons salt
2 tablespoons honey
50 g / 2 oz butter
100 g / 4 oz pearl onions

Rinse but do not soak the beans. Place them in a saucepan with all but 300 ml / ½ pint of the water, oil and salt. Bring to the boil and reduce the heat, then cover the pan and simmer until the beans are almost tender – about 1–1½ hours. Add more hot water to the pan as needed so as to keep the beans just covered while they are cooking. Drain, reserving about 300 ml / ½ pint of the cooking liquid.

Put the beans in an ovenproof casserole. Combine the reserved cooking liquid, honey and butter and stir until the butter melts. Pour this mixture over the beans, stir it in, then cover the casserole and bake in a cool oven (150 C, 300 F, gas 2) for 1 hour.

Heat the remaining 300 ml / ½ pint water to boiling point, add the onions and bring back to the boil.

Reduce the heat, cover and simmer for 5 minutes. Drain the onions, add them to the beans and re-cover the casserole. Cook for a further hour. **Serves 6–8**

Note Serve these beans instead of potatoes, rice or pasta, with your main dish. They can be cooked at the same time as meaty casseroles, stews or slow-cooked pot roasts. Alternatively they can be cooked in a slow cooker. Follow the manufacturer's instructions for cooking times.

Butter-Baked Beans

1 Beans which are not covered with liquid will dry out during cooking. Check the beans and top up with just enough hot water to cover them.

2 Bring the liquid back to the boil, then reduce the heat and continue simmering the beans.

Curried Butter Beans

2 rindless rashers streaky bacon, diced
1 onion, chopped
1 teaspoon curry powder
1 (283-g/10-oz) can cream of mushroom soup
2 tablespoons maple syrup or maple-flavoured syrup
2 tablespoons chilli sauce
2 (425-g/15-oz) cans butter beans, drained

Dry-fry the bacon until crisp, then drain it on absorbent kitchen paper and sauté the onion in the fat remaining in the pan. Stir in the curry powder, cook for a minute, then add the soup, syrup, chilli sauce and butter beans. Bring to the boil, cover the pan and reduce the heat, then simmer for 20 minutes. Finally stir in the crumbled bacon and serve. **Serves 4–6**

Creamy Creole Beans

25 g/1 oz butter
1 onion, chopped
1 green pepper, chopped
1 (300-g/10.6-oz) can tomato sauce
1 medium tomato, peeled and diced
$\frac{1}{2}$ teaspoon salt
$\frac{1}{4}$ teaspoon black pepper
$\frac{1}{2}$ teaspoon sugar
1 (425-g/15-oz) can butter beans, drained
75 g/3 oz full fat soft cheese, cubed

Melt the butter in a frying pan, add the onion and green pepper and cook until soft but not browned. Pour in the tomato sauce and add the tomato, salt, pepper and sugar. Bring to the boil, then cover the pan, reduce the heat and simmer for 10 minutes. Stir in the butter beans and cream cheese and heat through until the cheese has melted. **Serves 3–4**

Succotash

275 g/10 oz frozen sweet corn
1 (425-g/15-oz) can butter beans
25 g/1 oz butter
salt and freshly ground black pepper
1 tablespoon plain flour
150 ml/$\frac{1}{4}$ pint chicken stock
150 ml/$\frac{1}{4}$ pint milk or single cream

Mix the sweet corn and butter beans together in an ovenproof dish. Melt the butter in a saucepan, add seasoning to taste and the flour. Cook, stirring, for a minute then gradually add the stock and bring to the boil, still stirring. Remove from the heat and stir in the milk or cream. Pour this sauce over the bean mixture and bake in a moderate oven (180 C, 350 F, gas 4) for 30 minutes. **Serves 4**

Gingered Beans with Peaches

1 quantity Savoury White Beans (page 74)
150 ml/$\frac{1}{4}$ pint Spicy Tomato Sauce (page 108)
2 tablespoons brown sugar
$\frac{1}{2}$ teaspoon ginger
1 teaspoon prepared mustard
1 (410-g/14$\frac{1}{2}$-oz) can peach slices

Prepare the Savoury White Beans according to the recipe instructions. Drain the beans reserving 6 tablespoons of the cooking liquid. Mix the beans, reserved liquid, tomato sauce, brown sugar, ginger and mustard in a casserole, stir well and arrange the peach slices on top. Cover and bake in a cool oven (140 C, 275 F, gas 1) for 1 hour. **Serves 4**

Orange Baked Beans

350 g/12 oz haricot beans
1.95 litres/3¼ pints water
1 tablespoon oil
2 teaspoons salt
4 tablespoons concentrated tomato purée
2 tablespoons tomato ketchup
150 ml/¼ pint orange juice
½ teaspoon Worcestershire sauce

Rinse the beans, then place them in a saucepan and add the water, oil and salt. Bring to the boil, reduce the heat, then cover the pan and simmer until the beans are almost tender – about 1½–2 hours. Add hot water as needed to keep the beans just covered while they are cooking.

Drain the beans, reserving about 300 ml/½ pint of the cooking liquid. Transfer the beans to a casserole, then mix in the reserved cooking liquid, tomato purée, ketchup, orange juice, and Worcestershire sauce. Stir well, cover the casserole and bake in a cool oven (150 C, 300 F, gas 2) for 1 hour. **Serves 6–8**

Southern Baked Beans

450 g/1 lb haricot beans
2.25 litres/4 pints water
1 tablespoon oil
1 medium onion, sliced
1½ teaspoons salt
bay leaf
1 small red pepper, chopped
2 tablespoons molasses
4 tablespoons tomato ketchup
1 tablespoon prepared mustard
1 teaspoon Worcestershire sauce
½ teaspoon ginger
100 g/4 oz belly of pork rashers, thinly sliced
2 tablespoons brown sugar

Rinse but do not soak the beans. Transfer them to a large saucepan, then add the water, oil, onion, salt, bay leaf and red pepper. Bring to the boil, reduce the heat and cover the pan. Simmer until the beans are almost tender – about 1½–2 hours, checking the beans to make sure they do not dry out during cooking. Drain, reserving 300 ml/½ pint of the cooking liquid, then remove and discard the bay leaf.

Mix the reserved cooking liquid with the molasses, ketchup, mustard, Worcestershire sauce and ginger and mix well. Transfer the beans to a large ovenproof casserole and pour the molasses mixture over them, stirring well. Arrange the pork on top and sprinkle with brown sugar. Cover and bake in a cool oven (150 C, 300 F, gas 2) for 2 hours. **Serves 6–8**

Sweet and Sour Baked Beans

1 quantity Savoury White Beans (page 74)
1 (227-g/8-oz) can pineapple slices in natural juice
1 teaspoon cornflour
1 tablespoon soy sauce
2 tablespoons vinegar
2 tablespoons sugar
2 drops Tabasco sauce
½ medium green pepper, cut into strips

Prepare the Savoury White Beans according to the recipe instructions and drain them reserving the cooking liquid. Drain the pineapple, reserving the juice and cut the slices into chunks. Add the reserved cooking liquid to the juice to make it up to 250 ml/8 fl oz. Cream the cornflour with a little of the juice mixture, then stir it back into the liquid.

In a small saucepan, combine the cornflour mixture, soy sauce, vinegar, sugar and Tabasco sauce. Stir constantly over medium heat until the sauce boils, then remove from the heat. Combine the beans, green pepper strips and drained pineapple in an ovenproof casserole and pour the sauce over. Stir gently, cover and bake in a cool oven (140 C, 275 F, gas 1) for an hour. **Serves 4**

Western Beans

225 g/8 oz borlotti or red kidney beans
900 ml/1½ pints water
1 clove garlic, crushed
1 onion, chopped
25 g/1 oz butter
1 teaspoon salt
freshly ground black pepper

Soak the beans overnight. Drain them, discarding any which have not absorbed the water and place them in a saucepan with the water, garlic, onion, butter and salt. Season generously with pepper and bring to the boil. Reduce the heat, cover the pan and simmer for 1–1½ hours until the beans are tender.

Allow the cooked bean mixture to cool for 1 hour, then reheat it before serving. The cooling and standing process reduces excess moisture and improves the flavour of the dish. **Serves 4**

Confetti Beans

225 g/8 oz frozen cut green beans
1 (425-g/15-oz) can red kidney beans, drained
1 (425-g/15-oz) can butter beans
1 teaspoon Worcestershire sauce
¼ teaspoon pepper
½ teaspoon dry mustard
75 g/3 oz full fat soft cheese, cut into cubes

Cook the green beans according to the packet instructions and drain them. Heat the kidney and butter beans together, then drain them. Mix all the hot beans together in a saucepan, add the Worcestershire sauce, pepper, mustard and cheese. Heat gently, stirring occasionally until the cheese melts and serve immediately. **Serves 4–6**

Sweet and Sour Baked Beans served with grilled pork chops and broccoli

Chilli Beans

175 g/6 oz aduki or borlotti beans
900 ml/1½ pints water
½ teaspoon salt
1 tablespoon vegetable oil
1 small onion, chopped
4–6 tablespoons Green Chilli Sauce (page 108)
½–1 teaspoon chilli powder

Soak the beans overnight. Drain the beans and discard any that have not absorbed the water, then place them in a saucepan with the water and salt.

Heat the oil in a frying pan and add the onion. Cook until soft but not browned, then stir into the beans. Bring to the boil, reduce the heat and cover the pan. Simmer for about 1–1½ hours until the beans are tender.

Meanwhile, prepare the Green Chilli Sauce. Drain the beans, reserving the cooking liquid. Mix 3 tablespoons of the cooking liquid with the Green Chilli Sauce and chilli powder, then stir this mixture into the beans. Simmer for a further 30 minutes, stirring frequently and adding more of the reserved cooking liquid if necessary. **Serves 4**

Burgundy Bean Casserole

350 g/12 oz aduki beans
2 litres/3½ pints water
1 tablespoon oil
1 onion, chopped
2 teaspoons salt
150 ml/¼ pint Burgundy or full-bodied red wine
2 tablespoons soft brown sugar
150 ml/¼ pint soured cream

Rinse but do not soak the beans. Place them in a large saucepan with the water, oil, onion and salt. Bring to the boil, reduce the heat and cover the pan. Simmer until the beans are almost tender – about 1½–2 hours. Check several times during cooking, adding more hot water if necessary to keep the beans just covered.

Drain the beans, reserving the cooking liquid, then transfer them to an ovenproof casserole and add the wine, brown sugar and enough of the reserved cooking liquid to just cover the beans – about 300 ml/½ pint. Stir well. Cover and bake in a cool oven (150 C, 300 F, gas 2) for 2 hours. Uncover and bake for a further 30 minutes. Top the casserole with soured cream before serving. **Serves 6–8**

Swedish Bean Bake

350 g/12 oz aduki beans
2.25 litres/4 pints water
1 tablespoon oil
1½ teaspoons salt
1 cinnamon stick
6 tablespoons soft brown sugar
3 tablespoons cider vinegar
4 tablespoons dark golden syrup

Rinse the beans and mix them with the water, oil, salt and cinnamon stick in a saucepan. Bring to the boil, reduce the heat, then cover the pan and simmer until the beans are almost tender. This should take about 1½–2 hours. Add hot water as needed to keep the beans just covered while they are cooking.

Drain the cooked beans, reserving the cooking liquid. Transfer the beans to an ovenproof casserole and stir in the brown sugar, vinegar, syrup and enough of the reserved cooking liquid to just cover the beans. Cover the casserole and bake in a cool oven (150 C, 300 F, gas 2) for 2 hours. Uncover and bake for a further 30 minutes. Remove the cinnamon stick before serving. **Serves 6–8**

Note This is a sweet-tasting savoury bean dish – if you prefer accompaniments which are not as sweet as this, omit the golden syrup.

Jamaican Bean Pot

450 g/1 lb black beans
2.25 litres/4 pints water
1 onion, chopped
1 clove garlic, crushed
2 stalks celery, sliced
2 carrots, sliced
2 tablespoons oil
bay leaf
1½ teaspoons salt
1 tablespoon molasses
3 tablespoons brown sugar
3 tablespoons dark Jamaican rum
1 teaspoon dry mustard
pinch of dried thyme
2 tablespoons butter

Do not soak the beans. Rinse them, then place in a saucepan with the water. In a medium frying pan, fry the onion, garlic, celery and carrot in the oil until the onion is soft but not browned. Add the sautéed vegetables, bay leaf and salt to the beans and stir well. Bring to the boil, reduce the heat and cover the pan. Simmer until the beans are almost tender – about 1½–2 hours. Add more hot water if necessary to keep the beans just covered while they are cooking.

Drain the beans reserving the cooking liquid, then remove and discard the bay leaf. Mix the molasses, brown sugar, 2 tablespoons of the rum, dry mustard and thyme. Put the beans in a casserole and pour the molasses mixture over them. Add enough of the reserved cooking liquid to just cover the beans, then cover the casserole. Bake in a cool oven (150 C, 300 F, gas 2) for 2 hours. Uncover the casserole, dot with butter and cook for a further 30 minutes. Stir in the remaining rum just before serving. **Serves 6–8**

Savoury Beans with Rice

350 g/12 oz black-eye beans
900 ml/1½ pints water
1 clove garlic, crushed
bay leaf
½ teaspoon dried marjoram
salt to taste
¼ teaspoon black pepper
pinch of cayenne pepper
3 rashers rindless bacon
1 onion, chopped
250 ml/8 fl oz water
100 g/4 oz long-grain rice

Place the beans in a saucepan with the water, garlic, bay leaf, marjoram, salt, pepper and cayenne. Bring to the boil, then reduce the heat, cover the pan and simmer for 1–1½ hours until tender.

Dry-fry the bacon in a heavy-based saucepan until crisp, then remove it from the pan and drain on absorbent kitchen paper. Add the onion to the pan and cook until soft but not browned, then pour in the 250 ml/8 fl oz water, add the rice and a pinch of salt and bring to the boil. Reduce the heat, cover the pan and simmer gently for 15–20 minutes until all the water has been absorbed.

Drain the beans, discarding the bay leaf, and mix them into the rice. Serve immediately, topped with the crumbled bacon. **Serves 4**

Barbecue Beans

350 g/12 oz aduki, borlotti, kidney or butter beans
900 ml/1½ pints water
50 g/2 oz rindless streaky bacon
1 small onion, chopped
1 clove garlic, crushed
¼ teaspoon salt
2 tablespoons ketchup
1 tablespoon chilli sauce
2 teaspoons vinegar
1 tablespoon brown sugar
2 teaspoons prepared mustard
½ teaspoon salt
¼ teaspoon pepper

Cover the beans with cold water and leave them to soak overnight. Discard any that have not absorbed the water, then place the drained beans and measured water in a saucepan. Fry the bacon until crisp, drain it on absorbent kitchen paper and crumble it over the beans. Sauté the onion and garlic in the fat from the bacon until the onion is tender. Stir the sautéed onion mixture, crumbled bacon and salt into the beans. Bring to the boil, reduce the heat, then cover the pan and simmer the beans for 1–1½ hours or until they are just tender.

Drain and reserve the cooking liquid. Mix the ketchup, chilli sauce, vinegar, sugar, mustard, salt and pepper. Stir these seasonings into the beans, cover the pan and cook for a further 30 minutes, adding more cooking liquid as necessary. **Serves 4**

Barbecue Beans

Spanish Chick Peas

175 g/6 oz chick peas
900 ml/1½ pints water
1 tablespoon oil
1 teaspoon salt
25 g/1 oz butter
1 onion, chopped
1 clove garlic, crushed
1 green pepper, chopped
1 (397-g/14-oz) can chopped tomatoes
1 (340-g/12-oz) can sweet corn, drained
2 green chillies, chopped
¼ teaspoon dried oregano
generous pinch of ground cumin

Soak the chick peas overnight in cold water. Drain them, discarding any that have not absorbed the water, then place them in a medium saucepan with the measured water, oil and salt. Bring to the boil, reduce the heat and cover the pan. Simmer until the beans are tender – about 1–1½ hours. Drain the cooked beans and return them to the saucepan.

Melt the butter in a medium frying pan and sauté the onion, garlic and green pepper in it until the onion is soft but not browned. Add the tomatoes, corn, green chillies, oregano and cumin and stir well. Add the sautéed onion mixture to the beans and stir well. Cover and cook gently, stirring frequently, for 20 minutes. **Serves 4**

Note   Canned chick peas can be used instead of the dried ones. They should be drained and mixed with the sautéed mixture, then cooked as above.

Baked Lentils

225 g/8 oz lentils
600 ml/1 pint water
2 teaspoons oil
1 onion, chopped
1 teaspoon salt
1 (396-g/14-oz) can tomatoes, drained
1 green pepper, chopped
2 spring onions, chopped

Rinse the lentils and place them in a medium saucepan. Add the water, oil, onion and salt. Bring to the boil, reduce the heat and cover the pan, then simmer until the lentils are almost tender – about 30 minutes.

Dice the tomatoes. Combine the lentils with their cooking liquid, tomatoes, green pepper and spring onions in an ovenproof dish. Bake, uncovered, in a cool oven (150 C, 300 F, gas 2) for an hour. **Serves 4**

Serving suggestions These lentils are delicious with hot meat curries. If you prefer mild curries you can always add some of the curry spices to the lentils to complement the main dish.

Vegetables and Salads

In this chapter you will find recipes for fresh beans – French, runner and broad beans – as well as bean sprouts and dried beans. Many of the dishes are ideal as light accompaniments for the main dish, but with a little adaptation you may well be able to serve some of these salads for the first course.

If this is your first adventure with bean sprout salads, you are sure to be delighted with the crunchy texture they contribute to the meal. Try sprouting your own beans or lentils – just turn back to the introduction and read through the instructions. It's great fun watching them grow! If you're not that well organised don't worry – you can buy fresh bean sprouts in many good super-markets or greengrocers. Canned bean sprouts are widely available but they are not as good as fresh ones.

Salads made from dried beans are often best prepared in advance, dressed, then left in the re-frigerator to marinate and develop the flavours. Again, canned beans are particularly useful for salads as they do not require pre-cooking. Experiment with both dried and canned beans: once you have tried a few of the imaginative recipes in this chapter you are quite likely to feel inspired enough to create your own tasty bean salads.

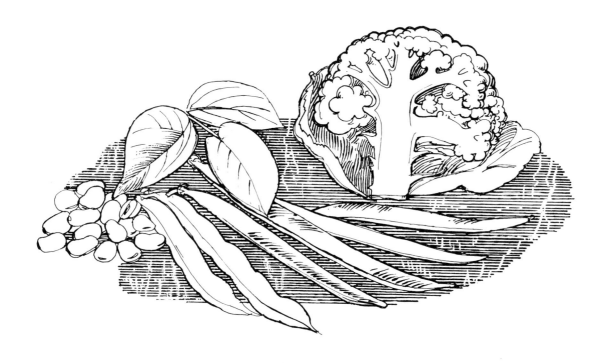

Green Bean Fritters

150 g/5 oz plain flour
¾ teaspoon salt
1 teaspoon baking powder
1 egg, separated
6 tablespoons milk
15 g/½ oz butter, melted
100 g/4 oz frozen cut French beans, cooked
100 g/4 oz carrots, lightly cooked and chopped
oil for deep frying

Sift the flour, salt and baking powder into a bowl. Make a well in the centre and add the egg yolk, milk and butter. Gradually stir the milk mixture into the dry ingredients to make a thick batter. Whisk the egg white until stiff and carefully fold it into the batter. Finally gently stir in the beans and carrots.

Meanwhile heat the oil to 180 C/350 F or until a cube of day-old bread turns golden in 1 minute. Drop spoonfuls of the batter carefully into the oil and cook the fritters, turning them occasionally until puffed and golden. Drain on absorbent kitchen paper and serve immediately. **Serves 4**

Serving suggestion Try serving these fritters as a simple starter. Arrange them in individual dishes and sprinkle grated Parmesan cheese on top. Alternatively, serve the fritters with a rich walnut and cream cheese sauce for a light vegetarian dish. Simply stir 50 g/2 oz finely chopped walnuts, 3–4 tablespoons natural yogurt and plenty of seasoning into 100 g/4 oz cream cheese, then chill before serving.

Stuffed Courgettes

4 large courgettes
50 g/2 oz butter
1 small onion, chopped
salt and freshly ground black pepper
50 g/2 oz cooked rice
25 g/1 oz roasted sesame seeds
100 g/4 oz cooked soya beans
50 g/2 oz fresh breadcrumbs
2 tablespoons chopped parsley
2 spring onions, chopped
4 slices processed cheese, halved

Cut the courgettes in half lengthways and carefully scoop out all the flesh to leave eight shells. Chop and reserve the flesh. Blanch the shells in boiling salted water for 4 minutes. Meanwhile, melt the butter, add the onion and cook until soft but not browned. Stir in a generous sprinkling of seasoning, the rice, sesame seeds, beans, reserved chopped courgette and bread-crumbs. Cook, stirring continuously, for a few minutes until the mixture is hot.

Stir in the parsley and spring onions and use a small spoon to fill the courgette shells with this mixture. Top each with a piece of cheese and cook under a hot grill for a few minutes. Serve immediately. **Serves 4–6**

Stuffed Courgettes

Stuffed Peppers

1 quantity Italian Salad Dressing (page 105)
4 medium green peppers
600 ml/1 pint water
½ teaspoon salt
350 g/12 oz long-grain rice
1 (300-g/10.6-oz) can tomato sauce
½ teaspoon dried basil
1 clove garlic, crushed
25 g/1 oz butter
1 onion, chopped
1 (425-g/15-oz) can red kidney beans
2 tablespoons chopped fresh parsley
4 slices Cheddar cheese

Prepare the Italian Salad Dressing according to the recipe instructions. Wash the peppers and cut a slice off the top of each, removing the stem. Remove the seeds and pith from inside the peppers, then blanch them in boiling salted water for 3 minutes. Drain the peppers upside down on absorbent kitchen paper.

Bring the measured water and salt to the boil, add the rice and simmer, covered, for about 15–20 minutes until the water is absorbed and the rice tender. Heat the tomato sauce, with the basil and garlic. Melt the butter in a frying pan, add the onion and cook until tender but not browned. Stir in the beans and parsley, then add the cooked rice and salad dressing.

Stand the peppers in a shallow ovenproof dish and fill them with the bean mixture. Pour the tomato sauce over them, allowing it to run down into the dish. Top each pepper with a slice of cheese and bake, uncovered, in a moderate oven (180 C, 350 F, gas 4) for 30 minutes. **Serves 4**

Fresh Vegetable Bake

225 g/8 oz French beans, trimmed, washed and cut into 2.5-cm/1-in pieces
2 carrots, thinly sliced
2 stalks celery, sliced
½ medium cauliflower, separated into florets
½ green or red pepper, cut into thin strips
2 courgettes, thinly sliced
225 g/8 oz shelled green peas
1 medium onion, sliced
2 tomatoes, peeled and cut into wedges
150 ml/¼ pint beef stock
2 tablespoons olive oil
2 cloves garlic, crushed
1 teaspoon salt
bay leaf
1 teaspoon dried dill weed
4 tablespoons grated Parmesan cheese

Layer all the vegetables in an ovenproof casserole. Heat the stock with the olive oil, garlic, salt, bay leaf and dill weed. When the liquid boils pour it over the vegetables. Cover the casserole and bake in a moderate oven (180 C, 350 F, gas 4) for 1 hour. Sprinkle the Parmesan cheese over and serve immediately. **Serves 6–8**

Variation

Vegetable Pie Cook the vegetables as above, layering them in a pie dish and omit the Parmesan cheese. Roll out a (368-g/13-oz) packet of puff pastry large enough to cover the pie. Sprinkle 100 g/4 oz grated Cheddar cheese over the vegetables, then top with the pastry. Cut a slit in the top of the pie to allow the steam to escape, brush with a little beaten egg or milk, then bake in a hot oven (220 C, 425 F, gas 7) for about 15 minutes until puffed and golden. Serve immediately.

French Bean Bake

225 g/8 oz frozen French beans
2 tablespoons oil
2 spring onions, chopped
225 g/8 oz mung bean sprouts or lentil sprouts
generous pinch of garlic salt
1 (283-g/10-oz) can cream of celery soup
50 g/2 oz fine fresh breadcrumbs
25 g/1 oz butter, melted
50 g/2 oz cashew nuts, chopped

Cook the French beans according to the packet instructions, then drain them. Heat the oil in a frying pan, add the beans, spring onions and bean or lentil sprouts. Sprinkle the garlic salt over them and stir-fry for 3 minutes.

Pour the soup over the vegetables, heat through and transfer to an ovenproof dish. Mix the breadcrumbs with the butter and nuts and sprinkle this over the beans. Place under a hot grill until crisp and golden on top. Serve immediately. **Serves 4**

French Beans with Blue Cheese

150 ml/¼ pint water
½ teaspoon salt
225 g/8 oz French beans, trimmed
50 g/2 oz butter
freshly ground black pepper
50 g/2 oz Danish blue cheese, crumbled
50 g/2 oz fresh breadcrumbs

Bring the water and salt to the boil and add the beans. Bring back to the boil, then reduce the heat, cover the pan and simmer until the beans are tender – about 10 minutes. Drain the beans and toss half the butter, pepper and blue cheese into them. Keep hot.

Melt the remaining butter in a small frying pan, add the breadcrumbs and cook, stirring, until they are golden brown. Sprinkle the crumbs over the beans and serve immediately. **Serves 3-4**

Green Beans Amandine

50 g/2 oz slivered almonds
675 g/1½ lb French beans
250 ml/8 fl oz water
3 tablespoons dry onion soup mix
1 teaspoon cornflour
1 tablespoon cold water

Dry-fry the almonds in a small frying pan over medium heat until they are golden, then set aside. Trim and wash the beans. Whisk the water and soup mix together in a saucepan and bring to the boil, stirring continuously. Add the beans, reduce the heat and cover the pan, then simmer for 10–15 minutes until the beans are just tender. Drain, reserving the cooking liquid.

Mix the cornflour to a smooth cream with the cold water, add it to the reserved cooking liquid and stir over medium heat until the mixture thickens. Return the beans to the pan and heat through for 3–5 minutes. Transfer to a serving dish and sprinkle the almonds over. Serve immediately. **Serves 4-6**

Devilled Green Beans

450 g/1 lb frozen cut French beans
25 g/1 oz butter
1 onion, chopped
1 green pepper, chopped
2 teaspoons plain flour
salt and freshly ground black pepper
1 tablespoon prepared mustard
2 egg yolks, beaten
300 ml/½ pint milk, warmed
2 tablespoons lemon juice

Cook the beans according to the instructions on the packet, drain and keep warm. Melt the butter in a medium frying pan, add the onion and green pepper and cook until the onion is soft but not browned. Sprinkle in the flour, salt and pepper and stir until smooth. Stir in the mustard, egg yolks and milk, then stir over low heat until the mixture is smooth and thickened, but do not boil. Stir in the lemon juice and pour the sauce over the beans. Serve immediately. **Serves 4-6**

Spinach and Beans

450 g/1 lb fresh spinach
2 rashers rindless streaky bacon
1 (425-g/15-oz) can borlotti beans, drained
salt and freshly ground black pepper to taste
2 tablespoons single cream

Wash, drain and trim the spinach, then chop it finely. Dry-fry the bacon until crisp, drain it on absorbent kitchen paper and toss the beans in the bacon fat remaining in the pan. Add the spinach and seasoning.

Cover the pan and cook for 5 minutes, then stir in the cream and heat through without boiling. Crumble the bacon over the mixture and serve immediately. **Serves 3–4**

Honeyed Lemon Beans

450 g/1 lb frozen cut French beans
25 g/1 oz butter
1 tablespoon water
2 tablespoons clear honey
½ teaspoon salt
¼ teaspoon paprika
½ teaspoon grated lemon rind
1 cooking apple, peeled, cored and diced
1 onion, chopped
1 teaspoon cornflour
1 tablespoon cold water

Cook the beans according to the instructions on the packet and drain them. Place the butter, water, honey, salt, paprika and lemon rind in a saucepan and heat through. Stir in the apple and onion and cook gently for about 10 minutes until the apple is soft. Blend the cornflour with the water and stir into the apple mixture. Add the beans, bring to the boil, then cover and cook gently for 5 minutes. Serve immediately. **Serves 3–4**

Broccoli and Chick Peas

350 g/12 oz fresh broccoli
150 ml/¼ pint water
½ teaspoon salt
1 (425-g/15-oz) can chick peas
2 tablespoons chopped canned pimiento
1 (396-g/14-oz) can artichoke hearts
1 teaspoon lemon juice
½ teaspoon dried basil
¼ teaspoon salt
freshly ground black pepper
50 g/2 oz butter

Wash and trim the broccoli and break it into small pieces. Bring the water and salt to the boil, add the broccoli, cover the pan and simmer until tender – about 10 minutes.

Drain the broccoli and return it to the pan. Add the chick peas, pimiento, artichoke hearts, lemon juice, basil, salt, pepper and butter, then toss gently until the butter melts. Continue cooking until heated through – about 10 minutes – then turn into a serving dish and serve immediately. **Serves 4–6**

Mexicali Vegetables

450 g/1 lb French beans
50 g/2 oz butter
1 clove garlic, crushed
2 carrots, grated
1 onion, chopped
2 stalks celery, diagonally sliced
4 tablespoons Green Chilli Sauce (page 108)
1 tablespoon prepared mustard
2 (425-g/15-oz) cans borlotti beans, drained

Trim the French beans and cut them into 2.5-cm/1-in pieces. Melt the butter in a large frying pan, add the garlic and cook for 1 minute. Stir in the green beans, carrots, onion and celery, then toss to mix and coat the vegetables in the butter. Cover and cook for 5 minutes.

Mix the Green Chilli Sauce and mustard into the vegetable mixture, add the borlotti beans and toss well. Cook, uncovered, until thoroughly heated – about 10 minutes. **Serves 6**

Broccoli and Chick Peas

Vegetable Stir-fry

450 g/1 lb French beans
2 tablespoons oil
4 stalks celery, sliced diagonally
3 spring onions, cut into 1-cm/½-in pieces
1½ teaspoons salt
1 teaspoon sugar
1 (225-g/8 oz) can water chestnuts, drained and sliced
150 ml/¼ pint chicken stock
1 tablespoon cornflour
2 tablespoons water
25 g/1 oz slivered almonds

Trim the French beans and cut them into 5-cm/2-in pieces. Heat a wok or frying pan, add the oil and heat for a few minutes. Add the French beans, celery and spring onions and stir-fry for 2 minutes. Add the salt, sugar, water chestnuts and chicken stock and continue to cook for a minute. Cover and cook for 10 minutes.

While the vegetables are cooking, blend the cornflour to a smooth cream with the water, then add to the vegetables and cook, stirring constantly over medium heat, until the beans are coated with a thin glaze. Turn the vegetables into a serving dish and sprinkle with slivered almonds. Serve immediately. **Serves 4-6**

Mangetouts and Bean Sprouts

225 g/8 oz mung bean or lentil sprouts
1 tablespoon cornflour
150 ml/¼ pint beef stock
1 tablespoon soy sauce
4 rashers rindless streaky bacon
2 stalks celery, sliced diagonally
1 small onion, sliced
100 g/4 oz button mushrooms, sliced
225 g/8 oz mangetouts

Wash and drain the bean or lentil sprouts. Mix the cornflour with the beef stock and soy sauce until smooth. Dry-fry the bacon until crisp, drain it on absorbent kitchen paper, then sauté the celery and onion in the fat remaining in the pan until the onion is tender but not browned. Add the mushrooms and mangetouts and stir-fry for 3 minutes.

Stir in the drained sprouts, stir well and pour in the beef stock. Stir over medium heat until boiling, then turn into a serving bowl. Crumble the bacon, sprinkle it over the vegetables and serve immediately. **Serves 4**

Marinated Vegetable and Shrimp Salad

225 g/8 oz Brussels sprouts, trimmed
225 g/8 oz broccoli, cut into small florets
½ small cauliflower, cut into small florets
225 g/8 oz frozen cut French beans, cooked and drained
50 g/2 oz black olives, stoned and sliced
1 (425-g/15-oz) can chick peas
6 tablespoons Tangy Lemon Dressing (page 105)
225 g/8 oz peeled shrimps
salt and freshly ground black pepper
1 small lettuce, shredded

Lightly cook the prepared fresh vegetables, then drain and mix them with the beans, olives and chick peas. Pour the Tangy Lemon Dressing over the salad and toss lightly. Refrigerate for 6 to 8 hours or overnight.

Stir the shrimps into the salad, then taste it and adjust the seasoning if necessary. Arrange the salad on a bed of shredded lettuce, either on one large platter or on individual plates. **Serves 6**

Italian Tuna Salad

2 (425-g/15-oz) cans cannellini beans
1 quantity Italian Salad Dressing (page 105)
3 spring onions, finely chopped
2 tablespoons chopped fresh parsley
50 g/2 oz stuffed olives, sliced
1 (198-g/7-oz) can tuna fish
4-6 large lettuce leaves

Drain the beans and mix them with the salad dressing, spring onions, parsley and olives. Toss well and chill for several hours. Drain the tuna fish and break it into chunks. Add the fish to the bean mixture and mix well. Serve the salad in the lettuce leaves on individual plates. **Serves 4-6**

Curried Turkey Salad

250 ml/8 fl oz water
1 chicken stock cube
pinch of garlic salt
pinch of onion salt
100 g/4 oz long-grain rice
100 g/4 oz mung bean or lentil sprouts
225 g/8 oz cooked turkey, diced
2 stalks celery, diced
½ medium green pepper, diced
3 spring onions, chopped
1 (396-g/14-oz) can artichoke hearts
2 teaspoons lemon juice
¼ teaspoon dried oregano
¼ teaspoon dried basil
pinch of dried dill weed
salt and freshly ground black pepper
dash of Tabasco sauce
½ teaspoon concentrated curry paste
150 ml/¼ pint mayonnaise

Bring the water to the boil in a small saucepan, add the stock cube, garlic salt and onion salt and stir until dissolved. Stir in the rice, reduce the heat, cover the pan and simmer for about 20 minutes. Wash and drain the sprouts. Combine the sprouts, turkey and freshly cooked rice in a large serving bowl. Mix in the celery, green pepper and spring onions. Drain and quarter the artichoke hearts and add them to the salad.

Mix the lemon juice, oregano, basil, dill weed, salt, black pepper, Tabasco sauce and curry paste together. Whisk this into the mayonnaise and continue to whisk until smooth. Pour the dressing over the salad and stir to mix, then refrigerate for at least 2 hours before serving. **Serves 4**

Polynesian Boats

1 ripe pineapple
1 (312-g/11-oz) can mandarin oranges
100 g/4 oz mung bean sprouts
175 g/6 oz cooked chicken, diced
1 spring onion, chopped
1 (228-g/8-oz) can water chestnuts
150 ml/¼ pint soured cream
3 tablespoons mayonnaise
1 tablespoon orange-flavoured liqueur such as
Curaçao or Grand Marnier
50 g/2 oz cashew nuts or hazelnuts

Cut the pineapple in half lengthwise with a long sharp knife, cutting through the leaves, then cut each half through lengthwise to make 4 wedges. Cut the pineapple fruit from the shell with a long sharp knife, then remove the core and eyes from it. Dice the fruit and drain it in a fine sieve with the mandarins. Reserve the juices for another use.

Wash and drain the bean sprouts. Combine the drained fruit, bean sprouts, chicken, spring onion and water chestnuts in a bowl. Stir the soured cream, mayonnaise and orange liqueur together, then carefully fold this dressing into the salad with the nuts. Carefully pile the salad into the pineapple boats and serve immediately. **Serves 4**

Note This salad can also be made with canned pineapple instead of fresh pineapple. Serve in lettuce cups.

Sunshine Salad

1 (425-g/15-oz) can cannellini beans, drained
½ quantity Sweet and Sour Honey Dressing (page 105)
or Yogurt Mayonnaise (page 106)
450 g/1 lb cooked chicken, diced
1 (340-g/12-oz) can sweet corn
100 g/4 oz small button mushrooms
1 medium avocado, peeled, stoned and diced
1 (425-g/15-oz) can peach slices, drained
4 spring onions, chopped
2 tablespoons chopped fresh parsley

Mix the beans with the dressing in a large bowl. Stir in the chicken, corn, mushrooms and avocado. Lastly add the peaches and onions and chill the salad for 30 minutes before spooning it into a serving dish. Sprinkle with chopped parsley just before serving. **Serves 6**

Salami and Rice Salad

450 ml/¾ pint water
1 teaspoon salt
225 g/8 oz long-grain rice
1 (425-g/15-oz) can red kidney beans, drained
100 g/4 oz shallots, chopped
225 g/8 oz salami, diced
1 small green pepper, diced
5–6 tablespoons Mustard French Dressing (page 104)
1 Iceberg lettuce, separated into leaves

Bring the water and salt to the boil. Add the rice, reduce the heat, then cover the pan and simmer for about 20 minutes, until the rice has absorbed the water. Mix the cooked rice, beans, shallots, salami and green pepper together and stir well. Pour the dressing over the salad and chill it for 2 hours before serving. Spoon the salad into large individual lettuce leaves. **Serves 4**

Polynesian Boats

Pepperoni and Lentil Salad

225 g/8 oz lentils
small strip of pared lemon rind
bay leaf
900 ml/1½ pints water
1 teaspoon salt
4 tablespoons Mustard French Dressing (page 104)
75 g/3 oz pepperoni, sliced
½ cucumber, peeled and diced
1 tomato, diced
50 g/2 oz black olives, stoned and sliced
2 tablespoons chopped fresh parsley
2 spring onions, chopped
GARNISH
½ lemon, cut into wedges
1 tomato, cut into wedges
fresh parsley sprigs

Mix the lentils, lemon rind, bay leaf, water and salt in a saucepan. Bring to the boil, reduce the heat and cover the pan. Simmer until the lentils are tender – about 30 minutes. Meanwhile, prepare the Mustard French Dressing, then drain the lentils, discarding the water, lemon rind and bay leaf.

In a salad bowl, combine the cooked lentils, pepperoni, cucumber, diced tomato, olives, parsley and spring onions. Pour the dressing over the salad and toss it in lightly. Chill for at least 2 hours, then serve garnished with lemon and tomato wedges and sprigs of parsley. **Serves 4–6**

Parisian Potato Salad

4 medium potatoes
350 g/12 oz French beans, cut into 2.5-cm/1-in pieces
100 g/4 oz cooked ham or roast beef, cut into strips
4 spring onions, chopped
3 radishes, sliced
½ quantity Vinaigrette Dressing (page 104)

Scrub but do not peel the potatoes. Cook them in boiling, salted water until just tender, then drain and cool them. Cook the French beans in boiling salted water until just tender.

Peel and slice the potatoes and arrange them in a glass serving bowl, layered with the beans and ham or beef, spring onions and radishes. Slowly pour the Vinaigrette Dressing over, allowing it to drizzle down between the layers. Chill for at least 4 hours. **Serves 4**

Hot Bean Salad

1 quantity Savoury White Beans (page 74)
6 rashers rindless streaky bacon
1 onion, chopped
150 ml/¼ pint vinegar
150 ml/¼ pint chicken stock
freshly ground black pepper
1 teaspoon sugar
1 egg yolk, lightly beaten

Prepare the Savoury White Beans according to the recipe instructions and keep hot. Dry-fry the bacon until crisp, then remove it from the pan and drain on absorbent kitchen paper. Add the onion to the fat remaining in the pan and cook until soft but not browned. Stir in the vinegar, chicken stock, a generous sprinkling of pepper and the sugar. Bring to the boil, then remove from the heat. Stir a little of the hot liquid into the egg yolk, then stir this back into the sauce and pour it over the beans. This salad tastes best served warm. **Serves 4–6**

Mixed Bean Salad

225 g/8 oz cut French beans, lightly cooked and
drained
1 (425-g/15-oz) can butter beans, drained
1 (425-g/15 oz) can red kidney beans, drained
1 (425-g/15-oz) can chick peas, drained
2 stalks celery, thinly sliced
1 green pepper, diced
1 small red pepper, chopped
1 onion, chopped
6 tablespoons corn oil
6 tablespoons vinegar
2 tablespoons caster sugar
1 teaspoon salt
½ teaspoon garlic salt
freshly ground black pepper

Mix all the drained beans, chick peas, celery, green and
red pepper and onion together in a bowl. Pour the oil
and vinegar into a covered jar and add the sugar, salt,
garlic salt and black pepper. Shake this mixture
vigorously for about a minute. Pour the dressing over
the beans and mix well. Cover and refrigerate for at
least 24 hours before serving. **Serves 8**

Orange Bean Salad

1 (425-g/15-oz) can red kidney beans, drained
½ quantity Sweet and Sour Honey Dressing (page 105)
1 (312-g/11-oz) can mandarin oranges, drained
225 g/8 oz French beans, cooked and cut into
2.5-cm/1-in pieces
4 shallots, chopped
1 large onion, thinly sliced
oil for deep frying
4 tablespoons chopped fresh parsley

Mix the kidney beans and Sweet and Sour Honey
Dressing with the mandarin oranges, French beans and
shallots. Toss gently and chill for 30 minutes. Meanwhile separate the onion slices into rings. Heat the oil to
180 C/350 F and fry the onion rings until golden. Toss
the parsley into the salad and serve garnished with the
crisp onion rings. **Serves 6–8**

Apple Bean Slaw

1 (425-g/15-oz) can butter beans, drained
½ medium white cabbage, finely shredded
1 large red dessert apple, cored and diced
50 g/2 oz Gruyère cheese, cubed
½ quantity Yogurt Mayonnaise (page 106)

Mix the butter beans, cabbage, apple and cheese in a
large bowl and pour the Yogurt Mayonnaise over. Stir
lightly to coat all the ingredients in the dressing, then
chill for 30 minutes before serving. **Serves 6**

Borlotti Pineapple Salad

1 (425-g/15-oz) can borlotti beans
1 green pepper, diced
2 spring onions, chopped
½ teaspoon dried dill weed
½ teaspoon salt
freshly ground black pepper
1 (227-g/8-oz) can pineapple slices, drained
½ quantity Sesame Seed Dressing (page 107)
1 crisp lettuce
4 sprigs fresh parsley

Mix the beans, green pepper and spring onions together. Add the dill weed and seasoning and stir well.
Reserve 2 pineapple slices and chop the remainder. Stir
the fruit into the beans. Pour the dressing over the salad
and mix well. Chill the salad for 30 minutes before
serving.

Arrange the lettuce leaves on four individual plates
and pile the salad on them. Slice horizontally through
the middle of each of the reserved pineapple slices and
twist them to form a garnish for each of the salads. Add a
sprig of parsley and serve immediately. **Serves 4**

Chilli Bean Salad

1 quantity Chilli Beans (page 80)
½ quantity Green Chilli Sauce (page 108)
4 tablespoons oil
1 teaspoon ground cumin
1 lettuce, shredded
1 avocado, peeled, stoned and diced
2 tomatoes, diced
50 g/2 oz black olives, stoned and sliced
100 g/4 oz cheese, grated

Prepare the beans and Green Chilli Sauce according to the recipe instructions. Mix the sauce, oil and cumin together and whisk vigorously. Arrange the lettuce, beans, avocado, tomatoes and olives in layers in a large shallow bowl and chill for 30 minutes.

Serve the cheese and dressing in small bowls to accompany the salad. **Serves 6–8**

Marinated Beans with Spinach

450 g/1 lb cooked black-eye beans
4 tablespoons chopped chives or spring onions
6 tablespoons oil
3 tablespoons lemon juice
1 teaspoon salt
225 g/8 oz fresh spinach, washed, trimmed and shredded
2 radishes, sliced to garnish

Mix the beans and chives or spring onions in a bowl. In a small jar or container with a tight-fitting lid, combine the oil, lemon juice and salt and shake vigorously for about a minute. Pour the dressing over the beans and stir gently, then chill them for 2 hours before serving.

Arrange the spinach on a platter and spoon the bean salad on top. Garnish with radish slices. **Serves 4–6**

Curried Succotash

1 (425-g/15-oz) can butter beans
275 g/10 oz frozen sweet corn, cooked
25 g/1 oz butter
1 onion, finely chopped
2 stalks celery, chopped
1 small green pepper, chopped
1 canned pimiento, chopped
3 tablespoons clear honey
8 tablespoons vinegar
4 tablespoons water
2 teaspoons curry powder
4 whole cloves
1 cinnamon stick

Mix the butter beans and sweet corn together in a bowl. Melt the butter in a pan, add the onion, celery and green pepper and cook until the onion is soft but not browned. Add the sautéed vegetables and pimiento to the beans and sweet corn and mix well.

In a small saucepan, combine the honey, vinegar, water, curry powder, cloves and cinnamon stick. Bring to the boil, reduce the heat, then cover the pan and simmer for 10 minutes. Strain the hot dressing over the salad and stir in. Chill for 6 hours or overnight before serving. **Serves 6**

Hong Kong Garden Salad

225 g/8 oz mung bean sprouts
½ cucumber, peeled and thinly sliced
1 avocado, peeled, stoned and diced
2 tablespoons chopped canned pimiento
1 tablespoon chopped chives
3 tablespoons Mustard French Dressing (page 104)

Wash and drain the bean sprouts. Combine them with the cucumber, avocado, pimiento and chives in a salad bowl and toss to mix. Pour the dressing over the salad, toss it thoroughly and chill for 30 minutes. **Serves 4**

Chilli Bean Salad

Macaroni Salad

225 g/8 oz elbow macaroni
1 (425-g/15-oz) can cannellini beans
225 g/8 oz frozen French beans, cooked and drained
1 red pepper, chopped
1 (396-g/14-oz) can artichoke hearts, drained
2 teaspoons lemon juice
¼ teaspoon dried oregano
¼ teaspoon dried basil
pinch of dried dill weed
salt and pepper to taste
1 drop Tabasco
4 tablespoons mayonnaise
50 g/2 oz black olives, stoned and sliced

Cook the macaroni in plenty of boiling salted water, then drain it and place in a bowl. Add the cannellini beans, French beans, red pepper and artichoke hearts.

Mix the lemon juice, oregano, basil, dill, salt, pepper and Tabasco together and whisk thoroughly. Beat this mixture into the mayonnaise until smooth. Pour the dressing over the salad and chill it for 2 hours. Stir the olives into the salad just before serving. **Serves 6**

Marinated Sauerkraut

1 (425-g/15-oz) can chick peas
1 (425-g/15-oz) can red kidney beans
2 stalks celery, chopped
1 green pepper, diced
1 tablespoon chopped canned pimiento
1 (450-g/1-lb) can sauerkraut, drained
1 tablespoon sugar
4 tablespoons oil
4 tablespoons vinegar
salt and freshly ground black pepper

Mix the chick peas with the red kidney beans and celery. Add the green pepper and pimiento and stir in the sauerkraut. Whisk the sugar, oil and vinegar together and season to taste, then pour this dressing over the salad. Chill for several hours before serving. **Serves 6–8**

Summer Salad

450 g/1 lb French or runner beans
175 g/6 oz shelled fresh green peas
100 g/4 oz fresh asparagus tips
1 cucumber, peeled and sliced
6 radishes, sliced
2 tablespoons chopped chives or spring onions
4 tablespoons Creamy Spinach Dressing (page 107)

Trim the French beans or string runner beans, then cut them into 2.5-cm/1-in lengths. Cook in salted boiling water until just tender. Cook the peas and asparagus together in boiling salted water until tender – about 10 minutes. Immediately they are cooked plunge all the vegetables into a large bowl of cold water, then drain them when cool and dry on absorbent kitchen paper.

In a salad bowl, combine the cooked vegetables with the cucumber, radishes and chives or spring onions. Pour the dressing over the salad, toss lightly and serve immediately. **Serves 4–6**

Variations

This salad can be made with canned vegetables. They do not require cooking but should be drained thoroughly. To use frozen vegetables, cook them according to the packet instructions, drain and cool them before tossing in the dressing.

Tangy Vegetable Salad

350 g/12 oz French beans, cut into 5-cm/2-in lengths
225 g/8 oz broccoli, cut into bite-sized florets
1 (396-g/14-oz) can artichoke hearts, drained and quartered
4 spring onions, chopped
½ quantity Yogurt Mayonnaise (page 106)

Cook the beans and broccoli very lightly in salted water – they should be crisp and definitely not overcooked. Drain the vegetables thoroughly, then mix them with the artichoke hearts and spring onions. Pour in the salad dressing and mix gently. Refrigerate for several hours or overnight. **Serves 4**

French Bean and Spinach Salad

225 g/8 oz fresh young spinach leaves
350 g/12 oz French beans, cooked
3 rashers rindless streaky bacon
½ teaspoon sugar
3 tablespoons cider vinegar
½ teaspoon salt
generous pinch of pepper

Wash and trim the spinach, then shred it finely and place it in a bowl. Drain the beans and toss them with the spinach. Dry-fry the bacon until it is crisp, then drain it on absorbent kitchen paper. Crumble the bacon over the beans.

Stir the sugar, vinegar, salt and pepper into the fat remaining in the pan. Bring to the boil, stirring constantly, then pour the hot dressing over the salad and toss it lightly. Serve immediately. **Serves 4–6**

Aubergine Salad

1 (227-g/8-oz) can red kidney beans, drained
1 (425-g/15-oz) can cannellini beans, drained
1 spring onion, chopped
2 tablespoons oil
1 clove garlic, crushed
1 green pepper, chopped
1 large aubergine, trimmed and cubed
1 tomato, peeled and diced
1 tablespoon chopped fresh parsley
4 tablespoons Italian Salad Dressing (page 105)

In a medium bowl, mix both types of bean with the onion and mix well. Heat the oil in a frying pan, add the garlic and green pepper and cook for 1 minute. Add the aubergine and cook, stirring constantly over medium heat, until the cubes are slightly browned. Stir in the tomato and parsley, then reduce the heat, cover the pan and simmer for 5 minutes.

Stir the aubergine and tomato mixture into the beans, pour the dressing over the salad and stir gently. Chill for 6 to 8 hours before serving. **Serves 4–6**

Bean Sprout Slaw

225 g/8 oz mung bean sprouts
2 carrots, coarsely grated
2 stalks celery, diced
1 quantity Yogurt Mayonnaise (page 106)

Wash and drain the bean sprouts, then mix them with the carrots and celery. Pour the dressing over the salad and stir until all the ingredients are thoroughly coated. Chill lightly until ready to serve. **Serves 4**

Spinach and Bean Sprout Salad

225 g/8 oz fresh young spinach leaves
225 g/8 oz mung bean or lentil sprouts
4 rashers lean rindless bacon
6 tablespoons Sweet and Sour Honey Dressing (page 105)

Wash and dry the spinach, then finely shred the leaves and transfer them to a salad bowl. Wash and drain the sprouts and add them to the spinach. Dry-fry the bacon until it is crisp, then drain it on absorbent kitchen paper. Crumble the bacon over the spinach and pour the dressing over the salad. Serve immediately. **Serves 4**

Salad Dressings and Sauces

Whatever the subject, no general cookery book is really complete without a short chapter of salad dressings and sauces, for they are often the simple recipes which make a perfect meal.

Here is a selection of salad dressings and a few sauces which are used throughout the book. The dressing is important in any salad recipe – particularly when beans are the main ingredient. Bean salads should be dressed and thoroughly tossed, then allowed to marinate, preferably for several hours, before serving. During the standing time the beans absorb flavour from the dressing and any other herbs or spices which have been added to the salad.

The recipe ideas range from an Italian Salad Dressing and a Tangy Lemon Dressing with variations, to a Green Chilli Sauce and a Creole Dipping Sauce – a collection of accompaniments which you will probably find useful for serving with many of your own favourite recipes as well as those suggested in this book.

Clockwise from the top: Green Bean Chow Chow (page 104), Green Chilli Sauce (page 108), Thousand Island Dressing (page 106), and Mustard French Dressing (page 104)

Green Bean Chow Chow

(Illustrated on page 102)

450 g/1 lb runner beans
1 small cauliflower
1 small cucumber, peeled and cubed
1 small green pepper, chopped
1 small onion, sliced
1 stalk celery, sliced
4 tablespoons salt
1.15 litres/2 pints white or cider vinegar
225 g/8 oz sugar
1 teaspoon dry mustard
pinch of turmeric
generous pinch of ground cloves
$\frac{1}{2}$ teaspoon ground black pepper

String the beans and cut them into 2.5-cm/1-in lengths. Break the cauliflower into small florets, trimming off any excess stalk. Layer all the vegetables in a bowl, sprinkling each layer with some of the salt. Leave to stand for 24 hours, then drain away all the liquid.

Pour the vinegar into a large saucepan, add the sugar, mustard, turmeric, cloves and pepper and heat gently to boiling point. Add the vegetables, bring back to the boil, then cover the pan, reduce the heat and simmer for 10 minutes.

Pack the vegetables and vinegar into heated wide-necked jars and cover them immediately with airtight lids. Allow this pickle to stand for at least a week before serving.

Vinaigrette Dressing

3 tablespoons red wine vinegar
8 tablespoons salad oil
1 clove garlic, crushed
$\frac{1}{2}$ teaspoon salt
$\frac{1}{4}$ teaspoon pepper
1 spring onion, chopped
3 tablespoons chopped fresh parsley

Combine all the ingredients in a large jar with a tight-fitting lid and shake vigorously for about a minute. This dressing can be stored in the refrigerator for 1 or 2 weeks.

Mustard French Dressing

(Illustrated on page 102)

150 ml/$\frac{1}{4}$ pint salad oil
2 tablespoons wine vinegar
1 tablespoon Dijon mustard
$\frac{1}{2}$ teaspoon salt
$\frac{1}{4}$ teaspoon freshly ground black pepper

Combine all the ingredients in a large jar with a tight-fitting lid and shake vigorously for about a minute. This dressing can be stored in the refrigerator for up to 3 or 4 weeks.

Sweet and Sour Honey Dressing

3 tablespoons clear honey
100 ml/4 fl oz vinegar
100 ml/4 fl oz oil
1 teaspoon salt
$\frac{1}{4}$ teaspoon pepper
2 tablespoons chopped spring onions

Combine all the ingredients in a large jar with a tight-fitting lid, then shake the dressing vigorously for about 3 minutes. This dressing can be stored in the refrigerator for 1 to 2 weeks.

Italian Salad Dressing

4 tablespoons oil
2 tablespoons wine vinegar
$\frac{1}{4}$ teaspoon dried oregano
$\frac{1}{4}$ teaspoon dried basil
generous pinch of dried dill weed
$\frac{1}{4}$ teaspoon salt
freshly ground black pepper
dash Tabasco sauce

Combine all the ingredients in a container with a tight-fitting lid and shake vigorously for about a minute. This dressing can be stored in the refrigerator for 3–4 weeks.

Tangy Lemon Dressing

2 tablespoons grated lemon rind
3 tablespoons lemon juice
6 tablespoons salad oil
1 clove garlic, crushed
$\frac{1}{4}$ teaspoon ground cumin
$\frac{1}{4}$ teaspoon dry mustard
$\frac{1}{4}$ teaspoon paprika
$\frac{1}{2}$ teaspoon salt
$\frac{1}{2}$ teaspoon sugar
pinch of cayenne pepper

Combine all the ingredients in a small container with a tight-fitting lid. Shake the dressing vigorously for about 1 minute. This dressing can be stored in the refrigerator for 3 to 4 weeks.

Variations

Orange Dressing Substitute the grated rind of 1 small orange for the lemon rind and use orange juice instead of the lemon juice.

Herb Dressing Omit the lemon rind, cumin and paprika, then add 2 tablespoons chopped mixed fresh herbs to the dressing.

Peanut Dressing Omit the lemon rind, cumin and paprika. Finely chop 50 g/2 oz roasted peanuts and add them to the dressing.

Tangy Tomato Dressing Omit the lemon rind, then add 2 teaspoons concentrated tomato purée to the dressing before shaking the ingredients together.

Yogurt Mayonnaise

150 ml/¼ pint mayonaise
2 tablespoons natural yogurt
½ teaspoon sugar
¼ teaspoon salt
1 spring onion, chopped

Combine all the ingredients in a small bowl and mix well with a whisk or fork. This dressing can be stored in the refrigerator for 1 to 2 weeks.

Green Mayonnaise

300 ml/½ pint mayonnaise
2 teaspoons lemon juice
2 tablespoons chopped parsley
2 tablespoons chopped spring onion
225 g/8 oz fresh spinach, trimmed and finely chopped
¼ teaspoon dried tarragon

Combine all the ingredients in a small bowl and stir well, then chill for at least 6 hours before use. This dressing can be stored in the refrigerator for a week.

Thousand Island Dressing

(Illustrated on page 102)

300 ml/½ pint mayonnaise
½ teaspoon Tabasco sauce
1 tablespoon pickle or relish
2 tablespoons chopped stuffed olives
1 spring onion, chopped
3 tablespoons chilli sauce (optional)

Combine all the ingredients in a small bowl and stir well. This dressing can be stored in the refrigerator for 1 to 2 weeks.

Sesame Seed Dressing

1 tablespoon sesame seeds
3 tablespoons vinegar
1 tablespoon soy sauce
1 tablespoon sugar
pinch of paprika
1 teaspoon prepared mustard
$\frac{1}{2}$ teaspoon salt
1 tablespoon chopped onion
6 tablespoons oil

Stir the sesame seeds over low heat in a heavy-based pan until golden, about 3–5 minutes. Watch the seeds carefully to prevent them from burning.

In a small bowl, combine the vinegar, soy sauce, sugar, paprika, mustard, salt and onion. Stir to dissolve the sugar, then slowly add the oil whisking continuously. When all the oil has been added, stir in the toasted sesame seeds. Use this dressing on the day it is made.

Creamy Spinach Dressing

2 tablespoons chopped fresh parsley
100 g/4 oz spinach, trimmed and chopped
2 spring onions, cut into 2.5-cm/1-in pieces
1 teaspoon prepared mustard
1 egg yolk
3 tablespoons vinegar
6 tablespoons oil

Place all the ingredients in a liquidiser and blend them together until smooth and creamy – about 2–3 minutes. This dressing can be stored in the refrigerator for 1–2 weeks.

Sesame Seed Dressing

1 Roast the sesame seeds in a heavy-based pan over low heat, stirring continuously to prevent them from burning.

2 Slowly add the oil to the vinegar mixture, whisking continuously. Lastly, add the roasted sesame seeds.

Green Chilli Sauce

(Illustrated on page 102)

1 (425-g/15-oz) can tomatoes, drained or 4 fresh
tomatoes, peeled
2 green chillies, chopped
2 spring onions, chopped
1 clove garlic, crushed
2 teaspoons chilli powder
$\frac{1}{4}$ teaspoon ground cumin
$\frac{1}{4}$ teaspoon dried oregano
$\frac{1}{2}$ teaspoon salt

Dice the tomatoes and place them in a saucepan with all the remaining ingredients. Cover and cook, simmering, for 10 minutes. Serve warm or chilled.

Creole Dipping Sauce

1 tablespoon oil
1 tablespoon finely chopped onion
1 clove garlic, crushed
2 tablespoons finely chopped green pepper
1 (227-g/8-oz) can chopped tomatoes
$\frac{1}{2}$ teaspoon salt
$\frac{1}{2}$ teaspoon sugar
$\frac{1}{4}$ teaspoon dried thyme

Heat the oil in a small saucepan, add the onion, garlic and green pepper and cook until the onion is soft but not browned. Stir in the remaining ingredients, cover the pan and simmer for 10 minutes. Serve warm.

Spicy Tomato Sauce

1 (425-g/15-oz) can chopped tomatoes
1 clove garlic, crushed
$\frac{1}{4}$ teaspoon dried basil
$\frac{1}{2}$ teaspoon dried oregano
$\frac{1}{4}$ teaspoon salt
1 teaspoon chilli powder

Combine all the ingredients in a medium saucepan. Bring to the boil, reduce the heat, then cover the pan and simmer the sauce for 10 minutes. Serve hot.

Marinara Sauce

1 tablespoon olive oil
1 clove garlic, crushed
1 (227-g/8-oz) can tomatoes
$\frac{1}{4}$ teaspoon salt
freshly ground black pepper
$\frac{1}{4}$ teaspoon dried oregano
pinch of dried basil
pinch of sugar
1 tablespoon chopped fresh parsley

Heat the oil in a medium saucepan. Sauté the garlic in the oil for about 1 minute. Add the remaining ingredients, breaking up the tomatoes with a fork. Cover the pan and simmer the sauce for 10 minutes.

Snacks and Sandwiches

Thinking up something different to eat can be very difficult when you're feeling really peckish or when you just don't have the time – or appetite – for a full-blown meal.

You could try, for example, an Oriental Pocket Sandwich, or a tasty open sandwich topped with cream cheese and some spicy beans. The snacks and sandwiches in this chapter are both simple and quick to prepare, but at the same time they are certainly worthy of serving to a hungry friend. Why not plan a simple informal supper menu around one of the lavishly filled sandwiches?

A quick read through the selection of recipes in this chapter will leave you full of ideas next time you feel hungry for a snack, as well as when you are faced with a starving member of the family!

Soya Bean Pâté

175 g/6 oz cooked soya beans
25 g/1 oz butter
1 small onion, finely chopped
2 tablespoons concentrated tomato purée
2 tablespoons chopped black olives
1 tablespoon sesame seeds
1 tablespoon chopped fresh parsley
$\frac{1}{2}$ teaspoon salt
a few crisp lettuce leaves

Mash the cooked soya beans with a potato masher until they are quite smooth. Melt the butter in a small frying pan, add the onion and cook until soft but not browned. Add the tomato purée, olives and onion to the beans. Roast the sesame seeds by stirring them constantly over low heat in a small heavy-based frying pan until lightly browned. Watch them carefully because the seeds will burn very easily. Stir the sesame seeds, parsley and salt into the bean mixture and mix well.

Serve spoonfuls of pâté on a few crisp lettuce leaves arranged on individual plates. Crisp toast, cocktail crackers or crispbreads may be served with it. Alternatively, the pâté may be spread on small crackers for serving with drinks. **Serves 6**

Roasted Beans

100 g/4 oz soya beans or chick peas
2 teaspoons oil
2 teaspoons salt

Soak the beans or chick peas overnight, then drain them and discard any which have not absorbed the water. Spread the beans out on a Swiss roll tin and bake in a cool oven (140 C, 275 F, gas 1) for 1 hour. Turn the beans several times to ensure even cooking.

Sprinkle the oil and salt over the beans and turn them several times to coat them evenly and lightly. Bake for a further 15–20 minutes until golden brown. Cool and store in an airtight container.

Cheese and Bacon Spread

1 (425-g/15-oz) can cannellini beans
3 rashers lean rindless bacon
50 g/2 oz pork sausagemeat
$\frac{1}{4}$ teaspoon Tabasco sauce
50 g/2 oz mature Cheddar cheese, grated

Reserve 4–6 tablespoons of the liquid from the can of beans. Mash the drained beans using a potato masher, adding enough of the reserved liquid as necessary to make a smooth spread.

Dry-fry the bacon in a small frying pan until crisp, then drain it on absorbent kitchen paper. Fry the sausagemeat in the same pan, breaking it up as it cooks. Drain any excess fat from the meat, then add it to the mashed beans together with the crumbled bacon and Tabasco sauce. Mix thoroughly and reheat the spread in the same pan. Transfer to an ovenproof serving dish or individual ramekins and top with the grated cheese. Place the dish under a heated grill until the cheese is bubbling and golden. Serve immediately. **Serves 4**

Top right: Mixed Chilli Fondue (page 65). *Clockwise from the top of the tray:* Tofu and Avocado Dip (page 47), Roasted Beans and Open Sandwiches (page 13)

Curried Butter Bean Dip

1 (425-g/15-oz) can butter beans
1 onion, finely chopped
1 clove garlic, crushed
6 tablespoons mayonnaise
150 ml/¼ pint soured cream
2 teaspoons dried dill weed
1 teaspoon curry paste
salt and freshly ground black pepper
assorted raw vegetables to dip; for example, sticks of
carrot and celery, cauliflower florets and radishes

Heat the butter beans with the liquid from the can. Add the onion and garlic, reduce the heat, then cover the pan and simmer for about 10 minutes or until the onion is soft. Transfer the bean mixture with any remaining cooking liquid to a liquidiser and blend until smooth. Leave to cool.

Add the mayonnaise, soured cream, dill weed and curry paste to the bean purée. Stir to mix well and chill for several hours or overnight. Taste and adjust the seasoning, then serve with the pieces of raw vegetable to dip. **Serves 6**

Variations

Bacon and Butter Bean Dip Add 100 g/4 oz crisp-fried, crumbled bacon to the dip and omit the curry paste.

Tuna and Butter Bean Dip Add 1 (198-g/7-oz) can tuna fish in oil, drained and flaked, to the dip and omit the curry paste.

Curried Chicken Dip Add 225 g/8 oz finely chopped cooked chicken to the dip.

Cheese and Bean Bakes

½ quantity Creamed Beans (page 74)
25 g/1 oz butter
1 small onion, finely chopped
salt
4 thick slices bread
100 g/4 oz mature Cheddar cheese

Prepare the beans according to the recipe instructions. Melt the butter in a small saucepan, add the onion and cook until soft but not browned. Add the beans and salt to taste. Heat through until bubbling, stirring occasionally to prevent the beans sticking.

Arrange the slices of bread on a baking tray and top them with the bean mixture. Sprinkle the grated cheese over and bake in a moderately hot oven (190 C, 375 F, gas 5) for about 15 minutes until golden brown and bubbling hot. **Serves 2–4**

Toasted Sandwiches

100 g/4 oz butter
1 small onion, finely chopped
2 tablespoons finely chopped green pepper
1 quantity Creamed Beans (page 74)
1 teaspoon chilli powder (optional)
12 slices bread
175 g/6 oz Cheddar cheese, sliced

Melt a quarter of the butter in a saucepan, add the onion and green pepper and cook, stirring constantly, over medium heat until the onion is soft but not browned. Stir in the beans and chilli powder (if used). Cook over low heat for 10 minutes.

Meanwhile, spread one side of each slice of bread with the remaining butter. Sandwich the cheese and bean mixture between the bread, buttered-side out. Cook the sandwiches under a hot grill, turning once, until golden brown on both sides. Serve immediately. **Serves 6**

Tofu Salad Sandwiches

100 g/4 oz fresh lentil or alfalfa sprouts (page 15)
450 g/1 lb tofu
3 tablespoons mayonnaise
1 tablespoon prepared mustard
1 teaspoon Worcestershire sauce
½ teaspoon salt
generous pinch of ground cumin
generous pinch of ground turmeric
¼ teaspoon paprika
1 spring onion, finely chopped
2 large carrots, coarsely grated
2 stalks celery, finely chopped
½ green pepper, finely chopped
100 g/4 oz butter
12 slices wholemeal bread

Rinse and dry the sprouts. Crumble the tofu with a fork, then stir in the mayonnaise, mustard and Worcestershire sauce. Add the salt, cumin, turmeric and paprika and mix well. Finally add the prepared vegetables and toss them thoroughly into the dressing.

Butter the bread and divide the prepared salad between six of the slices. Sprinkle the sprouts over the salad and top with the remaining bread. Press the sandwiches together lightly and cut them in half to serve. **Serves 3–6**

Note Tofu is a bland-tasting, versatile soya bean curd which can be used in both sweet and savoury dishes. It contains protein and very few calories, so is ideal for slimming or vegetarian diets. Most health food shops and oriental stores sell tofu and it is also available in long-life packs.

Italian Pitta Salad

100 g/4 oz Gruyère or Emmental cheese
100 g/4 oz Cheddar cheese
100 g/4 oz cooked chicken
100 g/4 oz cooked ham
1 (227-g/8-oz) can chick peas, drained
4–6 tablespoons Italian Salad Dressing (page 105)
1 spring onion, chopped
4 pieces pitta bread

Cut the cheese, chicken and ham into julienne strips and mix them together with the chick peas, salad dressing and spring onion. Toss gently to coat with the dressing.

Cut a pocket in each piece of pitta bread and carefully separate the sides of the bread. Stuff each pocket with the chick pea filling and serve immediately. **Serves 4**

Open Sandwiches

4 rashers lean rindless bacon
25 g/1 oz butter
1 small onion, finely chopped
1 (425-g/15-oz) can baked beans
2 tablespoons chilli sauce (optional)
100 g/4 oz full fat soft cheese
8 thick slices dark rye bread
2 spring onions, chopped

Dry-fry the bacon until the fat runs, then drain it on absorbent kitchen paper. Melt the butter in a saucepan, add the onion and cook until soft but not browned. Add the beans and chilli sauce (if used) and heat through stirring occasionally.

Spread the cheese on the rye bread and place it under a grill until hot but not browned. Top each slice with some of the baked beans. Crumble the bacon over each sandwich, garnish with a little chopped spring onion and serve immediately. **Serves 4**

Baking

Perhaps you never thought of beans in connection with any form of baking – well, here's your opportunity to experiment with breads and cakes made with beans.

In this chapter you will find a few basic recipes – Bean Purée and Shortcrust Pastry, for example – along with cake, flans and moist, light breads. But why bother to add beans to your baking, you may ask? One good answer is that puréed beans, mixed in with other basic baking ingredients, give soft breads and cakes which are both even in texture and exceptionally light.

Another advantage is the improved nutritional value which the beans contribute – many cakes and breads are often considered lacking in health-giving nourishment. Should you or your family regularly take a packed lunch to work or school, then home-baked bread is sure to add interest to your sandwiches. The breads in this chapter can be baked in quantity, then frozen so that you will always have a supply of delicious homemade bread available. Not only will your daily sandwich taste much better, but it will do you far more good than a couple of pieces of ready-sliced white bread!

Apple Cake (page 116)

Bean Purée

225 g/8 oz butter beans or borlotti beans
900 ml/1½ pints water
1 teaspoon salt
1 tablespoon oil

Soak the beans overnight. Drain them, discarding any which have not absorbed the water and place them in a saucepan with the measured water, salt and oil. Bring to the boil, reduce the heat and cover the pan. Simmer until the beans are tender – about 1–1½ hours.

Drain the beans and reserve the cooking liquid. Reduce small quantities of the beans to a smooth purée in a liquidiser. Add some of the reserved cooking liquid to each batch of beans and scrape the purée down from the sides of the liquidiser during processing.

Shortcrust Pastry

225 g/8 oz plain flour
pinch of salt
100 g/4 oz butter or margarine
about 2 tablespoons cold water

Sift the flour and salt into a bowl, add the butter or margarine, cut into chunks, and rub the fat in until the mixture resembles fine breadcrumbs. Sprinkle in the water and mix to form a short dough. Knead the pastry very quickly and lightly, then use as required.

Pastry flan case This quantity of pastry may be rolled out thinly and used to line a 23–25-cm/9–10-in flan dish or tin.

Apple Cake

(Illustrated on page 114)

350 g/12 oz cooking apples
100 g/4 oz butter or margarine
225 g/8 oz caster sugar
1 egg
225 g/8 oz Bean Purée made with pinto or borlotti beans (page 116)
175 g/6 oz plain flour
2 teaspoons baking powder
½ teaspoon salt
1 teaspoon ground cinnamon
¼ teaspoon ground cloves
½ teaspoon ground allspice
2 medium dessert apples
COFFEE ICING
450 g/1 lb icing sugar
50 g/2 oz butter or margarine, softened
pinch of salt
3–4 tablespoons strong black coffee, cooled
2 tablespoons lemon juice
50 g/2 oz pecan or walnut halves to decorate

Peel, core and slice the cooking apples, then cook them with 2 tablespoons water until reduced to a pulp. Cream the butter or margarine with the sugar until pale and creamy, then beat in the egg and stir in both the bean and apple purées.

Sift the flour with the baking powder, salt, cinnamon, cloves and allspice, then fold these dry ingredients into the cake mixture. Peel, core and dice one of the dessert apples and fold it into the cake. Spoon the mixture into three greased 16-cm/6½-in sandwich tins and spread out evenly. Bake in a moderate oven (180 C, 350 F, gas 4) for 30–40 minutes, then allow to cool in the tins for 10 minutes before transferring to a wire rack.

To make the coffee icing, sift the icing sugar into a bowl, add the softened butter or margarine and 2 tablespoons of the coffee. Beat thoroughly to make a smooth thick icing, adding more coffee if necessary. Sandwich the cakes together with most of the icing and spread a thick layer on top of the cake.

Halve, core and slice the remaining apple, dip it in the lemon juice and arrange the slices on top of the cake. Decorate with the pecan or walnut halves.

Brown Sugar Pie

1 quantity Shortcrust Pastry (opposite)
100 g/4 oz butter or margarine
300 g/11 oz soft brown sugar
3 eggs, separated
1 teaspoon vanilla essence
225 g/8 oz Bean Purée made with pinto or borlotti
beans (opposite)
pinch of cream of tartar

Prepare the pastry according to the recipe instructions, then roll it out and use it to line a 23-cm/9-in flan dish.

Cream the butter or margarine with 225 g/8 oz of the sugar until soft and creamy, then beat in the egg yolks. Stir the vanilla essence into the bean purée and mix into the creamed mixture. Pour this filling into the prepared flan case and bake in a moderate oven (180 C, 350 F, gas 4) for 45 minutes or until a knife inserted into the middle comes out clean.

Whisk the egg whites until stiff, then gradually whisk in the cream of tartar and remaining sugar and continue whisking until very stiff. Top the flan with the meringue, spreading it right up to the edges of the pastry. Bake for a further 5–10 minutes until the meringue is lightly browned. Allow to cool before serving. **Serves 6–8**

Harvest Pie

25-cm/10-in uncooked pastry flan case (opposite)
½ teaspoon salt
½ teaspoon cinnamon
1 teaspoon ground ginger
pinch of ground cloves
¼ teaspoon ground nutmeg
175 g/6 oz sugar
350 g/12 oz Bean Purée made with borlotti beans
(opposite)
3 eggs, lightly beaten
1 (170-g/6-oz) can evaporated milk
150 ml/¼ pint double cream, whipped

Prepare the flan case according to the recipe instructions. Stir the salt, spices and sugar into the bean purée, then gradually add the eggs and evaporated milk. Stir well and pour into the flan case.

Bake in a moderately hot oven (190 C, 375 F, gas 5) for 1 hour or until the flan is firmly set. Allow to cool, then chill before serving with whipped cream.

Colonial Bread

225 g/8 oz Bean Purée made with borlotti or pinto
beans (page 116)
250 ml/8 fl oz water
25 g/1 oz cornmeal
2 tablespoons sugar
1½ teaspoons salt
5 teaspoons oil
2 teaspoons dried yeast
3 tablespoons lukewarm water
50 g/2 oz wholemeal flour
50 g/2 oz rye flour
275 g/10 oz strong plain flour

Prepare the bean purée according to the recipe instructions. Bring the water to the boil, remove from the heat
and stir in the cornmeal, all but 1 teaspoon of the sugar,
salt, bean purée and oil. Allow to cool until just
lukewarm. Dissolve the yeast in the lukewarm water
with the remaining sugar and leave to stand in a warm
place until frothy.

Combine the bean purée mixture with the yeast
liquid and stir in the flours to make a stiff dough. Turn
out on to a floured surface and knead until smooth and
elastic. Return the dough to the lightly-floured bowl,
cover and leave in a warm place until doubled in size –
about 1½ hours.

Lightly knead the dough and place it in a 1-kg/2-lb
loaf tin. Cover and leave to rise for about 45 minutes in
a warm place or until the dough has risen to the top of
the tin.

Bake in a moderate oven (190 C, 375 F, gas 5) for
about 45 minutes, until golden brown. When tapped on
the base, the cooked bread should sound hollow. Cool
on a wire rack.

Bean Bread with Dill

225 g/8 oz Bean Purée made with cannellini beans
(page 116)
25 g/1 oz butter
1 tablespoon grated onion
1 teaspoon salt
2 teaspoons dried dill weed
2 teaspoons dried yeast
250 ml/8 fl oz lukewarm water
1½ tablespoons sugar
450 g/1 lb strong plain flour
1 egg, lightly beaten
1 teaspoon coarse salt
1½ tablespoons grated Parmesan cheese
1 tablespoon chopped parsley

Prepare the Bean Purée according to the recipe instructions. Melt the butter in a frying pan, add the onion and
cook for a few minutes. Stir in the Bean Purée, salt and
dill weed. Remove from the heat and allow to cool.

Dissolve the yeast in the lukewarm water and stir in
the sugar. Add the cooled bean mixture to the yeast
liquid and stir it into the flour to make a stiff dough.
Turn the dough out on to a lightly floured surface and
knead until smooth and elastic. Return it to the floured
bowl, cover and leave in a warm place until doubled in
bulk – about 1½ hours.

Lightly knead the dough, then place it in a greased
1-kg/2-lb loaf tin. Make a few diagonal slits across the
top of the bread and brush with a little beaten egg. Mix
the salt, cheese and parsley and sprinkle over the loaf.
Cover and leave in a warm place until the dough rises to
the top of the tin – about 30–40 minutes. Bake in a
moderate oven (190 C, 375 F, gas 5) for 30–40 minutes
until golden brown. When turned upside down and
lightly tapped the loaf should sound hollow. Cool on a
wire rack.

Corned Beef Puffs

1 tablespoon oil
1 small onion, chopped
175 g/6 oz cooked black-eye beans
1 medium potato, cooked and diced
50 g/2 oz white cabbage, shredded
1 (200-g/7-oz) can corned beef, diced
salt and freshly ground black pepper
1 (368-g/13-oz) packet puff pastry
beaten egg or milk to glaze

Heat the oil in a small frying pan, add the onion and cook until soft but not browned. Stir in the beans, potato, cabbage and beef, then add the seasoning and stir well. Cook this filling for about 10 minutes, stirring frequently until the cabbage is just softened. Remove from the heat and allow to cool.

Roll out the pastry very thinly and cut out 10–12 circles, each measuring 10 cm/4 in. in diameter. Divide the filling between the pastry circles, brush the edges with a little water and fold the pastry over the filling to meet in the middle or on one side. Press the edges together with a fork to seal them in a pasty shape.

Place the puffs on a baking tray and brush them with a little beaten egg or milk. Bake in a hot oven (220 C, 425 F, gas 7) for 10–15 minutes, until well puffed and golden brown. Serve hot or warm.

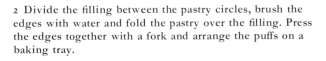

Corned Beef Puffs

1 Roll out the pastry and cut out 10–12 circles measuring 10 cm/4 in. in diameter. Use the rim of a small basin or plate as a guide.

2 Divide the filling between the pastry circles, brush the edges with water and fold the pastry over the filling. Press the edges together with a fork and arrange the puffs on a baking tray.

Courgette Bread

3 eggs
350 g/12 oz caster sugar
250 ml/8 fl oz oil
100 g/4 oz courgettes, grated
1 teaspoon vanilla essence
225 g/8 oz Bean Purée made with borlotti or pinto
beans (page 116)
225 g/8 oz plain flour
1 teaspoon salt
1 teaspoon bicarbonate of soda
2½ teaspoons baking powder
2 teaspoons ground cinnamon

Beat the eggs with the sugar and oil until well mixed. Add the courgettes, vanilla essence and Bean Purée. Sift the flour, salt, bicarbonate of soda, baking powder and cinnamon together, then stir these dry ingredients into the egg mixture. Beat the mixture thoroughly, divide it equally between two greased 1-kg/2-lb loaf tins and bake in a moderate oven (180 C, 350 F, gas 4) for 1–1¼ hours or until a skewer inserted into the middle of the loaf comes out clean. Cool on a wire rack.

Spicy Bean Scones

225 g/8 oz plain flour
3 teaspoons baking powder
1 teaspoon salt
75 g/3 oz butter or margarine
100 g/4 oz cooked red kidney beans, chopped
2 tablespoons chilli sauce (optional)
1 teaspoon Worcestershire sauce
4–6 tablespoons milk

Sift the flour, baking powder and salt into a bowl. Rub the butter or margarine in until the mixture resembles fine breadcrumbs, then stir in the beans. Mix the chilli sauce (if used) with the Worcestershire sauce and milk. Stir the milk mixture into the dry ingredients, adding a little extra milk if necessary to make a soft dough.

Knead lightly, then roll out to 1-cm/½-in thick and cut out about 2.5-cm/2-in rounds. Place the scones on greased baking trays and bake in a hot oven (230 C, 450 F, gas 8) for 10–12 minutes. Transfer the scones to a wire rack and serve warm.

Index